"Theresa Saldana is the countess of Heaven in my heart and the angel of America in my dreams. Theresa Saldana is a soulmate to me. My conception of the girl I long to be with most. I have psychedelic fantasies of romance about her in springtime—enchanting visions of our walking together through the gardens of magnificent palaces of Heaven."
—from the Diary of Arthur Jackson

"I must not visit any cinema to indulge in amusement or nostalgia until Theresa Saldana precedes me into eternity first, so that she can be with me in spirit when I watch a film in a cinema. I will only see a film before Theresa's death if Theresa Saldana herself is in it."
—from the Diary of Arthur Jackson

OBSESSED
The Anatomy of a Stalker

OBSESSED

The Anatomy of a Stalker

**RONALD MARKMAN, M.D., J.D.,
AND RON LaBRECQUE**

AVON BOOKS ◆ NEW YORK

AVON BOOKS
A division of
The Hearst Corporation
1350 Avenue of the Americas
New York, New York 10019

Copyright © 1994 by Ronald Markman and Ron LaBrecque
Front cover photo courtesy of Bettman Archive
Published by arrangement with the authors
Library of Congress Catalog Card Number: 93-46928
ISBN: 0-380-76650-7

Published in hardcover by William Morrow and Company, Inc.; for information address Permissions Department, William Morrow and Company, Inc., 1350 Avenue of the Americas, New York, New York 10019.

The William Morrow edition contains the following Library of Congress Cataloging in Publication Data:

Markman, Ronald,
    Obsessed : the stalking of Theresa Saldana / Ronald Markman and Ron LaBrecque.
        p.   cm.
    Includes index.
    1. Jackson, Arthur, 1935—Mental health.   2. Saldana, Theresa—Assassination attempt, 1982.   3. Stalking—Case studies.   4. Forensic psychiatry—United States—Case studies.   5. Insane.   Criminal and dangerous—Case studies.   I. LaBrecque, Ron.   II. Title.
RA1151.M293   1994   93-46928
364.1'555'092—dc20   CIP
[B]

First Avon Books Printing: July 1995

AVON TRADEMARK REG. U.S. PAT. OFF. AND IN OTHER COUNTRIES, MARCA REGISTRADA, HECHO EN U.S.A.

Printed in the U.S.A.

RA   10 9 8 7 6 5 4 3 2 1

To David and Michael
upon their graduations as they embark on their future

and to the memory of
Chester S. Weinerman,
poet, lawyer, editor

OBSESSED

The Anatomy of a Stalker

Contents

Contents

Introduction

This book is a journey into the psychologically distorted world of Arthur Jackson, a man with chronic mental illness who is now in his late fifties, and who carries within himself the potential to commit great violence. His life represents the failures of government institutions to properly deal with him, bypassing opportunities that once might have checked his murderous impulses or later might have protected others from him.

Since Jackson's adolescence in a coastal city of Scotland, when symptoms of his mental illness, schizophrenia, first became manifest, his life has been a daily exhibition of abnormal thinking and behavior. Those troubled years, now totaling well over four decades, have been punctuated by occasional outbursts of deadly acts committed by Jackson.

Through his bizarre interpretation of the world around him, Arthur Jackson has created a complicated, highly personalized philosophy which guides his aberrant behavior. The unusual patterns of thought that form the framework of his strange existence can seem incomprehensibly irrational to a normal person. His unshakeable obsessions were decades in the making. Ultimately, his internal compulsions led him from Scotland to California. There, with a brutal and near-fatal knife attack on a young actress named Theresa Saldana, he joined a growing list of mentally ill people achieving notoriety through highly public acts of violence.

A variety of government agencies that had contact with Jackson throughout his life, from mental health services to law enforcement, might have dealt with him differently and, as a result, prevented that tragedy as well as others about which authorities have since learned.

Jackson's experiences reveal dilemmas both of social policy and law that arise in the attempt to effectively deal with the violent mentally ill. Our prison systems offer virtually no treatment for psychologically disturbed patient-inmates. Civil procedures to involuntarily hospitalize people who may desperately be in need of such care are even more cumbersome and inadequate than the criminal justice system.

If systemic problems have not been enough to complicate the matters involving Arthur Jackson, some participants have displayed questionable judgment. A lingering question is whether a California prosecutor, by following a course in which the pursuit of justice was seemingly affected by political concerns, created the possibility of future problems with this eternally troubled man for authorities in the United States and the United Kingdom. As a result, British prosecutors have been blocked, for a time at least, from implementing what may be the best long-term solution now possible to counter the threat that Jackson now poses to other people.

In too many instances the law offers a weak barrier against people like Jackson who are dangerous to others. Opposing legal viewpoints, each founded on valid principle, clash. Too often, dangerous mentally ill people cannot even be lawfully confined. The question arises whether to incarcerate those who have committed acts of violence in a prison or to confine them in a true hospital. Legal debate becomes complex. What are the constitutional rights of the mentally ill defendant? How do we protect society and, specifically, innocent victims from people like Jackson? He is, it is not to be forgotten, a man neither deterred by the threat of punishment nor guided by a moral compass that even remotely resembles normalcy.

The progress of Jackson's mental illness has been

well charted but its origins remain a scientific mystery, although great progress toward its control through drug therapies has been achieved. A PBS *Frontline* documentary in 1990, titled "Broken Minds," referred to the "enigma" of schizophrenia. Paul McHugh, M.D., of Johns Hopkins Hospital, said, "The whole capacity of the individual to relate to the world has been devastated by the illness, and we don't understand why."

There is no doubt that Arthur Jackson's craziness is deeply imbedded. That everyone is best served if he remains safely confined is indisputable. Law, politics, and public policy, however, have thus far impeded a satisfactory, lasting solution.

This book is possible because a number of people generously provided time to discuss in detail their involvement with Jackson. The authors particularly express their gratitude to Mrs. Valerie Howard of London; Los Angeles County prosecutors Susan Gruber and William Hodgman; Los Angeles Municipal Court Judge Michael Knight; defense attorneys Steven Moyer and Norman Kava; Los Angeles County District Attorney Senior Investigator Dennis Stults; Detective Chief Inspector Douglas Harrison of Scotland Yard, now retired; former Los Angeles County District Attorney Ira Reiner; juror Geraldine Wolfe; and Inspector David Smith of the Aberdeen police; and to Dorothy Harris for suggesting the title.

Arthur Jackson, even in the mental byways of his schizophrenia, remembers in exacting detail his travels and experiences, although his perspective is skewed. Hundreds of pages of Jackson's handwritten notes, diaries, and letters, plus court, medical, and law enforcement documents, fill out a sad record of this man's life and of the harmful effects he has had on others.

An extensive record of trial transcripts and documents from both law enforcement and medical agencies was used in the research. Many of the observations in the book are derived from Dr. Markman's examinations of, and interviews with, Arthur Jackson. These encounters span an eleven-year period, beginning shortly after Jackson's arrest for attacking Saldana. While Saldana, truly an innocent victim of a madman, declined to be interviewed, her security consultant, Gavin de Becker, did respond to some inquiries from Dr. Markman, clarifying some positions taken by him and his client. The authors are indebted to Robert Shuman, their editor at William Morrow, for his caring and expert work on the manuscript.

CHAPTER ONE

|❚❚❚❚|

Aberdeen

The seeds of doom regarding the chartered nature of my fate were planted on the day I was born. I assume that I was appointed by Karma to serve in the capacity of a ransom for the redemption of souls, the final installment of the ransom being paid on the night I die in "D" block at Alcatraz, or in the gas chamber at San Quentin.

—FROM THE DIARY OF ARTHUR JACKSON, 1980

Aberdeen, Scotland is an ancient place lying at the foot of the Grampian Mountains, "approached along the top of rugged sea-cliffs by a route once guarded by Dunnottar Castle," according to Henry W. Meikle, "His Majesty's Historiographer in Scotland." The harbor has a rich history as a shelter for fishing boats, whose crews navigate out into the North Sea searching for catches of whitefish. Many of the city's finest buildings are strong constructions of locally quarried "pale granite." This is a city of institutions enriched by tradition. The university was founded nearly five hundred years ago and its library established not long afterward. The establishment of Aberdeen Hospital

5

with six beds in 1742, Meikle wrote, "helped mark the start of public medicine in Great Britain."

Such heritage would leave an imprint on Arthur Jackson, born in Aberdeen on August 28, 1935. As a son of this city, he would dabble in its history and develop an attachment to its old places. The truth is, though, that he would always be a stranger to others there.

Jackson is a schizophrenic, an heir to lifelong mental illness as a member of an emotionally troubled and psychologically disturbed family. His psychological makeup was probably volatile from the beginning of his life because of the presence of a genetic component predisposing him to schizophrenia. Medical researchers now believe that the origins of this mental disease are, in part, transmitted by the body's genes, the "blueprint" for all development. Schizophrenia, however, still holds many mysteries for science to solve, and Jackson's life is an exhibition of the disease's most troubling enigmas. Schizophrenia affects people in varying degrees of intensity, driving a few to violence. Arthur Jackson would be one of those few so affected in the most extreme fashion.

Enough is known of the illness to understand that the world around the schizophrenic can greatly affect the extent of the disease's development in an individual. Jackson's parents provided neither affectionate nurturing nor a steady course for him as he grew older. This inadequate parenting allowed no strengthening of his weak mental foundation. From birth, Arthur Jackson was a child whose potential for adaptive qualities was limited because of the schizophrenia. Without positive parental interaction, there was virtually no chance for any normal psychological growth within him. The most significant ill effect of his family situation was that Jackson was never able to develop a strong ego that would provide him with a sense of emotional security and positive identity.

His father, James Jackson, was an alcoholic whose

occupations were variously listed as paper packer and laborer. He was an absentee parent who divorced his wife in 1944, when Arthur was nine years old, after thirteen years of marriage. James Jackson was apparently a benign character whose skill-less parenting consisted largely of ignoring his son. Before the divorce, he might be seen leaning against a wall of the family apartment playing the violin quite expertly even though drunk. "That's my father," Jackson said to a grammar-school friend making his first visit to the Jackson home.

After moving away from his wife and son, the senior Jackson sought treatment for his alcoholism at the Royal Aberdeen Mental Hospital. The effort at rehabilitation failed. Thereafter, he maintained limited contact with Arthur and provided no financial support for the boy or his mother. Arthur Jackson would, nonetheless, later remember his father with a certain fondness, saying, "I suppose he couldn't help taking a drink and I still quite like him."

Jackson never knew his sister, a year younger, who was confined all of her life to the Woodlands Institution for Mental Defectives near Aberdeen. She had been diagnosed as a "congenital idiot," a phrase then used to medically describe a person retarded from birth, although such terminology is now dated. Unless there had been a significant misdiagnosis, this meant that Jackson's sister either was born with brain damage or suffered brain damage during birth. There is also the possibility that she was an autistic child. "Idiot" was then the medically accepted term for the severest degree of retardation, a condition today labeled as "profound." As a boy, Jackson's limited understanding of his sister's condition caused him worry about his own potential mental problems, adding another aggravating element to his predisposition for abnormal self-absorption and concentration on personal defects, real or imagined.

Jackson's mother, Jean, who was thirty-two years old when Arthur was born, displayed characteristics of schizophrenia but was never diagnosed or treated by her doctors. She lived on the fringes of normalcy, subsisting on government welfare payments and maintaining few relationships with others. She appears to have been a pathologically self-centered person, overwhelmed by the demands of marriage and motherhood, and emotionally ill equipped to cope with them. Because she was undoubtedly someone preoccupied with her own difficulties, her ability to relate to or communicate with others was severely impaired. Her son's ego development was negatively affected because she was a person more likely only to "take" from a relationship, unable to give nurturing in return. In Arthur Jackson's case, the psychological damage was so great that, eventually, he would deteriorate to the point where he would be unable to differentiate between the fantasy erupting from his unconscious and the reality of the world around him.

A mentally disturbed mother can promote normal development in a child, provided that she offers continual emotional support, such as touching and tenderness. Jean Jackson appears to have been a woman who maintained a "global withdrawal" from those around her. Still, Jackson would one day tell doctors that he was fond of her despite their frequent arguments.

Arthur Jackson grew up in Aberdeen's public housing projects. When he was five years old, he lived temporarily in the city's poorhouse while his mother was being treated at the Woodend Hospital pneumonia ward. The same situation of displacement for Jackson arose the following year when his mother was treated for another physical illness at Central School Hospital.

Jean Jackson moved periodically, once when the slum buildings in her neighborhood were cleared to make way for new public housing. As a result of this transience, Arthur changed schools frequently. By the time he dropped out of school permanently at age fourteen, not yet finished with eighth grade, he had attended nine different ones. When he was older he said, "I have often wondered why we moved about so much. I think that is why my education is so poor."

Robert Anderson, a boyhood friend who grew up to become an Aberdeen jeweler, recalled that Jackson was largely "shunned by the other children." Jackson never even mentioned to Anderson that he had a sister. As the two boys grew older, Anderson recognized that Jackson was strange, but felt that he "made up for it in other ways. He was brilliant artistically." The young Arthur Jackson appreciated things of beauty, and developed a special interest in historic architecture.

When Jackson was eleven, he moved in with his maternal grandmother in Aberdeen so that he could attend a school near her home. One of his hobbies about this time was sketching ancient Scottish and English castles. He studied photographs in books at the library to use as guides for his artwork.

He did have some childhood acquaintances and accompanied them on outings. He later wrote that as a ten-year-old, he would spend a typical Aberdeen weekend at the movies. His diary records with precision one particular weekend. Friday night he went to the Playhouse, a city movie theater, and watched a Don Ameche film, *That Night in Rio*. On Saturday he was at the "Mickey Mouse Club" at the Odeon, another movie theater, watching popular serials including *Hopalong Cassidy* and *Flash Gordon*. During intermission the children participated in a community songfest. One popular vocal was "This Is the Army, Mr. Jones."

From time to time Jackson expressed some affection for others, although it always took on an unusual cast. He later described one such relationship in his diary:

Fiona, who was the first love in my life. She arrived at Ashley Road School, Aberdeen, Scotland, on January 9, 1946. Born in Quebec, she spent some time in the eastern United States before coming to Britain at the end of the war. Was there a karmic reason as to why Fiona had been destined to have such an emotional impact on my life (love at first sight) on that January morning she walked into my classroom . . . my dream of love failed. Not that we didn't try. It was cruel fate. Was there also a voodoo curse which would jinx all future love relationships in my life, connected with my having unwittingly caused Fiona's doll to become decomposed by leaving it out all night in the back garden of her house at 32 Fountainhall Road, Aberdeen, (circa autumn 1947) with the result that the damp morning air destroyed its fibre? Did my personality begin deteriorating from then onwards, or was I, like I said earlier, doomed from the day I was born?

As a younger child he received good grades in school and was not perceived by teachers as particularly unusual. His schizophrenia would not have produced noticeable symptoms when he was still a boy. Later in elementary school he scored in the mid-eighties on an IQ test, which placed him on the low end of normal. The repeated moving, creating a lack of consistency and stability in his life, explains the inferior testing scores.

In fact, Jackson's innate intelligence is high, but his mental disease blocked normal learning performance as he grew older, though his mental disorder does not directly diminish the capability of his intellect. Memory, mathematical skills, knowledge of current events, and other strengths of the mind are generally unaffected by schizophrenia.

He wasn't getting proper guidance at home, however, and the frequent school changes left little opportunity for teachers to have a lasting, positive impact. Thus, at an early age, Arthur Jackson was already slipping through society's safety nets.

Had Jackson had a different boyhood in a less dysfunctional family, or more constant contact with other stabilizing forces, there is the possibility that his life would have taken another, more acceptable course and his behavior would not have become totally guided by mental instability. His idiosyncratic thinking might not have evolved to the degree that it did. With guidance, his energies might have been productively focused on art, the theater, or writing, creative ventures for which he showed both interest and talent.

Jackson was fascinated with the United States and its popular culture. When he was about eleven years old he superimposed a U.S. map over an Aberdeen city map, memorizing the details of state lines and their congruence with city streets and landmarks. He would then, from memory, announce to acquaintances that when crossing a particular Aberdeen street he was actually going from "Kansas to Nebraska" or whatever geographical substitution his revised map of Aberdeen revealed to him. One person who saw this map described it as "beautiful. He was very meticulous in the way he would write and the entire map was beautifully engraved."

As he grew older, his prolific writings became more florid and excessively detailed, using a richness of language that was sometimes sophisticated, although certainly unusual because of its emphasis on his obsessions. The prose is sometimes advanced in its grammar and vocabulary, but the content always descends into the convolutions of his fantasies.

When he was young, he was capable of some normal accomplishment. In eighth grade, he successfully directed a school play. When he was a little older he conducted a city-wide campaign to save an old and architecturally important Aberdeen church from demolition. His boyhood friend, Anderson, recalled that Jackson demonstrated a number of "positive traits" before the schizophrenia took hold.

Once the direction of a severe mental illness is estab-

lished, however, usually in preadolescent years in cases
of schizophrenia, little can be done to change the mental damage inflicted to that point. Proper therapy might
keep the malady under control, but the illness cannot
be reversed or eliminated.

Typical of the disease, Jackson's schizophrenia began
to show symptoms when he was about fifteen years old.
He became unusually preoccupied with masturbation,
which he had been practicing for about a year and
which he believed had already ruined his life by destroying his character. He had picked up this notion
from reading articles about such sexual behavior, perhaps in religious tracts. He became abnormally obsessed with this issue. This was an early, significant
sign of his mental deterioration. Concern over such activity is normal for teenage boys, but there is a delinea-
tion between normalcy and a descent into debilitating
abnormality. Anxiety from any cause can be a positive
symptom if it motivates someone to function at his or
her best. At the other extreme, anxiety results in dysfunction by freezing someone into obsessional preoccupation.

Jackson unquestionably crossed the line into abnormality. In most young males, concern about excessive
sexual exploration is self-limiting. In Arthur Jackson,
such worry became all-consuming, controlling almost
all of his waking thoughts as he looked for magical
"cures." He effectively converted his sexual preoccupation into an illness of its own.

He perceived this practice of self-gratification as a
deficiency in his character, and he spent his time trying
to find ways to improve himself. He thought he could
overcome such moral and physical "imperfection" by
making dramatic changes in his life. He had always
been a nonsocializing outsider in school. "To force myself to mix with people," he explained in his diary, he
joined a youth club. Jackson, though, lacking initiative
and self-confidence, found this new attempt at interac-

tion with others dissatisfying. He went to dances but did not find them pleasurable. His experiment failed and he moved on to a series of other attempts at personal growth. He joined a bodybuilding class. He does not record in his diary whether he pursued this with any diligence, but it is evident that he soon abandoned that activity for another. He diagnosed himself as having an "inferiority complex" and purchased a mailorder self-improvement course that promised to build self-esteem through a special diet and advice pamphlets. Nothing Jackson tried altered his deep-rooted negative self-image.

As a teenager, Jackson held a variety of jobs, including that of a messenger. He was usually fired for poor performance or an inability to get along with his fellow workers. His first job was apparently as a busboy at Aberdeen's Braemar Hotel and lasted only three days. On all of his jobs he imagined that fellow workers laughed at him and deliberately tried to torment him. While it may be true that he was the butt of some teasing, his illness-diminished self-esteem would have led him to react to whatever may have been said much more intensely than a normal adolescent would have. Also, a schizophrenic can presume that highly personal meaning is hidden in the outwardly neutral comments of others.

Jackson was seventeen years old in the summer of 1952 when he went to his family doctor, identified in surviving records only by his last name, Pollock. Jackson was convinced that he had discovered a cure for his troubled emotional existence, telling the physician that he wanted to be castrated. "I feel that the scrotum operation is the only thing left. It is the only thing which would purify my mind," he said. He further hoped that surgeons would "scrape the dirt off my brain." Jackson was not speaking metaphorically.

Aware that his patient's problems were probably entirely psychological, the doctor sought to assess the ex-

tent of Jackson's self-understanding. He asked the boy
why he thought he couldn't hold a job. Jackson answered vaguely, shrugging his shoulders, "giving the
impression that there was no reason at all," the doctor concluded.

A few months later, on October 14, encouraged to
do so by Dr. Pollock, Jackson went to the psychiatric
clinic at the Aberdeen Royal Infirmary. The seriousness
of his condition was evident, and he was advised to
seek treatment at a residential mental institution.

Kingseat Hospital, one of two major mental facilities
serving Aberdeen, is fifteen miles and a forty-minute
bus ride north into the beautiful and serene countryside.
Three days after his examination at the Royal Infirmary,
Jackson arrived at the multibuilding facility of one
thousand beds, which sprawls over pleasant grounds.
Kingseat is a tranquil, rural place where patients live
in dormitory-style buildings. This institution, however,
would be anything but soothing for Jackson, who would
encounter psychiatric treatment apparently administered
with conscientiousness but better left to another era of
medicine.

In his entrance forms, Jackson listed his occupation
as an ironmongery (ironware) shop assistant, although
there is no other record indicating that he actually had
ever held such a job. He classified his religion as Prot-
estant. Then he signed a document that read:

> I hereby request to be admitted to Kingseat
> Mental Hospital, Newmacher, as a Voluntary Pa-
> tient, and understand that I may leave the Hospital
> upon giving you three days' clear notice. I under-
> take to leave the Mental Hospital when requested
> to do so.
>
> I also consent to electrical, insulin or other
> method of treatment which may be thought neces-
> sary by the Medical Staff of the Hospital.
>
> I understand that an assurance has not been

given that the treatment will be administered by a particular Practitioner.

Entrance to the public hospital was not allowed without review and approval by the commissioner for the General Board of Control in Edinburgh. This supervision was to ensure that the prospective patient's admittance was, indeed, truly voluntary, and not a violation of Jackson's right not to be unjustly committed against his will.

A physical examination showed that Jackson was fit. He weighed 159 pounds and his medical history revealed that he had contracted only the usual childhood diseases. He had not previously been diagnosed as having any specific psychiatric illness. The doctor filling out the hospital admission form noted that Jackson was neither suicidal nor dangerous to others.

Jackson's primary complaint to Kingseat Hospital doctors, as he had told his family physician that summer, concerned his masturbation. "It is sapping my mental strength," he said during one of the first consultations. This belief was a widespread myth of common wisdom, but Jackson was more susceptible than normally developing boys to succumbing to the notion that he could be creating actual, debilitating weaknesses within himself.

A psychiatrist wrote of Jackson that day, "He regards the masturbation as being some form of wasting disease and feels that up to now it has wrecked his life. He says that as a result of this he feels inferior to other people in all respects and that it is gradually ruining his mind. The onset of his worry and preoccupation over this matter was occasioned by reading some articles about the subject from which he gained the impression that excessive masturbation resulted in weakness of will and character and often resulted in complete ruination of life."

Jackson allowed that he had attempted to engage in

social activities with girls, but insisted he had no intention of any "serious" interaction with females. He announced proudly to the psychiatrist that he did not "smoke, drink, or go with women. It is the only way that I can purify myself." He said that he had had "minor" homosexual experiences with other boys when he was twelve years old.

The doctors described Jackson as "garrulous," a young man who talked about stage work and proposed that after leaving the hospital he might go to London to seek a career in the theater. Asked why he was attracted to such work, he replied, "I don't know, but I just feel there is more of a force towards that within me."

"The patient would seem quite attached to the mother," a hospital psychiatrist noted.

Jackson seemed to be aware to some degree that his psychological disturbances were abnormal and that he needed treatment. He could not, however, understand precisely what was wrong. He expressed his worry that he may have been afflicted with the same mental disorder as his younger sister, although he still had little knowledge or understanding of what that was.

He did not appear tense or anxious during his preliminary interview with a psychiatrist, but was absolutely unsmiling throughout their conversation. "The boy is a heavy, serious looking youth, his brows puckered and his hair close cropped," the examining physician wrote. The doctor thought that Jackson "gave the impression of carrying the world's worries upon his shoulders. . . . He discussed his complaints without any embarrassment whatsoever and is astonishingly frank." Another psychiatrist wrote that although Jackson did not appear depressed, he found "the hopelessness of his utterances" remarkable. Jackson, for example, said that "in every respect" he felt inferior to other people. His comments to Kingseat doctors displayed distinct, hallmark signals of schizophrenia, particularly because of the great dissimilarity between his thoughts and the emotions that accompanied them.

The initial prognosis was not positive. At the end of the admission document, a psychiatrist wrote, ''The diagnosis in this case is thought to be that of schizophrenia simplex. Owing to the grossly inadequate prepsychotic personality the outlook with treatment is poor.'' In the initial examinations, Kingseat psychiatrists found no evidence of hallucination or ''ideas of influence.'' Sometimes also referred to as ''ideas of reference,'' this is an archaic term for a process called *projection*, when a patient attributes to others thoughts or feelings he himself has imagined. The process also involves a patient attributing personal significance to the neutral remarks of others. While the Kingseat doctors did not observe this in their initial sessions, such patterns of thinking have been present throughout Jackson's life and eventually would be a major psychotic catalyst for the imagined relationships that would be at the core of the tragedies to come.

Schizophrenia is a term known to most people but widely misused and misunderstood. Commonly, the disease is confused with multiple-personality condition, an entirely different disorder. Schizophrenia is a form of psychosis, a condition that embraces several major mental illnesses in which an individual's emotional, behavioral, or thought functions are significantly distorted. A psychotic can perceive the world around him or her in a distorted way and still behave in a relatively normal fashion. A psychotic may also act abnormally in response to the misperceptions.

The normal processes of thinking and retention of memory in the human brain are miraculous phenomena. When they falter, as in schizophrenia, the resulting distortions are even more mysterious to understand. There are various forms of schizophrenia, including catatonic, disorganized, and paranoid. For example, a paranoid individual is highly suspicious and jealous without adequate cause and can act on those delusions. A delusion is a misinterpretation of events in one's environment, such as witnessing two unknown people whispering to each other and concluding that they are plotting to kill you.

Hallucinations are the severest form of mental decompensation in schizophrenia and can be auditory, visual, tactile, or olfactory. Someone who is hallucinating is experiencing a perception without a stimulus, such as hearing words being spoken when the room is actually silent, or seeing bugs or animals when nothing is there.

Drugs, including amphetamines, cocaine, LSD, and PCP, can bring on symptoms indistinguishable from schizophrenia when the chemical agents affect the central nervous system. As some of these compounds were developed in the 1960s, researchers hoped that by studying drug-induced symptoms in subjects they might reach a better understanding of schizophrenia, but this goal has not yet been accomplished.

Schizophrenia marks the failure of an individual to adapt to the stresses that confront every human being in daily life. The weaker one's ego, the more stressful simple events in life become. In the schizophrenic, having to get up, get dressed, and catch a bus may be overwhelming, producing other symptoms to the point that the individual is unable to function.

This syndrome was initially called *dementia praecox*, a phrase developed by the pioneering psychiatrist Emil Kraeplin in 1896. *Dementia* defined a chronic brain disorder and *praecox* referred to preadolescence. About 1911, another member of the first schools of psychiatry, Eugen Bleuler, introduced the term *schizophrenia*, which, literally translated, means "split-mindedness." Bleuler refined the method of diagnosing schizophrenia by classifying the malady as a mental disease that combines four hallmark symptoms, evolving prior to puberty and leading to a chronic psychological deterioration over one's life. Bleuler's diagnostic standard continues to be used by psychiatrists today. He established a means of identifying schizophrenia's existence in his patients by determining whether the "four A's" were present: loose association, autism, ambivalence, and affect disruption.

Loose association, the benchmark thought disorder of schizophrenia, means that the patient makes bizarre connections between things that normal people do not link, pairing disparate objects of his imagination, such as in Jackson's concern that his masturbation was a result of dirt physically adhering to his brain. Jackson's thought process transformed the metaphorical "dirty mind" into an actuality.

Autism, directly related to loose association, defines the mind's self-protective phenomena of turning its focus inward egocentrically while at the same time avoiding as much emotional contact as possible with other human beings. The condition allows the schizophrenic to avoid the paralyzing anxiety arising out of normal social contact. This is quite different from individuals who might be termed "loners," those who merely have difficulty relating to others and feel uncomfortable in social situations. An autistic person goes a step beyond and is sufficiently withdrawn to be totally preoccupied with his internal thought process, seeming to daydream for most of his waking hours.

Ambivalence is something everyone feels at one time or another. In a schizophrenic it is the complete inability to tolerate opposite feelings simultaneously toward the same object. The average person can have a range of feelings toward someone, but the schizophrenic cannot love and hate at the same time. If both feelings are tugging at the schizophrenic mind, the result is even further mental deterioration, producing a greater clinical decompensation.

Affect disruption occurs when the emotional reaction of a person relates abnormally to a thought. A death, which would routinely evoke sadness in a normal person, can, for example, elicit laughter, a lack of concern, or inappropriate expressions of joy in a schizophrenic. The posture the schizophrenic takes is totally divorced from the event itself.

While knowledge is still limited about schizophrenia's makeup, scientists believe that the genetic component causes an alteration in the brain's chemistry, resulting in abnormal reactions in the organ's "circuitry." For unknown reasons, the symptoms suffered by schizophrenics do vary from patient to patient.

The best estimates available indicate that approximately 1 to 2 percent of the total world population suffers from the disease. In the United States, for example, with a population of about 258 million people, some 2.5 to 5 million individuals are schizophrenic. A hereditary link has been well documented by statistical analyses of families. When one parent is schizophrenic, the odds that a child will develop the disease appears to be about 16 percent, which is a significantly higher risk factor than for children of nonschizophrenic parents. Recent studies indicate that when both parents are afflicted the chance that the children of that union will also develop schizophrenia rises to about 54 percent. Jackson's familial background apparently predestined him to the condition. Because mental illness in his family also resulted in less than adequate parenting for him, opportunities to check the ravages of the disease were lost. Of course, the emergence of schizophrenia does not mean the parents have failed.

In the early 1950s, in the United States at least, harsh methods of treatment for schizophrenia were being replaced by newly developed and effective drugs. Antipsychotic drug therapies were coming into wide use in the United States. At Kingseat Hospital, where the newest methods had not yet been introduced, Jackson underwent intensive and sometimes primitive treatment consisting of numerous physician-induced insulin comas, electroshock therapy, and some limited administration of medications.

Insulin coma treatment, later replaced by electric shock treatment, was developed in the early 1930s when doctors noted that schizophrenics psychologically improved after a coma. The purpose of artificially inducing coma in a person was to create an electrical disturbance in the brain by reducing the patient's blood sugar to a level that alters brain electrical activity. The dynamics of disrupting the electrical circuits in the brain in this manner are similar to those found in naturally induced seizures. The experience is dramatic, lasting several hours. The theory underpinning the procedure postulated that the violent upset to the body's rhythms disorganized the patient's crazy thinking, which led to the creation of a more rational thought process.

Shock treatments, then administered with little control other than physical restraint by hospital attendants, could produce potentially harmful side effects. A patient's convulsions could be strong enough to fracture bones. Sometimes as many as four strong hospital aides would be required to hold a patient down during treatment. Patients were also restrained by straitjackets or tied down with sheets. Eventually a muscle-paralyzing agent called Anectine, related to curare, would be used to prevent injuries by minimizing body movement during the procedure. This antidote to one of the most dangerous side effects, however, wasn't used until after the time Jackson was at Kingseat.

The shock treatments Jackson received would likely have been sufficiently traumatic and mentally disruptive to him so that he probably had no conscious memory of them immediately afterward. He might also have lost his memory of events just prior to the treatments, a common phenomenon. In most cases, though, the memory slowly returns. With insulin coma, the several-hour period in which the patient sinks into a hypoglycemic state, characterized by a sometimes terrifying feeling of losing control, is particularly unpleasant.

Within five days of his admission to Kingseat, Jackson was receiving almost daily treatments, a rather quick start of procedures so serious in nature. Indeed, this is testament to the extent of psychological disturbance that hospital staff members must have witnessed in their new patient, particularly evidenced by his bizarre comments. "I would not marry," he told a psychiatrist quite seriously, because "you know yourself that marriage leads to TB."

Jackson undoubtedly found the Kingseat experience extremely unpleasant, fortifying his resolve to end it. Being a teenager surrounded by crazy adults in a hospital setting was certainly disconcerting. Although he had expressed bizarre desires, he would not have viewed himself as so severely disturbed as his fellow patients. Even so, he admitted himself to Kingseat because every psychiatrically disturbed individual embodies some traits of normalcy, no matter how small, that produce awareness of the illness present within. Jackson's schizophrenic preoccupations were a major part of his life and he recognized that he was different from others. This drove him to seek a cure for his troubles and gave him a willingness to put himself in the hands of doctors who might alter his future, which he viewed as bleak.

He viewed medical science as a means of providing solutions to his problems as he saw them. For a time he probably acquiesced to the harsh shock treatments administered by hospital physicians because he thought that they were merely doing what he had previously requested of his family doctor, actually ridding his brain of real debris. In time, though, he grew weary of the daily physical punishment and mental confusion to which he was subjected by the treatments.

Why doctors at Kingseat used both insulin and electric shock on Jackson is unknown. By the early 1950s insulin coma was rarely administered in American hospitals. The more than fifty comas induced in Jackson is a staggering figure. Jackson's hospital records fill page after page, documenting in cold numbers an extraordinary record of intensive treatment. The records suggest that doctors hardly had an opportunity to properly evaluate whether their routine was producing improvement in their patient. A determination of whether a shock-treatment patient has improved cannot be made until the procedures are stopped for a time. Medical records indicate that Jackson's treatments were virtually continuous.

A review of Jackson's therapy provides a glaring example of the difference between psychiatric procedure in the United States and in Great Britain at the time. The psychoanalytic teachings of Sigmund Freud played a major role in the understanding of psychiatric illness in the United States. In Great Britain, the psychoanalytic movement was relatively small, and physical therapies were seen as the primary means to treat major mental disorders.

Certainly, a seventeen-year-old with the beginning symptoms of schizophrenia entering a mental institution today in either the United States or Great Britain receives treatment far different from what Jackson was subjected to then.

Modern therapy begins with a neuroleptic, an antipsychotic tranquilizer. Such drugs are effective in bringing schizophrenic symptoms under control by acting as antianxiety agents. Anxiety is the foundation for all psychiatric symptoms and illnesses. In the majority of people, the anxiety level stays within a normal range and allows an individual to achieve an acceptable solution to the problem causing the tension; it might heighten concentration when answering test questions, for instance.

Other psychiatric symptoms form when, for various reasons, anxiety breaks through those boundaries of normalcy. Anxiety is the direct result of a confrontation between the ego and an individual's environment or unconscious mind. It is a condition that cannot be long-standing or free-floating. As an example, an individual might have an unconscious thought that spontaneously springs into his awareness, such as wanting to kill a parent. If the anxiety this thought produces is not adequately resolved, a symptom will substitute, perhaps as a compulsion not to step on any cracks in the sidewalk because the person has remembered the childhood saying "Step on a crack, break your mother's back." The substitute symptoms create dysfunction when the person's waking hours are preoccupied with them.

Research has also shown that behavior is controlled by the biochemical reactions of neurotransmitters in the brain, such as noradrenalin, serotonin, and dopamine. Antipsychotic tranquilizers are now known to affect the concentrations and interrelationships of these substances.

One of the most widely used neuroleptics today continues to be Thorazine (generically chlorpromazine and called Largactil in Great Britain), one of the earliest drugs of this kind to be marketed, and introduced in the United States in 1954. This drug, first developed by a French pharmaceutical company, and which acts on the central nervous system, was not yet available to Jackson's Scottish doctors when he was at Kingseat. Use of the drug for treating psychiatric illness was pioneered by an American pharmaceutical company, SmithKline and French Laboratories, and its use in the United States was a step ahead of the rest of the world. Initially, the drug was quite expensive, which would have hindered its distribution. Additionally, innovative medical knowledge, although available in technical literature, was not immediately accepted outside its area of origin, and advances in U.S. psychiatry would not necessarily have been accepted by doctors in Great Britain.

Uncomfortable and debilitating side effects are limiting factors to wonder drugs like Thorazine. Commonly they can be nuisances to the patient, and can include blurred vision, muscle stiffness, and tremors. Sometimes, though, they can be so debilitating, such as when the drug induces a zombielike state, that a patient will refuse to take the medication.

It is reasonable to believe that properly administered drugs would have checked, but not cured, the teenage Jackson's deepening schizophrenia. He followed a classic pattern. Unchecked, the disease blossoms. If, however, the craziness can be curbed to some degree through medication and the patient begins to act in a relatively normal fashion, a certain amount of positive mental conditioning takes place over time, reaching a point when medication can be stopped. A common example of this process occurs when a person sets an alarm clock to wake up earlier than usual in the morning. In time, an individual's internal body clock causes awakening before the alarm goes off. The substitution of normal behavior for psychotic behavior can have a similar effect on the functioning of a schizophrenic.

Over the months that Jackson received treatment at Kingseat, there was little or no indication of sustained improvement. At times he became violent and impulsive, sometimes breaking windows. He was unable to tell doctors why he acted destructively.

Not surprisingly, given the extreme discomfort of the therapy, Jackson tried to run away. The hospital log of January 10, 1953, recounts that "at about 12.20 P.M. he suddenly jumped out of his chair, and, head down, charged out of south ward passage-way onto the institutional grounds." He slipped and fell on the lawn, giving a hospital aide enough time to catch up and restrain him. After being returned to his ward, he exhibited "extreme tension . . . [and] . . . auditorily hallucinated." Such episodes led to Jackson's designation as a "dangerous patient."

Typical was the afternoon of February 25, 1953, during his nineteenth week at the hospital. When he became uncontrollable, hospital aides forcefully restrained him while a doctor injected him with amobarbitol, then a new, quick-acting sedative being used in clinical trials. Hospital records state that "[Jackson] became quieter and more manageable but still auditorily hallucinated, bewildered by his surroundings and showing marked evidence of thought disturbance."

"What sort of hospital is this?" he asked a doctor after the sedative took effect. "How long have I been here? I must have been pretty bad!"

Doctors believed that their patient's disorientation may have been a side effect of "considerable amounts" of electroconvulsive therapy, administered in an attempt to decrease his anxiety. Through his continued preoccupation with sexual problems, "to a morbid and pathological degree," the doctors could see that Jackson's underlying anxiety was persisting and was coupled with signs of increasing paranoia.

The doctors tried to better understand Jackson by analyzing the writing he did during his hospital stay. His works were incoherent, poorly spelled treatises:

> I can shut aurotoc [sic] when in a dream even. But previously my [sleep willpower] of checking it "maracursly" has dropped on wet dreams because lately my mind has been constantly obsessed by sex ideas and general depression. . . . I would let myself down—and into a horrible mental obsession if I was to commit self-abuse, so I avoid it—because masturbation is a sure thing to lead to mental weakness . . . so future sex life is half planned and half mystery to me.

Whether doctors were taking the right course with this patient, and would eventually have succeeded in guiding him toward some normalcy, became a moot point when Jackson's mother intervened.

Throughout her son's stay at Kingseat, Jean Jackson had caused difficulty for hospital staff. Several times on visiting days she claimed to supervisors that her son had been "beaten up by the nursing staff." Her charges were investigated and reported to be groundless, presumably the creation of her own mental disturbances rather than the product of actual observations by her. A Kingseat psychiatrist wrote that "she has been seen several times on visiting days when she produced the most bizarre and unrealistic claims. . . . The opinion of the senior psychiatrists who saw her was that she herself was mentally unwell and she certainly had no insight into her son's psychotic behavior."

Then, on March 4, four and a half months after her son had entered the hospital, she arrived at the institution and insisted to him that he leave. Doctors tried to persuade her to agree to his "certification," which would have allowed him to be confined against his will, but she was adamantly opposed to that. The doctors realized that she was also mentally disturbed, and reasoning with her was not possible. They noted in Jackson's file after she left that she had exhibited "even less insight than the patient."

Jean Jackson demanded that Arthur fill out the requisite form giving the hospital advance formal notice of his departure, to take place three days later.

On March 7, Jackson, who was legally free to leave no matter what the doctors believed was best for him, walked away from Kingseat. The doctors there never saw him again as a patient. Jackson returned to live with his mother in a city-subsidized apartment. Kingseat psychiatrists decided not to attempt any follow-up—to encourage Jackson to return for more treatment—because of the "lack of cooperation from this family."

Three days after his hospital departure, Kingseat's deputy physician superintendent wrote to Dr. Pollock, Jackson's family physician, to report that "A full course of deep insulin therapy was commenced which, however, had no effect on the course of his illness and he deteriorated during that time.''

Jackson's hospital treatment was probably beneficial initially, even with the repeated shock treatments, which were begun almost immediately. A mental disorder usually evolves through the combination of external and internally created stress. In Jackson's case, external stresses included his difficulties in confronting peers, school problems, and the troubled relationships at home. Accordingly, a locked hospital unit is therapeutic not because it keeps the patient in but because it blocks the outside from reaching the patient. Regardless of whether a patient is given any other treatment, the hospitalization itself can effect a transient improvement.

True, lasting progress would have required long-term follow-up therapy to prevent further damage to Arthur Jackson's schizophrenically impaired thought process. Because of Jackson's aversion to further treatment, the years following his ill-advised release from Kingseat Hospital would be marked by his continuing mental deterioration.

In his writings he expressed the sense that the unusual emotional drives within him were inherited and concluded that he was neither responsible for them nor in control of them. As a teenager he had attempted to fight the inner drives, but as he approached his twenties he came to accept them more and more. He explained the turmoil he felt through his bizarre interpretation of the world around him. Most disturbing is that the pursuit of his delusions was too often accompanied by a surprising lack of awareness or concern on the part of those in contact with him, many of whom could have caused a more positive redirection of his life. Instead, as he grew older, the focus of his interests became increasingly bizarre, and intellectual curiosity was transformed into psychiatric obsession.

As a boy, Jackson had been interested in American

culture, and that fascination was concentrated on American movies. He went to Aberdeen's movie theaters regularly. Beginning in his teenage years, he would sit in the Aberdeen library, off in a secluded corner by himself, reading books about Hollywood, hour after hour.

Bits of film information are strangely incorporated into his often impenetrable logic. He weaves unrelated people, places, and events into complex relationships that convey deep, religious meaning only to himself. His reveries bubble and stew and spill out in interminable writings. His diaries cover the minutiae of his daily existence and the cosmic scope of his delusions. Unquestionably, he is a man propelled by strange forces within his psyche.

At the spiritual center of Jackson's ramblings is an American bank robber named Joseph Cretzer, who was killed by guards during an inmate-inspired riot in the federal penitentiary on San Francisco's Alcatraz Island on May 4, 1946.

Alcatraz was then the most notorious prison in the United States, perched ominously on a stone outcropping cut off from the city by the strong tidal currents running through San Francisco Bay. The country's most dangerous criminals were incarcerated on "the rock," a place legendarily invulnerable to escape, reached only by ferry, the dangerous waters presumably trapping even the strongest swimmer who might consider that route to freedom.

Jackson had just turned eleven when he first heard about the Alcatraz uprising. In September, a month after his birthday and about four months after the incident, Jackson and his mother were at the Odeon Cinema to see a rerun of a 1940 George Raft picture, *The House Across the Bay*. He later wrote:

> The scene which lingers in my memory the most is at the end of the film, where the principal

character in the story, played by George Raft, slowly sinks under the waves of San Francisco Bay—not far from Alcatraz, the lights of which are viewed through the night darkness—with a haunted look of death in his eyes.

A newsreel report about the Alcatraz revolt of the previous May accompanied the movie. One scene that was compelling to Jackson showed "all the cell doors on the upper tiers of 'D' block automatically sliding open at the press of a button."

The penitentiary images made enough of an impression on him that the fascination he had held for castles transformed itself into an interest in prisons. His study of French penal colonies, as well as U.S. and English prisons, he later wrote, "became more engrossing, almost to the point of fixation."

Three years after seeing the newsreel, which had referred only to unnamed convicts, Jackson learned about Cretzer when "I read a serialized narrative in a Sunday newspaper about ex-Warden James Johnston's stewardship at Alcatraz."

What triggered Arthur Jackson's obsession with Joseph Cretzer cannot be known. Learning of Cretzer's death was, however, an important psychological catalyst in Jackson's disease-distorted logic. He felt a commonality with the dead convict that was certainly not based on any reality. This illusion of a profound relationship with someone he never met became central to his being. His musings of a personal connection to Cretzer became the foundation of his mysterious mental tapestry, and eventually resulted in terror for others.

Jackson calculated that he had been "a 10-year-old, 6,000 miles away in Aberdeen, Scotland," attending the Saturday movie matinee during Cretzer's "countdown to death . . . in the tunnel at Alcatraz." He estimated the time at which "Cretzer went berserk and started shooting at the captive guards imprisoned inside cells 403 and 402 of 'C' block.'' He pinpointed the moment the convict had been shot to death by prison guards, so that he could compare it to his own activities at that precise time.

This matchup was important to him because he came to believe that details of Cretzer's life and death revealed his own destiny. He would later theorize in his diary that as a ten-year-old, ''symptoms of emotional maladjustment and psychic disturbance leading to personality disorder had already begun developing.'' He then observed that he had been ''too young to be aware that anything was wrong—living what seemed at the time, and in retrospect, a normal, more or less happy childhood. (They say ignorance is bliss, and it sure as hell was back then. . . .)''

He came to believe that somehow Cretzer's spirit had contacted him ''on an unconscious level,'' and later wrote:

> My theory propounds the possibility that Cretzer's soul must have had very urgent reasons to link up with someone still alive. Regarding the karmic factor, I can only assume that Cretzer and I knew each other in a previous life, most likely as Knights of the realm in medieval England.

He imagined that he and Cretzer had fought side by side at the pivotal Battle of Hastings in 1066. Psychiatrists and others would later learn from Jackson and his diaries that Jackson routinely ''discovered'' obscure connections between himself and others on whom his imagination focused. For example, Jackson thought it significant that both he and Cretzer had schoolteachers whose first name was Lillian. So, too, with other coincidences Jackson noted. Cretzer was part American Indian, and Jackson ''felt an attraction to an [Asian] Indian girl'' who was a grammar-school classmate. On the day the bank robber was killed at Alcatraz by prison guards, Jackson had gone to the movies with three brothers whose last name was Banks.

Thoughts of Cretzer were present throughout Jackson's teenage years, although he apparently did not mention his fixation on the bank robber to the psychiatrists at Kingseat Hospital.

Some months after his release from that mental institution, for reasons not documented, Jackson's mother sent him to live with relatives in Canada. Psychiatrists and investigators would later learn little about this interim period in his life. His eighteen months or so with family apparently passed uneventfully. For certain, though, his schizophrenia was, at best, only dormant during this time, possibly contained by a more normal day-to-day existence established by his relatives in contrast to the insecurity that shrouded his life in Aberdeen.

The dynamics of his disease did not allow him to follow routine for long. Cretzer, and all the madness his presence in Jackson's addled imagination personified, would again come to the forefront of Jackson's existence.

CHAPTER TWO

❘❚❚❚❘

America

Following a period of living with his relatives, Arthur Jackson became "restless," as he later described his feelings. In January 1955, in the midst of a Canadian winter, he decided to leave. Traveling by bus and carrying his British passport, he crossed the border into the United States without the slightest difficulty and traveled directly to New York City.

He obtained a department store stockroom job, which he did not keep for long, never even noting the store's name in his diary. The U.S. Immigration and Naturalization Service classified him as a resident alien, a designation that made him eligible for the military draft, although he was still a British citizen. Within a few months of his arrival, Jackson received his notice of induction into the United States Army. He was nineteen years old. A little more than two years had passed since his unwise departure from Kingseat Hospital in Aberdeen.

In preinduction examinations, government doctors either did not detect any mental problems or minimized what they observed. In hindsight, Jackson's ability to slip through this process, even though the army medical review was probably not comprehensive, is remarkable, but not necessarily attributable to the misfeasance of the examiners. Even when not in treatment and taking prescribed antipsychotic drugs, schizophrenics can, at times, function in a controlled manner. People untrained in medicine or psychology might not recognize some behavior as having a foundation of mental disorder.

There have been celebrated cases of mental deterioration going unnoticed. Howard Hughes, the wealthy industrialist who as a young man had also tried his hand at movie production in Hollywood, is one example of a well-known man whose mental illness was not recognized until his symptoms were painfully obvious and his entire existence had become a bizarre expression of his distorted thinking. His psychiatrically induced phobias and rituals are well documented in the biography *Empire*, written by Philadelphia journalists Donald L. Barlett and James B. Steele. The authors describe Hughes's complete isolation from others except for a few trusted aides. They recount his obsessions, such as his fear of germs, which, for example, led him to write elaborate and lengthy memos describing how a can of fruit was to be opened and to spend hours each day methodically wiping every square inch of his telephone with Kleenex.

Another example of a mentally ill public figure is James Forrestal, the distinguished secretary of defense in the Truman administration, who was gripped by a paranoid psychosis during a several-month period in which he met regularly with the President of the United States, fellow members of the Cabinet, and other important people in Washington. Forrestal didn't seek medical help in the early stages of his illness and came late to treatment which, had it been administered sooner, likely would have been beneficial. Through experience and training a psychiatrist would have noticed what others did not by being attuned to the nuances of an individual's sensitivity, suspiciousness, or abnormal emotional reaction to events. When Forrestal's symptoms had progressed to a great degree, he was finally admitted to the Bethesda Naval Hospital in nearby Maryland. Not long after, early one May morning in

1949, he committed suicide by jumping off the roof of the facility.

Jackson, typically, offered no information about his psychiatric history during his preinduction examination by army doctors. Mental patients do not often freely divulge their medical history when questioned about their backgrounds. He never mentioned his four and a half months in Kingseat Hospital or the troubling, obsessive, idiosyncratic thoughts that had flowed through his mind for years, such as his ruminations about Cretzer.

Jackson presumably was able to maintain a facade of normalcy during those military physicals. Mental disorders are not static conditions. They can modulate up and down. A person can appear extremely psychotic in the morning and by nightfall be able to carry on a rational conversation which had been beyond his reach just hours before. Because Jackson's symptoms had been evident to other doctors for years, his successful passage through the army entrance examinations is puzzling. Jackson's condition was so pronounced that even a physician not trained in psychiatry should, in a comprehensive review, have been able to notice the mental abnormality. In those years, however, army induction physicals were cursory, assembly-line exercises, and little emphasis was placed on looking for psychiatric conditions. Additionally, Jackson wanted to enter the army, which would have given him additional incentive to control his behavior. By remaining passive during the induction examination he drew little attention to himself. The less he talked, the lower the risk that others might observe symptoms of his mental disorder.

In Jackson's case, a government system of review created to solve problems, to prevent human disasters, was woefully inadequate. Jackson's mental illness, had it been properly diagnosed during the preinduction procedures, was pronounced enough to make him ineligible for military service. The proper diagnosis was not made. Jackson was sworn in as a U.S. Army private, ID number US 51 358 034.

Just as he was beginning his time in the army, an obsession that, at least to Jackson's conscious mind, had lain dormant for the previous six years was revived when he unexpectedly came upon a picture of Joseph Cretzer:

> . . . on Sunday morning, May 15th, 1955 . . . at Coney Island . . . we visited the "Chamber of Horrors" where . . . I set eyes on a photograph of Cretzer. He is shown lying side by side with Coy and Hubbard, on a slab inside the San Francisco morgue. This was the most significant stage in the hitherto dormant evolutive process. Now, an actual psychic impression had been made.

The deep emotion he felt at these revelatory moments was stored in his memory and brewed with other strange thoughts for decades. In this instance, Jackson saw a similarity between the photograph of Cretzer lying dead after being shot by prison guards and a death mask of the Egyptian King Tutankhamen, also on display in the amusement park exhibit. This comparison, he believed, infused this moment with even greater mystical meaning, in his last hours as a civilian before beginning his army basic training at Fort Dix in New Jersey.

Once on the military base, Jackson continued his futile attempt to conform to the world around him, but he was incapable of doing so. He rebelled against the authority of military discipline and consistently refused to follow directions. Finally, in August, he was given a special court-martial and convicted of insubordination for disobeying an officer's routine order. The root of his behavior, his schizophrenia, was still unrecognized by his military superiors. His contentious view of any authority figure arose from his distorted perception that commands from others were completely demeaning. A simple direction from a superior, a meaningless part of the day for other soldiers, could be viewed by Jackson as an assault on his dignity, part of a vast conspiracy to control him through what he deemed to be unfair persecution.

Jackson's disobedience was mistakenly viewed by superiors as an ordinary matter of discipline, easily corrected with punishment of the offender. He received a suspended six-month sentence in an army jail upon his court-martial conviction. His punishment was limited to a fifty-two-dollar-a-month deduction from his pay for several months. Then he was determined to be fit for duty and was returned to his unit to continue training.

The purpose of military performance ratings may rest more in satisfying a paper-oriented bureaucracy than in genuine evaluation. The likelihood is that in Jackson's case the records represent an inflated level of accomplishment. During basic training he received two conduct and efficiency ratings. On September 8, about three months after entering the military, his conduct was adjudged "satisfactory" and his efficiency rating was "excellent." On November 9, both his conduct and efficiency ratings were "excellent," and he was rated "skilled" as a "light weapons man." Since objective standards of firing range scores are used for the weapons ratings, he no doubt earned those designations. History's most famous example of a mentally disturbed man who became proficient with a gun through military training is Lee Harvey Oswald, whose Marine Corps marksmanship proved deadly in 1963 when he assassinated President John F. Kennedy in Dallas.

Less likely is that Jackson truly achieved excellence in conduct and overall efficiency, particularly considering his court-martial. In the absence of noticeably egregious behavior, and given Jackson's capability to exhibit periods of normalcy, training officers probably took the easy path of moving him along in order to meet personnel quotas. Given Jackson's mental instability, there is little surprise that the promise of his training review ratings was unmet when he began active duty. He couldn't sustain even a semblance of normalcy for long.

In November, he was sent to Germany to join other American troops stationed in Europe. Once there, problems erupted anew. Twice he underwent a disciplinary proceeding called an "Article 15," less severe than a court-martial. In no instance up to this point did there appear to be any insight on the part of army officers that Jackson's inability to conform to military regimentation was the result of a disturbed mental condition.

Instead, according to an army document, "All actions were the result of disrespect and not following orders." His problems, according to the rigid and narrow parameters of army thinking, were due to his "'individualism,' and his resistance, hostility, and unwillingness to follow orders."

Because of his poor duty performance, Jackson was transferred from platoon to platoon. His paranoia was stirred. He complained that others were "picking on me," and "harassing me." As was possibly the case in Aberdeen when he encountered problems on his teenage jobs, he might well have been the target of ridicule to some degree. Even more so than before, though, his markedly lower self-image would have led him to experience abnormal sensitivity to any negative comments directed at him, and his schizophrenia would have allowed his mind to effortlessly create the perception of disparagement against him that didn't exist at all.

His commanding officers, no doubt unschooled in detecting mental illness, variously described him as a "shirker," and an "individualist." One of Jackson's battery commanders wrote that Jackson "hasn't faintly resembled a soldier," complaining that the inductee never completed his share of work and never properly prepared for inspections.

Finally, some of Jackson's superiors came to recognize that Jackson was no mere disciplinary problem. And, facing another court-martial for disobeying orders from an officer, Jackson at last admitted to having had psychiatric treatment before entering the army.

Army doctors did a more complete search of his background. They sought information from medical sources in Aberdeen. On April 13, 1956, Dr. R.A.Y. Stewart, acting physician superintendent of Kingseat Hospital, responded to Capt. William B. Rudemiller, M.C., division neuropsychiatrist in the medical detachment of the 2nd Armored Division Artillery in Germany. In a two-page letter, Dr. Stewart recounted the disappointing five months Jackson had spent at Kingseat in the winter of 1952–53, concluding, "Though I have never seen the patient, it seems obvious from his records that he was suffering from an acute schizophrenic illness superimposed on a rather inadequate personality, handicapped by an unsatisfactory upbringing and poor personal environment."

With this information, Jackson's commanding officer finally concluded that this troubled soldier would be unable to continue satisfactorily in the military. He requested that Jackson be placed in a military hospital as a prerequisite to "elimination from service." On June 7, 1956, exactly a year after his induction, Jackson began treatment as an outpatient of Lt. Col. Donald V. Leddy at the U.S. Army Hospital, Landstuhl, Germany.

Army psychiatrists now correctly diagnosed Jackson as schizophrenic, describing his disease as "chronic, moderate, manifested by seriousness, preoccupation, withdrawal, autistic thinking, and lack of insight."

A battery of psychological tests, they said, supported their further conclusion, wrong as this part of the diagnosis was, that his schizophrenia was "largely in remission at this time." Their prediction for the future was accurate, though. The doctors concluded that "this man's contact with reality is tenuous and that it is questionable whether or not he will be able to finish out his tour of duty."

On June 18, Jackson was admitted as a patient into the army hospital at Landstuhl. Because he was not viewed to be dangerous to himself or others, and therefore did not require physical confinement, he was placed in an open ward. Given Jackson's known history to that date, the decision not to confine him was reasonable. In his interviews with doctors and other hospital staff members, his memory seemed good and his responses to questions were not alarming. He expressed concern that the psychiatric evaluation might injure his military career as well as expose him to deportation from the United States.

"I want to stay on good terms with the Department of Justice," he told a psychiatrist. "I know I'm not subversive and we can just forget the rest," he said, apparently referring to the disciplinary problems that had led to his placement in the hospital. The doctor wrote afterward in his notes, "It would seem that much is running through his mind, but not being expressed."

In an interview with an army psychiatric social work technician, Jackson "looked unduly serious and preoccupied, as well as tense; his facial expression was somewhat rigid and he did not smile; expressed his feelings at great length; said that when he was 17 he had made a mistake by entering a Scottish mental hospital because now people are prejudiced about his mental health."

Jackson concluded that life in the U.S. Army was difficult for him because he didn't know much about America or "American ways. But I am learning." He expressed his opinion that his problem with his platoon sergeant was that the superior officer "doesn't like an alien who thinks about anything but doing what he is told to do." Jackson said that he liked to think about artistic things such as paintings, theater, journalism, and music. These interests, he believed, made him different from other men in his outfit "[who] are the brawny type." He confessed that he wanted to do anything necessary to become a U.S. citizen, "so I won't be an alien and feel different."

Following the preliminary examinations, Jackson was transferred to the army hospital at Frankfurt, where he was initially placed in a locked ward, a confinement against which he rebelled. He complained that he did not deserve to be forcibly restricted. When doctors learned that he had been in an open ward at Landstuhl, they quickly moved him to a similar unit in their facility. Jackson reacted happily to the change. The doctors noted that in the open ward he was "no management problem," although he remained secluded from other patients. Jackson stated over and over again to doctors that he should be returned to duty because only then would he be able to "prove himself."

As Jackson tried to win release from the hospital, medical personnel witnessed increasingly abnormal behavior in their patient. He was mysterious and unexplaining when he announced that he knew what his mistakes had been. He became belligerent and tried threats, saying he would "use all of my influence" to be returned to active duty. The doctors, of course, recognized that the threats were empty and a further reflection of his deep emotional problems. On August 14, he was transferred to Walter Reed Army Medical Center in Washington, D.C.

There, he was observed to be "moderately hostile, rigid, tense, and very serious." Jackson vigorously denied that he had any serious mental illness and tried to rationalize his predicament. He called his stay at Kingseat Hospital a "minor incident." He seemed well oriented but "demonstrated marked persecutory ideation and constantly complained of being harassed and picked on." He said he thought the army was "just intolerable,'' and that he was entitled to his rights ''as an individual.''

He continued his practice of meticulous research of subjects that interested him. He asked a nurse to bring him a series of articles on mental health from the hospital medical library. When he could, he signed out of his ward and spent hours in the library taking notes from books. Nurses were at a loss to explain what he did with the notes or what he was studying because he did not bring anything back to the ward after these research excursions.

Even though he had been there only a short time and observation had been limited, Walter Reed doctors concluded that Jackson was not ill enough to be denied a weekend pass, routinely given to recovering patients. The pass allowed Jackson to leave the facility without restriction and travel without notifying anyone of his destination. Just two weeks after his transfer from Germany, Jackson signed out on a weekend pass and went to New York City, probably by train from Washington's Union Station. He took a room at the YMCA. What the doctors did not know, because Jackson had never mentioned it, was that their new patient was harboring what he called a ''lovesickness'' for an army colleague in Germany. He later would intimate to a psychiatrist that this was a man whom he had admired from afar. Jackson may never have spoken to the other soldier. He wrote about feeling tormented by memories of the man once he had been returned to the United States.

Alone in his New York hotel room, dwelling on thoughts of the soldier, he became anxious and despondent. He had purchased some sleeping pills and attempted suicide with an overdose. This was the only documented actual suicide try in Jackson's life. He took thirty tablets of Sleepeez and twenty-eight tablets of Nytol, both popular, over-the-counter sedatives. The pills made him sick, and when he began to vomit he called the hotel front desk for help. He was taken by ambulance to St. Vincent's Hospital, where he received emergency-room treatment. When the procedure was finished and he was recovering, the army was notified by the hospital that Jackson was there.

The following day he was brought to the U.S. Army Hospital at Fort Jay in New Jersey. His physical condition was not serious, and that same day he was again transferred to another army hospital, this one at Valley Forge in Pennsylvania. Doctors there found him to be well oriented and cooperative, but still expressing hostility and suspicion.

By the third day following the suicide attempt, Jackson was talking expansively to a nurse about his problems. He was contrite about trying to kill himself. He described the act as impulsive, and he expressed no further desire to commit suicide. Doctors, however, continued to classify him as suicidal and medicated him with Thorazine, which meant that finally Arthur Jackson was receiving appropriate psychiatric medication. Now considered to be dangerous to himself, he was placed in a locked psychiatric ward where he could be more closely monitored. Reacting to the confinement, Jackson became reclusive, refusing to attend any recreational activities. He spent each day sitting alone, avoiding contact with other patients.

Although the treatment was adequate, the diagnostic basis on which the treatment was administered appears to have been inaccurate in concluding that Jackson's problems were not deep-rooted. An army psychiatrist who had examined Jackson on August 29, two days after the suicide attempt and one day after Jackson's twenty-second birthday, wrote, "the man is 'odd' but seems less so when considered in light of what is normal for his background of culture and upbringing. He strikes me as mostly immature and impulsive though he is forming what seems to be a broad philosophy of life. Must take precautions. . . .''

Therefore, because the medical personnel seemed to have been most concerned with just his temporary suicidal ideation, and were not aware of the more serious nature of his chronic condition, a beneficial long-term therapeutic program was not instituted.

Three weeks after the suicide attempt in New York, Jackson was back at Walter Reed Army Medical Center in Washington, D.C.

Typical of Jackson's dysfunctional family, contacts from relatives were extremely limited and could hardly have offered him any sustaining support or sense of affection. An uncle called the hospital in late August to perfunctorily check on the young man's condition but offered no messages for his nephew. In October, Jackson's mother sent a letter to an army official asking about her son's condition. Jackson worried that her contact with government officials had been inappropriate, and would somehow jeopardize him. He did agree that she should be informed of his condition.

Unsurprisingly, army doctors ultimately concluded that Jackson was unfit for further military service. Remarkably, though, the same doctors also determined that Jackson had the capacity to lead a fully functional, relatively normal life in civilian society. One wrote that Jackson had "only slight incapacitation for social and industrial adaptation, due to symptoms of irritability, hostility, and a tendency toward feelings of persecution." Jackson, these military psychiatrists said, could meld into the general population following standard, modest psychotherapy.

This optimistic assessment of Jackson's potential for future success, assuredly invalid, must be viewed in light of the dual bureaucratic role sometimes played by military doctors. They were required to be concerned with proper patient treatment during Jackson's crisis period, of course. However, the effect of their diagnosis on continuing government financial responsibility for Jackson was also probably considered. Army docu-

ments concerning Jackson's mental state hint that officials were careful to avoid a determination that would
have required Jackson to become a continuing responsibility of the government because of a chronic psychiatric condition, making him eligible for long-term
disability payments and government-subsidized medical care.

As a requisite prelude to his discharge, Jackson was
given a complete medical examination on February 1,
1957. Each of many items in his physical evaluation
was marked "normal." At the end of the list, the box
labeled "psychiatric" was checked "abnormal." On
the recommendation of a three-doctor evaluation panel,
he was discharged by the end of the month. He was
deemed eligible for Social Security disability payments.

With a succession of traumas behind him and now
free of obligations, Jackson once again pursued his obsessions and delusions. He used his army discharge pay
to travel across the United States, headed for Los
Angeles.

Once there, he scoured microfilm newspaper archives
at the Los Angeles Public Library, making copies of
ten-year-old articles about the Alcatraz riot and Cretzer's gunshot death. A May 4, 1946, United Press dispatch, which he read in microfilm copies of the *Los
Angeles Times*, reported details of the bloody conclusion to the prison uprising:

> The three-day battle of Alcatraz Island Federal
> Prison ended today in a final blaze of gunfire after
> three convict ringleaders—Joseph Paul Cretzer,
> Bernard Paul Coy and Marvin Franklin Hub-
> bard—had been killed and all their fellow rebels
> in blood-spattered Cell Block C captured.
>
> Federal Prison Director James V. Bennett de-
> clared that Coy was killed "probably last eve-
> ning," Cretzer "somewhat later," and Hubbard
> about 8 A.M. today during the final attack by Alca-

traz and Leavenworth [federal prison] sharpshoot-
ers. . . . The three rebel chieftains were found in
death, stiff and cold, beside their guns.

The article went on to refer to the uprising as a
"futile, tragic mutiny," an episode of violence in which
two guards were killed and fourteen others wounded.
As Jackson studied the newspaper pages, he saw a short
biography of Cretzer, which read in its entirety:

Joseph Paul Cretzer, 34, believed to be the
leader of the Alcatraz Prison break attempt and
rioting, is well known to Federal authorities in
Los Angeles as the nation's No. 1 bank robber.
Cretzer is serving a life sentence at "The
Rock" in San Francisco Bay for second degree
murder and bank robbery.
The desperado was sentenced to McNeil Island
Federal Penitentiary after he had pleaded guilty
to the $2700 robbery of the Ambassador branch
of the Security First National Bank on Nov. 29,
1935, the $6400 robbery March 2, 1936, of the
Melrose Bronson Ave. branch of the Bank of
America and the hold-up of the Seaboard National
Bank at Wilshire Blvd. and Vermont Ave. July
1, 1936, when $200 was taken.
Cretzer was sentenced to 25 years in prison by
U.S. Judge Ralph E. Jenney in January 1940.
While in the County Jail waiting transportation to
prison an attempted escape was balked when it
was learned that he had fashioned a handcuff key
from wood fiber and a spoon.

Accompanying the news reports were a number of
photographs that made deep impressions on Jackson,
including a picture that depicted tiered rows of cells
inside the prison and another showing the Alcatraz
Prison ferry docking at Army Pier in San Francisco

with two prison guards standing over the blanket-covered
bodies of the three dead convicts. Particularly affecting
to Jackson was a mug shot of Cretzer, the first time he
had ever seen a picture of the man alive. The photograph he had seen at Coney Island was a "death mask"
image, taken after Cretzer had been killed. All this was
fuel for Jackson's newfound notion that he had a "karmic obligation to free Cretzer's soul," as well as his
own, so both men could "be released and live together
in the hereafter." He later wrote about the emotions he
had experienced as he sat in the Los Angeles Public
Library and read the old newspapers:

> I remember feeling, to a moderate degree, spiri-
> tually lost, alone, and a trifle disoriented at the
> time, and seeing a live photo of Cretzer, which I
> hadn't come across prior to this fascinating time
> almost as if his psychic personality was finally
> communicating to me a sense of reawakening in
> my karmic memory.

As he continued his travels, Jackson lived meagerly
on his Social Security payments and infrequent, menial
odd jobs, none of which he could keep for more than
a few days. One such job was in a department store
warehouse in Los Angeles. After this, he never held a
job again. He joined the YMCA in Los Angeles in the
fall of 1958 and for a year visited regularly, "for
body-building 'work-outs' with weights," exercise that
harkened back to his futile teenage efforts at self-
improvement.

From time to time, he came into contact with law
enforcement authorities.

Arrested by Los Angeles police in February of 1959
for possession of a concealed weapon, a "locking-blade
knife," he was later convicted and served a ninety-day
sentence at the county jail, located downtown in the
Hall of Justice. Upon his release, he was transferred to

the custody of the Immigration and Naturalization Service because he was a British citizen and still classified as a resident alien in the United States. While considering deportation proceedings, officials at the INS wrote to Jean Jackson in Aberdeen asking permission to obtain family medical records from Scotland. Her response to an Aberdeen doctor served only to emphasize the disordered upbringing she had provided to her son.

> 78 Skeene Square
> Aberdeen
> Feb 17th 58

To Dr. Milne,
   Regarding Arthur Jackson, The Emigration in New York asked my son for permission to send a letter to you regarding his history from home life, his conduct and treatment. He went into the Hospital Voluntarily with a Common Teenage Complaint And he has never been insane, only when he was under treatment and they cannot deport my son Because of such a trifling Complaint. It was not my son's fault or mine that he never got his discharge. It depends on what you say to the Emigration while I wait results.

> Yours (s) J. S. Jackson

There is one thing I must mention, I never took my son out of Hospital through lack of insight. That is one thing we both possess, and that is Insight.

Jackson was released from the hospital after a time, but not deported. He continued his wanderings in the West and focused some of his attention on historic architecture.

   When I resided in the U.S. my concern about the architectural heritage (changing skylines and vanishing landmarks) was confined exclusively to American cities, and can be traced back to May 1955, when I watched steel-helmeted workmen with electric drills noisily dismantling New York's famous Third Avenue elevated railway in the upper East Side, around 116th Street.

In 1961, he wrote a letter to President John F. Kennedy complaining about the environment and specifically mentioning his annoyance that "proper respect" was not being shown to a structure in Los Angeles that he claimed had significant architectural history. This would be the first time, but not the last, that Jackson's bizarre letter writing, filled with aggressively toned language, would bring him to the attention of law-enforcement authorities.

Jackson mailed the letter to the White House, where it was passed on to the Secret Service for review. Jackson had demanded that a government official be sent from Washington, D.C., to Los Angeles to look into the architectural matter that concerned him. The president's security agents found passages woven into the rambling message that they interpreted to be threats against Kennedy, then in the first year of his administration.

Because Jackson had made reference to his British citizenship, the Secret Service contacted the Immigration and Naturalization Service which, not for the first time confronting a problem with this man, initiated proceedings with California officials to have Jackson admitted to Patton State Hospital in San Bernardino for psychiatric examination. There, his chronic schizophrenia was once again diagnosed.

Jackson, now twenty-five years old, was designated by the government to be an "undesirable alien," eligible for deportation, the strongest action U.S. authorities could take against him. Unlike now, threatening a president was not then a federal crime. He was held for a time at the INS detention center at El Centro, in California's southern desert region, and then deported to Scotland. U.S. authorities had moved the problem of Arthur Jackson into the jurisdiction of another government, but only for a time. He would one day return to America.

Scottish authorities, reacting to the deportation, required that Jackson be examined by psychiatrists once he was home in Aberdeen. In June of 1961, Jackson met with a doctor at the Ross Clinic, part of Aberdeen's network of public mental health facilities. Jackson explained that he had been deported because of his "unusual ideas." After an hour-long interview, the doctor concluded that his patient was a "paranoid schizophrenic."

As part of his government-mandated review of Jackson, the doctor also interviewed Jean Jackson, whom he found to be "a rather simple, sincere sort of person. She describes some rather bizarre habits [her son] has, such as buying his own food in addition to his normal meals. He refuses to go anywhere without his mother." The psychiatrist noted that his patient dressed in a "bizarre fashion," his outfits always including his U.S. Army fatigue jacket.

Jackson was asked by the psychiatrist to voluntarily admit himself to a mental hospital for treatment. He refused. The doctor wrote to a colleague that perhaps this patient should be confined against his will. "I think we may well have to admit him under certificate," he wrote, but added, however, that "there is no immediate urgency about this." In the meantime, the psychiatrist wanted Jackson to visit a physician who was taking blood samples from schizophrenics as part of a study to discover the disease's unknown causes. "To this end I am asking him to return as an out-patient on Monday and we will consider thereafter his admission."

Jackson did not return to the clinic to participate in that medical research nor was he either willingly or involuntarily admitted to a mental institution afterward. He just continued to drift through the bizarre, isolated world of his delusions:

I don't want to be reincarnated but I'll return to earth periodically on a space time machine. It will be a paradise in heaven.

He spent much of his time in the Aberdeen central library, sitting alone and reading in the spacious reference room. Aberdeen, a city of 350,000, had nine library branches, some closer to where Jackson lived, although he invariably took the fifteen-minute bus ride downtown to the main branch, adjacent to St. Mark's Cathedral.

He was an orderly patron, bothering no one else, usually requiring only an admonition at 8:00 P.M. to leave because closing time had arrived. The librarians, who invariably described him as eccentric, saw him as a miserly character who did not leave for meals all day long, nor did they ever see him bring any food with him. He was always one of the first patrons to arrive in the morning and among the last to leave at night.

One librarian recalled that Jackson was "interested in everything American." His daily reference works were piled on a worktable on which he had first carefully spread a newspaper to completely cover the wood. These volumes always included *The Motion Picture Directory, Webster's New World Dictionary of the American Language*, and a one-volume American encyclopedia. Each day he took extensive notes, cut them into sections, and pasted them into a scrapbook.

He rarely conversed with anyone, including the librarians. Once he did get especially angry when an out-of-date reference book was taken off the shelves. If someone approached, he would use his body and arms to shroud whatever work was before him. He relished privacy and quiet and was particularly annoyed during school examination periods when more students than usual filled the study tables. The proximity of others in this public place seemed to unduly unnerve him, and he became upset even when someone walked by him.

His requests of librarians were so infrequent that they

would remember for years the time that he asked if they had a reference work to determine the number of people who had committed suicide by jumping off the Golden Gate Bridge in San Francisco. The question's relation to Joseph Cretzer is clear. Alcatraz is easily visible from the span of the bridge, high above the tidal waters below. This information request is noteworthy in its revelation that Jackson, at least temporarily, apparently was contemplating suicide as a means to his mission concerning Cretzer. Jackson probably would not have asked the question if the Golden Gate Bridge, notorious for the number of suicides committed there, were not near the site of the prison where Cretzer died. The time would come when an elaborate scenario he would envision for his death would, as a matter of "principle," preclude suicide.

Jackson would often disappear from Aberdeen for the summer months, usually traveling to London where he most often stayed in Salvation Army hostels. Little is known about how he otherwise spent his time in England during these visits. Paranoid people are fantasizers and dreamers. One of Jackson's wishes was to return to America, and London was the common port of departure from Great Britain. Furthermore, since his limited education allowed him to achieve little in Aberdeen, it is possible he also thought of London as a place to seek his fortune. Certainly, he pursued his compulsions there. During a February 1965 visit he had an experience that he later deemed to be an "initiation ceremony," intended to unite him with Joseph Cretzer "in spiritual brotherhood."

[This] involved my yielding to an irresistible, manic-depressive obsession to type out an identification card bearing Joseph Cretzer's name and particulars of his prison registration status, together with his criminal record. Over a three day period . . . I was permitted the use of the student's union office, containing typewriters for students, inside the University of London, just off Russell Square. Here, I would spend hours endeavoring to arrange a correct formula of statistical details on several blank, postcard-sized cards. Alas, it was hopeless. I had to give up in the end. No matter how diligently I kept trying, there was always some damn thing or another which failed to meet my high standards of neurotic, Virgo-style perfection.

The travels he claimed to have made were remarkable, and might seem unlikely were it not for his frugality. Some of these trips are documented. On December 31, 1965, he left by train from Waterloo Station in London, later boarding a ship to Rio de Janeiro, arriving, he said, on January 14, 1966. He traveled throughout South America and eventually arrived in Miami, moving northwest to New Orleans, then further west through Texas, and south into Mexico.

Again he illegally entered the United States, this time crossing at the Mexican border into California. Moving up the Pacific coast, he headed for San Francisco and its magnificent views of the bay where no doubt he stared at Alcatraz Island, no longer home to a functioning prison. In 1963, U.S. Attorney General Robert F. Kennedy had ordered the facility phased out of the federal penitentiary system. The last prisoners were transferred from the island to other institutions. During Jackson's 1966 visit to San Francisco, Alcatraz was a deserted place and the subject of numerous proposals for its future use.

During that visit, Jackson's thoughts of Cretzer revived an old compulsion. He once again attempted to create an "identification card" bearing Cretzer's name and vital statistics, similar to the one on which he had labored the year before in London. He often "took liberties with other people's typewriters," he wrote, and did so once more in San Francisco. Discovered trespassing in an office at the Drake Hotel, he was escorted out of the building. When he moved to a nearby office building, he was again discovered and city police were called. When they determined that Jackson was an illegal alien, he was detained and transferred into the custody of the INS. In November 1966, Arthur Jackson was once again deported from the United States and flown home to Scotland.

From then until his last days in Aberdeen, he lived almost exclusively with his mother in her welfare apartment at 9 School Drive. The city-owned apartment was in a four-unit complex in the east end of town, one of several such buildings called "council housing estates," interspersed among high-rise buildings. They were meager accommodations, to be sure, but clean and comfortable with a small patch of grass out front.

From time to time, Jackson broached his strange thoughts to others. One doctor's report from 1967 reads: "He wishes to have superficial blood vessels removed from the [eyelid]. He believes the eye is the mirror of the soul and, therefore, the blood vessels were disfiguring his soul, and he wished to make the world better. He wished to have a mole removed because he believed it was sapping his strength, and he was going to purgatory for misdemeanors in previous lives. But he was convinced that there would be a beautiful paradise at the end of it all. And he, at that time, believed he was being punished because he's an idealist."

There are numerous records of his encounters with doctors over the years in Aberdeen, whom he often consulted for minor problems, such as one visit about the irregular growth of his toenails. The doctor in that instance later referred to his patient as "this very strange man." Jackson believed that each of the common problems that troubled him represented a far more serious condition than it actually did.

Some of his encounters began to include emotional outbursts of abnormal intensity. In 1970, for example, Jackson became annoyed when his doctor did not act quickly to remove a mole from his forehead. First, Jackson threatened to sue the doctor. Then he told the physician that had he been his superior in the army he would have had him court-martialed. Invariably, when these sorts of confrontations occurred, Jackson's mother reinforced her son's obsessions. One day, Jean Jackson called the doctor and demanded that he perform the minor surgery because the mole was "weakening" her son. This correlation between a perceived physical malady and the reduction of spiritual or moral strength was similar to the thought process Jackson had employed when he had worried about his masturbation as a teenager.

The doctor in this case, L. Stankler, a consultant dermatologist at the Aberdeen Royal Infirmary, was concerned enough about Jackson's threats and apparent instability to seek advice from the Medical Protection Society Limited in London.

A regional secretary of the society wrote back saying, "I have come to the conclusion that I am sure you would be wiser to refer Mr. Jackson to your plastic surgeon colleague for him to remove the lesion ... it is likely that Mr. Jackson is able to give a valid consent and ... if you explain to him that he might be left with a residual somewhat unsightly scar, and he still agrees to your performing the operation, then you would have an adequate defence should he seek to complain against you later.... nevertheless if he was dissatisfied in any way, I have no doubt he could become a real nuisance and at least you would possibly be bombarded with long letters. It is conceivable I suppose that an unfavorable result could precipitate an acute schizophrenic episode and I am sure you would not wish to be involved in the wrangles that might ensue...."

A plastic surgeon eventually performed the outpatient operation on Jackson.

For nearly two decades, Jackson was periodically in contact with doctors who reviewed his eligibility for government disability benefits. There is no indication during that time that anyone noted that he was a potentially dangerous man. In one typical report, this one written after a 1974 examination, a divisional medical officer for the Department of Health and Social Security confirmed that Jackson is "incapable of work ... A long history of schizophrenia ... he is withdrawn and solitary and could not face any employment stress in his present state."

In the mid-1970s, in an application for a "sickness benefit" from the Scottish Home and Health Department, Jackson reported that he was living alone and "engaged in writing a book." A clerk noted, "He presents a slim man of reasonably good physique who expressed his rather odd opinions in good English."

During all these years, Jackson is known to have been involved in only one socially and personally constructive endeavor, probably the last outwardly positive act of his life. Interested in architecture and spurred by his library readings, he became involved in an effort to preserve an old church in Aberdeen, St. Nicholas, scheduled for demolition in an urban redevelopment project. According to an acquaintance, Jackson offered a spirited and intelligent defense on behalf of the building and was even quoted by the local newspaper and appeared in a television interview. He recalled the event in his diary:

> I have been an outspoken opponent of what I call "the rape and bastardization of Britain" ... A keen preservationist, I wrote to a number of organisations, mostly newspaper offices, protesting against the steady destruction of the nation's architectural heritage. The protest, or campaign, began in earnest in May, 1969, when I contacted the *Daily Mail* and Princess Margaret. Then, in November 1969, her Majesty The Queen.

Unlike his letter to President Kennedy, which had contained threatening passages and resulted in his first

deportation from the United States, his letter to the
queen was probably more focused on the architectural
problem and not so rambling or alarming as to force a
reaction from the authorities. This expression of normalcy was, by now in his life, an aberration for Jackson. As the 1970s passed, life's circumstances
continued to lead him downward.

He did have acquaintances with whom he conversed
from time to time, all of them dating back to his childhood. As an adult, he was incapable of engaging in
new relationships. One person who talked with Jackson
from time to time was his boyhood friend and neighbor,
Robert Anderson, who would occasionally pass Jackson
on the street or encounter him at the library.

Anderson recognized that Jackson was mentally ill
and sometimes avoided engaging him in conversation
because the discussions could grow tedious. Once a talk
began, Jackson would go on for hours unless Anderson
forced an end to the visit. Jackson's demeanor was always placid, often making reference to the "memoirs"
he was writing. Mostly, Jackson would reminisce, "living in the past." Jackson's schizophrenic temperament
made it easy for Anderson to avoid him when he
wanted to. If Anderson did not initiate an encounter
by making deliberate eye contact or saying something,
Jackson would just pass him by, never taking the initiative to begin a conversation.

Jackson interpreted the expression of even the modicum
of emotional warmth that starting a conversation required
as a demeaning act of submission. His lack of self-esteem
was so great that he found it devastating to put himself
in any position he deemed weak. Thus, he created a barrier with every human being he encountered. His self-
respect was so fragile that he could interpret offering eye
contact to an acquaintance as losing a battle of wills.

Anderson, who had more contact with Jackson than
probably anyone else in Aberdeen outside of a few
members of Jackson's family, wondered where he ob-

tained his money. Jackson never seemed to have much, but the source of what he did spend was still a mystery to Anderson. Once on a trip to London he was surprised to meet Jackson in a chance street encounter. Jackson's money was apparently mostly used for travel, not possessions. His clothes, "meager garments," as Anderson described them, had a "shoddy" look but were always "tidy, pressed and looked after."

Later, when Jackson became notorious in his hometown, a shopkeeper would recall to one reporter how Jackson occasionally came into the store in disheveled dress, "weird-looking," spending an inordinate amount of time shopping, usually making only simple purchases, such as a single apple.

Hints that Jackson had a potential for violence were rare but not unknown during these years. An Aberdeen woman had a nasty encounter with Jackson in the mid-1970s. The seemingly benign behavior witnessed by the Aberdeen librarians was not the experience of this woman, who worked in the kitchen of a decrepit men's hostel where Jackson was temporarily living. Late one evening, Jackson, who had just returned to the hostel, demanded food. The woman told him the kitchen was closed for the night. Jackson pulled a knife and threatened her, but he was soon overpowered by another male boarder who evicted him from the premises.

It is impossible to judge in retrospect what Jackson might have done had the other man not intervened. The incident did have violent potential. Jackson's paranoia had become more pronounced as he grew older, and with these changes came the increasing unpredictability of his behavior. In this instance in the hostel kitchen, he was not acting out in response to schizophrenic delusions. However inappropriately, he was attempting to meet the real need of his hunger. Police were not notified, since such violent encounters were common at the hostel.

Through complaints to the local government housing agency, mostly made by letter, Jackson pursued a feud

with a neighbor, a man named Smith who lived in the
apartment directly above Jackson and his mother. Jackson
accused Smith of purposefully making noise to annoy him
and his mother. One tactic used by Smith, Jackson said,
was to throw food out of his window to attract screeching
seagulls. The seagulls in this seaport city *are* loud and
make noise constantly. Jackson, no doubt, was bothered
by the birds. It is equally certain that Smith was an innocent target of Jackson's delusions. Jackson, though, was
convinced otherwise, and wrote:

> Smith is like a para-sorcerer or wizard of mis-
> chief. He is possessed with a demonic compulsion
> to cause distractions. Smith is allied with the Hous-
> ing Department. He is capable of communicating
> bad feelings without performing actual acts.

Jackson obtained a lawyer, Frank LeFevre, known as
one of the top defense attorneys in the city, to help him
pursue a lawsuit against Smith. LeFevre didn't think the
case was viable. He thought that if Smith was, indeed, a
noisy neighbor, Jackson might have had a remedy under
the Scottish "law of nuisance," but that would have
required the landlord, the City of Aberdeen, to obtain
the equivalent of an injunction against Smith. Lefevre
quickly concluded that the problem was largely confined to Jackson's imagination. Jackson tried to convince LeFevre that this was a "blockbuster" of a case
because he believed both he and his mother had been
victims of long-term abuse:

> As for my mother, her worst phase was the
> first year, 1974. She already had a nervous heart
> condition, to begin with, and therefore the effect
> of hearing this vindictive monster (Smith) drop-
> ping heavy objects onto the floor above her,
> which sounded like bombs, at for example 3
> o'clock in the morning—several times during the

night—caused cardiac shocks. I too had to endure
these same tortures for years.

Jackson couldn't afford a lawyer, but he was eligible
for aid under the Scottish state legal advice system.
LeFevre, in order to be paid, was required to submit a
report on the likelihood of success, a potential result
which he viewed as virtually nonexistent. "We would
never have been able to go the distance of a court
action because that would have involved another legal
aid certificate," LeFevre said.

Jackson presented "sheaves of writing" to LeFevre,
displaying an "ability to print in such a way almost as if
it was done by machine." The lawyer found their conversations mystifying. "He would break off and say something like, 'I remember the night I sat in a café on the
south end of Majorca and Elvis Presley was singing "Little Wooden Heart" on the jukebox. It was one of the
most memorable evenings of my life.' Then he would go
on again and some other pop tune would be introduced."

A law school friend of LeFevre who had attended
grammar school with Jackson told the lawyer that he
remembered his classmate as a "brooding, introspec-
tive child."

Occasionally, Jackson would call LeFevre and berate
him for not moving forward on the case. The lawyer
later said that "the thing died a death probably because
of my discouragement and our [law firm's] lack of iner-
tia to do what he wanted."

After a time, Jackson stopped contact with the lawyer
altogether. In the troubling days soon to arrive for Jackson, he would put aside worries about aggravating
neighbors and noisy seagulls to pursue other, more dangerous obsessions.

CHAPTER THREE

❙❙❙❙❙❙

The Movies

> *Theresa Saldana is the countess of Heaven in my heart and the angel of America in my dreams. Theresa Saldana is a soulmate to me. My conception of the girl I long to be with most. I have psychedelic fantasies of romance about her in springtime—enchanting visions of our walking together through the gardens of magnificent palaces in Heaven.*
>
> —DIARY OF ARTHUR JACKSON, 1980

Arthur Jackson, forty-five years old in 1980, psychologically was a man dangling from the edge of a cliff. Then his fingerhold gave way. The last bit of normalcy to which he could cling disappeared, and he plunged into a mental abyss.

On October 7, Jean Jackson died of cancer at Woodend Hospital. She was seventy-seven years old. The next day her son went to the city registrar to officially record his mother's passing. The document hints that her own upbringing had been less than secure and might be viewed as a precursor to her son's problems. Her father's name was "unknown."

The death of Jean Jackson was a psychological catalyst for Arthur, a monumental event accelerating his deepest descent into a madness from which he could never escape. Jackson's father, whom he had seen rarely in the years since the divorce, had died in 1974. There is no indication that Jackson even took special notice of his father's death. Indeed, his reaction to his mother's death was not a matter of normal grief, of painfully feeling an important loss as others might experience the death of someone they loved. The link to reality that Jean Jackson had provided her son was tenuous at best. From the beginning, the fragile connection between them had been a terribly weak foundation for self-esteem. Even at its best, Jackson's relationship with his mother only resembled normalcy. Still, her passing marked the disappearance of his only shared emotional relationship with another person, including other relatives in Aberdeen from whom he was distant.

The emotional devastation accompanying his mother's death was aggravated in Arthur Jackson by two other deaths that soon followed, which apparently aided in destroying whatever was left of his sanity. On March 14, 1981, one of Jackson's aunts, Margaret Milne, died. In April, an Aberdeen man with whom Jackson may have only imagined a homosexual relationship was killed in an automobile crash. Jackson came to believe that the dead man, to whom he had been attracted, was now communicating to him from the grave.

Given the turmoil of his life, almost anything could have triggered a turn to an ugly, new course for this emotionally fragile man. He had no faculty for coping reasonably with life's stresses, which now must have appeared to be mounting furiously against him.

As it happened, it was a movie that captured Arthur Jackson's peculiar imagination. He was spurred to action, which he believed would bring spiritual satisfaction into his empty existence.

He was conditioned to respond intensely to what he saw on the screen. In his memory was an extensive catalogue of film release dates, actors, plots, and titles. In 1974, he had written to the actor Gregory Peck, then president of the Screen Actors Guild, commenting about his suicide attempt and other details of his life. He never received an answer. Still, he perceived a deep affinity with Hollywood and its people, and now he would build on that foundation, continuing to incorporate its heroes and villains into his own fantasy world in a new and dangerous manner.

Jackson frequently attended films at both of Aberdeen's movie theaters. On January 24, 1981, a Saturday evening a little less than three months after his mother's death, he went to the Queen's Cinema, where two movies were showing. The film that probably attracted him to the theater that night was the featured movie, *Cruising*, starring Al Pacino. The lead character is a New York City policeman who poses as a homosexual while working undercover during an investigation.

The second movie, though, would be the one to have a permanent impact on him. In turn, the result of Jackson's fascination with this film would be pain for others, scarring their lives forever.

Defiance was an American production, starring Jan-Michael Vincent, a handsome, tough-jawed man who portrayed a soft-spoken but hard-hitting local hero. The cast included Art Carney, Danny Aiello, and a dark-haired young woman, Theresa Saldana, at the threshold of a movie-acting career.

Saldana was a New Yorker, an adopted child who later told *Parade* magazine that she had been lovingly raised as a "Puerto Rican-Italian." She was twenty-six years old when *Defiance* arrived at the Queen's Cinema in Aberdeen. Saldana had had small parts in two previous movies, *Nunzio* and *I Wanna Hold Your Hand*, both produced in 1978. *Defiance* was her first costarring role, playing the heroine opposite Vincent.

Defiance had been ready for release the previous March, but its distribution had been delayed. The movie's scenes of gang violence had fed into a simmering controversy in which the film's critics accused the movie's producers of glorifying street crime. The mediocre film offered a superficial look at its one-dimensional antagonists. The good were saintly and the bad were unremittingly evil. *Daily Variety* said the movie is "much more than a mindless action feature, but not quite the sociological exercise needed to attract the more sophisticated filmgoer."

This stark dichotomy between the good and bad characters was shallow storytelling at best, but profoundly revealing to Jackson. He saw much of his own life portrayed on the screen. Indeed, he believed that many autobiographical elements contained in the letter he had sent seven years before to Gregory Peck had been introduced into the screenplay without his permission.

Jan-Michael Vincent played Tommy, a merchant marine who decides to live temporarily in a neighborhood on New York's Lower East Side, which is being terrorized by a Hispanic gang called "The Souls." Tommy begins a romantic relationship with Marsha (Saldana), who comforts him after he is hurt in a gang attack. Jackson especially identified with this moment because it reminded him of an encounter he had had with a victim of street violence. As he watched the movie, he remembered lying in the emergency room at St. Vincent's Hospital in New York in 1956, waiting to be treated for his sleeping pill overdose. Next to him at the hospital was a man who had been beaten, a "mayhem victim," as Jackson described him.

After a dramatic moment in the film, in which Tommy decides not to leave his adopted neighborhood after all, he rallies residents, whom police never seem to help, to rise up and defeat The Souls.

Messages within the film received only by Jackson through schizophrenic symbolism caused him to feel an emotional connection to the actors. He related the film's characters, their words, and their experiences, however tangentially, to moments in his life. The psychotic process of "projection" took over as he watched, and he began to attribute intimate, truth-bearing personal significance to the fiction that he was viewing on the screen.

The movie provided Jackson with several key pieces to the psychotic jigsaw puzzle he had been constructing in his mind for decades. No psychiatric clinician can be sure of the precise interpretation Jackson gave to each element. A normal person pieces together a jigsaw puzzle with visual and intuitive thinking, but deals with only one surface. In Jackson's distorted thought process, the puzzle, in a sense, has pictures on *both* sides of the pieces, which interlock in strange ways only he can visualize.

Such multilayered thinking already had been demonstrated by Jackson when he mentally superimposed a map of the United States on an Aberdeen street map. This psychological phenomenon, called "ideas of reference," happens when a schizophrenic takes an event and, regardless of its actual connections to the world, delusionally reinterprets its meaning.

In some respects, Jackson's identification with Tommy, and his belief that Tommy's life paralleled his own, is easily understood. Tommy was an organizer, a decent man who enjoyed being an outsider, just as Jackson viewed himself in counterposition to society. Almost any connection is plausible in a paranoid thought process. Later, Jackson would reveal to psychiatrists some of the unusual connections he made between his life and what he saw in *Defiance*.

One member of the cast was named Montana, which Jackson linked to Cretzer's birthplace. Another actor was named Lopez, also the last name of a man imprisoned with Cretzer at Alcatraz. Jackson had once taken the middle name of Joseph, in Cretzer's honor, later changing it to Richard, for King Richard the Lion-Hearted. An actor in the movie named Richard brought this symbolism to the fore. Jackson, who grew up in the working-class seaport town of Aberdeen, also might have envisioned himself as a hearty, free-roving merchant marine traveling from port to port, like Tommy.

Stark, unambiguous relationships of love and hate are established in the schizophrenic mind, and Jackson may have reacted negatively to Saldana when he first watched her performance. Early in the film, Saldana's character makes a derogatory reference to homosexuals, no doubt stirring Jackson's self-hatred concerning his rarely discussed sexual leanings. In his diaries he expresses fear that others will think he is homosexual because he has never kissed a woman romantically.

When in the movie Tommy is disturbed by neighbors making noise, a problem he readily solves through intimidation, Jackson was able to compare that with his upset at his neighbor in Aberdeen, perhaps wishing that he could solve his ''problem'' as effectively as the screen hero did.

Tommy is an outsider befriended by Marsha, a woman who becomes his lover and constant source of support. Marsha personified a fantasy of Jackson's, that someone would lovingly take care of him. He dreamed of such a relationship but never saw it fulfilled in the slightest. Tommy was a movie hero, brave and respected by the neighborhood, receiving the kind of adulation that Jackson never knew.

Sometimes Jackson combined symbols. He likened his strong attraction to Saldana to his feelings about the army colleague in Germany who had held an ''emotional power'' over him in 1955, bringing on the ''lovesickness'' that had led to the suicide attempt. Jackson, on some level, may have come to view Saldana as an ''obtainable'' substitute for that distant soldier.

Jackson's mystical attraction to Saldana quickly became an overpowering component of his being. This strange new romance of his combined with his decades-old fixation on Cretzer. His schizophrenia had driven him beyond seeking mere temporal stability in his life; he had become fixated on achieving eternal bliss of cosmic proportions, and a plan of action to accomplish that began to form in his mind. Jackson discarded any lingering thoughts of suicide. Now, there was another way for him to reach heaven to be united with Cretzer, for a reunion with "loved ones" and a mating with Saldana, all of which would happen, he believed, only if he followed a pre-scribed manifestation of his spirituality.

Jackson's "love" for Saldana would not be expressed in a common fashion. Because of his dementia, his display of affection would not be gentle. Arthur Jackson would confirm his love for Theresa Saldana by killing her.

Importantly, in his view, this would result in a state-administered execution, freeing his soul to join Saldana, Cretzer, and others in Heaven. About forty-eight hours after seeing *Defiance*, Jackson's new plan had fully transformed into an uncontrollable obsession.

Although the love for the figure of obsession is in a twisted, fantasy form, there can be the realization within the schizophrenic that actual fulfillment of a normal relationship is either hopeless or insignificant. There may have been that spark of insight in Jackson. There-fore, he chose the only relationship he believed he had the ability to enforce, one in an idealized afterlife.

His intent was not a malicious, hateful desire to murder the actress, a woman he had never even seen in person. From a psychological point of view, his love was infantile, metaphysical in nature, and not a mature form of desire or lust. Essentially, it could be termed an infatuation, psy-chiatrically ignited by the death of his mother.

Jackson was no doubt familiar with Hollywood's best-known version of a disturbed mother-son relationship. The psychological dynamics propelling Jackson are similar to those which pushed the character Norman Bates in Alfred Hitchcock's classic *Psycho*. For much of the movie, the audience is led to believe that Bates's mother is alive. Finally, the audience learns that she is dead, that it has been Norman Bates himself dressed in her clothes and talking to himself. Before the secret is revealed, the viewer believes that the mother is diabolically controlling her son. In a sense, she is, but from the grave.

To a normal person, the symbolism Jackson has drawn on to connect himself to Saldana appears remote and illogical in the extreme. From the viewpoint of the schizophrenic, such links, as tenuous as they may be in reality, take on a durability and an intellectual soundness unassailable by the outside world. Common among the mentally ill who become dangerously obsessed with others is a firm belief that intimate relationships, created only in the imagination, actually exist.

Robert Bardo was a nineteen-year-old Tucson resident whose schizophrenically induced obsession with the television actress Rebecca Schaeffer brought him to Los Angeles in the summer of 1989. Bardo had previously been infatuated with Samantha Smith, a schoolgirl from Maine who became famous when she embarked on a goodwill peace trip to the Soviet Union in the 1980s. Samantha Smith later was killed in a plane crash in Maine, and Bardo transferred his obsession with her to Rebecca Schaeffer, merely by watching the young actress on television. The connection Bardo made between Smith and Schaeffer was flimsy for all but the abnormal mind. Schaeffer was the costar of a television situation comedy called *My Sister Sam*. Her character's name was Samantha. This, according to psychological theory, is a prime example of the phenomenon of "loose association," one of the primary characteristics of schizophrenia.

According to testimony during a five-week, nonjury trial before a judge in Los Angeles in 1991, Bardo had spent two years trying to communicate with Schaeffer from Arizona, all without success. Then he came to California to find her. He obtained her address from a private detective. The investigator had obtained it from records of the California Department of Motor Vehicles. One July day in 1989, Bardo went to Schaeffer's apartment building in the Fairfax section of the city.

When she came to the door, he shot and killed her. She was twenty-one years old. Convicted of murder in the first degree, Bardo was sentenced to life in prison without the possibility of parole.

Bardo and others fall into a relatively new category of deviant, the so-called celebrity stalker. The psychological underpinnings of their actions are not new. Rudolph Valentino was beset by stalkers, as were famous people before him in history. Celebrity stalkers today constitute a growing phenomenon, their pursuits made simpler by ease of mobility.

The omnipresence of celebrity in our society has led to an increase in behavior that threatens those who are well known, not the least reason being the sense of familiarity intensive media attention produces. Some stalkers are driven, in part, by the knowledge that completion of their mission could result in their own celebrity. President Reagan's would-be assassin, John Hinckley, whose motive was to impress an actress, may be the most infamous of this category in recent decades.

Whether these disturbed people stalk movie stars or well-known politicians, there are psychological commonalities among them. They are usually people on the fringes of society who have no significant sense of self, people whose lives are often insubstantial. They come to believe that their attachment to a well-known individual will make them whole persons, both improving their importance in the eyes of others and enriching their abysmal self-images. In the psychotic individual, this concept of importance by association is a world apart from the more common act of "name-dropping" employed by many people in conversation. The comedian David Letterman and the actress Sharon Gless have both been subjects of persistent stalkers in highly publicized cases, and are just two examples of a growing cadre of the famous whose lives are beset by psychologically disturbed people.

The increase of celebrity-stalking feeds a new branch

of mental health service that has sprung up around the problem. As with other societal maladies, more government and insurance money becomes available, and a new "industry" forms to take advantage. As has happened in the treatment of alcoholism, the curbing of sexual harassment in the workplace, and other issues, sometimes joining the field of true experts are people of limited experience and little specialized knowledge who drain funding without providing useful services or products in return. In this new arena, attempts have been made to profile stalkers by creating objective parameters for identifying them, when the truth is that beyond general psychiatric principles, these attempts rarely produce meaningful results.

The dangerousness of known stalkers is calculated by using the same standards used to predict the potential harm that might be posed by people with a wide variety of other psychiatric conditions, such as child molesters. Still, predicting behavior, particularly dangerous behavior, is a most inexact science.

The popular belief, fostered to a large degree by the superficial television "tabloid news" program portrayals of stalkers, is that the attainment of fame is the primary goal of the stalker. The underlying motivation for taking violent or unusually intrusive action against a celebrity is, however, usually much more strangely complicated. Most stalkers of celebrities view fame for themselves as a secondary benefit of their actions.

Arthur Jackson, often categorized as a celebrity stalker, does not neatly fit the description. Jackson's goal was not to achieve notoriety for himself. To this day, he does not seek celebrity. He expresses disinterest in the publicity that has surrounded him. Nor did he seek out Saldana because she was famous. When Jackson viewed *Defiance*, she was a young actress working her way up, not a well-known Hollywood figure. Her appearance on a movie screen may have given her a larger-than-life aura in Jackson's eyes, but she was not then a celebrity.

Jackson's thought process does involve a consistent, internal logic, however crazy that thought pattern may appear to others. The identification with the bank robber Cretzer, the rage against the neighbor he believed was purposely annoying him, and his obsession with Saldana are part of a schizophrenic continuum now extending over nearly forty-five years of his life. In 1981 when he went to see *Defiance*, he possessed enough self-awareness to know that in real life, as an unattractive, undesirable forty-five-year-old man, he was never going to ''get the girl,'' as movie heroes do.

There is a common misconception that crazy people ''snap'' at their particular moments of acting out. The process of psychological deterioration, however, is more subtle. Psychotics are usually pushed to abnormal behavior by things seemingly unrelated to their aberrant behavior. The nature of Jackson's illness is unpredictably erratic; it is an up-and-down condition in which he can demonstrate lucidity one moment and bizarreness the next.

Jackson's desire to kill Saldana became an uncontrollable compulsion on which he focused exclusively for months.

I am determined to fulfill the sacred mission, come what may. Suicide has always filled me with a sense of dread. It also has a stigma of dishonor about it. While on the other hand, the state execution seems to convey the awe-inspiring impression of possessing the ceremonial military style honor about it in comparison. Remember, not only am I desperate to get out of this world but also the angels of heaven are anxious to get me out.

In September of 1981, in anticipation of his trip to the United States to search for Saldana, he applied for a British passport. The application required references and Jackson listed Aberdeen lawyer Frank LeFevre, his boyhood acquaintance Robert Anderson, and a distant cousin named Mark Westbrook, whom he rarely saw. LeFevre and Anderson didn't learn until much later that they had been listed. Westbrook, at Jackson's request, signed the passport application to verify that the photograph of Jackson was a "true likeness" of the man, as required by British law. Remarkably, the safeguards of bureaucratic records failed again. No one reviewing the application, apparently, noticed any record of Jackson's two previous deportations from the United States. The passport was approved and issued.

By this time, several months had passed since Jackson's decision to go to America and hunt Saldana. The intensity of purpose propelling him had not diminished in the slightest, a psychological demonstration of the depth of his obsession.

He saw Saldana in another movie, this time director Martin Scorsese's award-winning *Raging Bull*. She appeared briefly, uttering only one line of dialogue. For Saldana, being cast by the perfectionist Scorsese, acclaimed as one of the best movie directors of his generation, had been an important career boost.

During the months that Jackson refined the plans for his "mission," he was rarely sidetracked by other interests. Yet the occasional diversion from his "work" concerning Saldana was no less self-possessed:

> In association with my cultural and political views I have since the 17th of [October], bestowed on myself an unofficial title or ideological nickname. So now it can be revealed that I am the phantom writer of Kings College, Aberdeen, who penned "right wing" propaganda on the wall of the K.C. library toilet and signed them "Richard the Loyal-heart." ... replies were penned by three or four students—obviously in a rage—one of whom called me a "fascist bastard." Contrary to being offended, I was philosophically amused, because I know deep down I am not a chauvinistic type at all.

In October, Arthur Jackson made formal his "mission." He began to write a document, a petition for execution, intended to guide U.S. officials in their dealings with him once he had achieved his obsessive goal with Saldana. In the document's seven legal-size pages, filled with his careful, tiny printing and tens of thousands of words, Jackson gave details of his plan and his expectations of punishment. On his first day of composition, he wrote only one paragraph:

> St. Raphael and United Nations Day,
> October 24, 1981 A SOLEMN PETITION
> TO THE GOVERNMENT OF THE
> UNITED STATES OF AMERICA
> It is on behalf of I, Arthur Richard Jackson, a British subject and citizen of the United Kingdom— and on behalf of any other interested parties—that I be granted the right, under due process of law, to be sentenced to death, following a conviction having been brought against me in court involving a capital crime, and that I also be granted, by special request, the opportunity of being executed at a penal institution, or similar establishment (former penitentiary), of my own choice, and the date of execution is of my own choice.

Subsequent paragraphs and pages, each segment dated according to the day on which it was written, were added over the next six weeks. Jackson wrote without a hint of doubt that his proposal would be perfectly acceptable to the United States government. He used the past tense, as though his murderous attack on Saldana had already taken place.

> ... because ... the desire within me to start a new life in another world is an overwhelming one, combined with a recently adopted policy of mine ... to substitute the long-held idea of committing

> suicide with the far better plan of enlisting ... judicial sources to mercifully put me to death instead, you can understand why it was necessary for me to commit any conclusive acts of fatalistically justifiable homicide in the United States of America rather than in the Kingdom of Britain, due in part to the former having since 1976 reintroduced the death penalty (whereas the latter abolished it in 1965) and due in part to America being my favorite country.

He did concern himself with the possibility that he might be denied his desired elaborate execution because of his diminished mental state, but he never thought that he would fail to kill Saldana.

> The initial plan is that I assassinate the victim, most probably in New York—if not then, possibly in Los Angeles—on or about the fourth week of January 1982.

He offered a rationale for authorities not to categorize him as mentally ill once he was captured.

> Maybe you will think it is schizophrenia but I think it is an allergy syndrome or I suffer from neurasthenia. . . . They would be interfering with destiny if they tried to term [me] schizophrenic and block the petition.

Jackson represented a lethal combination of traits. He was an intelligent schizophrenic, a man smart enough to overcome virtually any obstacle between him and his goal. If he chose to attack without attracting attention from others, and then escape into obscurity, he had the capacity to do that.

> A final point to appreciate manifests itself when you realize that I need never have volunteered

to surrender and make incriminating statements against myself at all. I could, if I had wanted to, simply have remained free and carried my dark secrets with me to the grave. . . .

The spiritual permutations of his plan demanded specific details for the execution. As a boy, he had sought to exorcise imagined demons by having a surgeon scrape the dirt from his brain. Now, as a deranged adult, he wrote with precision and passion the prescription for the ultimate cure to his problems:

An indoor execution conveys an atmosphere of spiritual warmth and spiritualistic stateliness. The chair is also an important factor. By being shot from the back of the head by a Springfield 30.06 rifle, the same type of weapon which killed Cretzer, while strapped down to a chair, combines the traditional American method along with the manner in which Cretzer met his death at Alcatraz in May, 1946. I have given this combined method a name—I call it the Alcatraz Coronation, because you are seated on the throne of death and crowned by bullets—a maximum of six and a minimum of four. All fired by one marksman. The execution weapon can be mounted on a tripod and be equipped with a telescopic sight to ensure none of the shots go off target and in the TV camera crews, press photographers or spectators on the front side of me. . . . Regarding the chair, this has to be a replica of the type used for electrocution and gassing executions. . . . Each of the six shots should be fired at intervals of five seconds and in accordance with my religious principles, at least one of them should be seen to emerge out of the front of my head, preferably around the optical vicinity . . . to obtain this traumatic exorcistic effect.

The fulfillment of the petition's grand plan, Jackson believed, had universal and eternal implications. Still, there were matters seemingly mundane and petty that grew large in his vision and with which he had to deal. For one, he determined that he would require a hair transplant following his arrest. He believed that his receding hairline made him a "degraded man, a non-entity, a freak, an inferior specimen according to my documents with regard to how life will be in heaven." Although his petition scheduled the execution to take place on June 12 or June 24, 1982, he was willing to delay it for three months to allow time for his new hair to grow in.

> Every man should possess a complete set of hair to truly be a complete personality comparable to that of a mane belonging to a male lion as a symbol not only of masculinity but of kingliness. A complete head of hair is therefore an emblem of sacred dignity and the crown of a king which makes a man worthy of being a Knight of St. Michael the Archangel in the Kingdom of Heaven. The pathetic sight of men with receding hairlines or more extensive baldness is obscene and masochistic.

Jackson was sensitive about governmental hierarchy. He knew that Alcatraz had been a federal prison and therefore concluded that he needed to be arrested by federal authorities and tried in a federal court. A large manila envelope in which he placed his petition was marked, "For the Attention of U.S. Federal Authorities Only. City, County or State Authorities Have Not My Permission To Open This Envelope." He finished his petition on December 5.

That done, he turned his attention to getting to the United States in preparation for killing Saldana on January 24, 1982, the one-year anniversary of his seeing *Defiance*.

He purchased a new diary. The opening page was

inscribed with his name. In the space for his address, he printed, ''C/O The Office of Michael The Archangel and Vice-President of Heaven.''

He conducted research for his mission at the Aberdeen Public Library. One day he took a Manhattan telephone directory from a shelf, looked up ''T. Saldana,'' and took note of the West Twenty-fifth Street address and telephone number.

From his disability pension, which amounted to about sixty-five dollars a month, he had saved enough to make his journey. He left Aberdeen for London on December 14.

On New Year's Day, 1982, he boarded a British Airways jet at London's Heathrow Airport and flew to Kennedy International Airport in New York City.

Records of his previous deportations from America some twenty years before were no doubt logged somewhere in government files, along with tons of other paper documents from the precomputer era. Jackson had been categorized as an ''undesirable alien'' by the United States government sixteen years before when he had been deported for the second time. The immigration officers on duty New Year's Day at the busy New York airport where Jackson landed, however, had nothing in their lists of persona non grata to warn them that this British visitor actually was a person who ought to be turned away. Jackson's passport was readily stamped, allowing his entry into the United States.

Arthur Jackson passed through United States Customs quickly and simply. He made his way to Manhattan by subway and got an inexpensive hotel room late on the night of his arrival. His pursuit of salvation through the death of Theresa Saldana would begin in earnest the next morning.

CHAPTER FOUR

❘❘❘❘❘

The Search

In Manhattan, Arthur Jackson obtained some stationery from the New York Statler Hotel. For the next two and a half months he would continue his diary, filling page after page with his extraordinarily small lettering, recounting a bedeviled journey across America.

Already possessing a telephone-directory address for Saldana in New York City, he assumed that locating his prey would be easy. He was confident that he would complete his mission later in the month as planned.

In the meantime, he set out to obtain a handgun, the implement he deemed the most "humane" with which to kill Saldana. Many times, in several cities, he contemplated surprising a lone policeman and killing him by stabbing him with a knife or a blow to the head with a hammer, so that he could then steal his weapon. In each instance, he decided against such action, not out of any apprehension of needlessly killing someone but out of calculation that the attempt might fail.

In New York, he concluded that he would probably not succeed because policemen there were too "tough." In Philadelphia, he made the erroneous assumption that because the city was known as the place of "brotherly love," the policemen would be gentler. When a patrolman there ejected him from the downtown bus station, accusing Jackson of loitering, he wrote in his diary that he wanted to kill the police officer.

That strong reaction is an example of the rigidity of schizophrenic thinking: a thought process that can deal only in absolutes and extremes. The "insult" from the policeman led Jackson to view him, morally, as a mortal enemy. The only way he could conceive of dealing with such a foe was in the extreme. Usually, most people can verbally finesse situations of confrontation, but Jackson was capable of only an infantlike, out-of-control, extremely violent reaction to being challenged.

A popular-culture example of such unwavering thinking is the paranoid, pyschotic gangster portrayed by the actor Joe Pesci in the movie *Goodfellas*. This character shoots and kills a young man for a slight, *perceived* insult interpolated from a comment innocently uttered by the unlucky victim. For Jackson and that movie character, who was based on a real person eventually murdered by his fellow mafiosi, the slightest insult is interpreted as a devastating, humiliating attack on the ego. The only way these men can overcome the subjugation they feel is to be in complete and God-like final control of the other person.

Arthur Jackson, counteracting the impoverished self-image his psychological damage has wrought, had assumed a morally superior perspective toward the rest of the world. As inner forces propelled him toward his goal, he was an entity emotionally isolated from the rest of humanity, traveling through a space and a time of his own strange creation. His daily, written account of his activities mixed the reporting of insignificant details of each hour with his cosmic, philosophical rantings. His mind seemed to be racing at triple speed. He appeared to work hard at the writing in order that his transcription might keep pace with his ceaseless introspection and self-important commentary on virtually everything that he observed. He often included a notation of the precise time that events occurred, even decidedly unmomentous happenings. Traveling by bus, napping in public places, and touring on foot the cities he visited, he was always physically close to other people. But for all the true linkage he made to any other person he encountered, though, he might as well have been in an uninhabited void.

He began his latest American journey at the Port Authority Bus Terminal in New York City, where he bought a Greyhound "Ameripass" ticket which allowed him unlimited travel. Then, Arthur Jackson headed west.

He spent two weeks in San Francisco. Since his last visit there in 1966, the federal government had turned Alcatraz Island into a penal museum, leaving the once-abandoned penitentiary buildings intact. Twice, Jackson took the National Park Service ferry to Alcatraz for the guided tour of the former prison, which by then had not held an inmate for nearly twenty years. He was solidifying his spiritual link with Cretzer, who had died there thirty-five years earlier.

On January 19, he was forty miles south of San Francisco in San Jose, visiting the Winchester House, a tourist attraction because of the odd architecture of the multiroom structure. Afterward, he wrote about an incident there that seemed to mark a rare occasion on which he responded in a normal fashion to another human being:

> 6:56 P.M., opened letter slot in doorway ... supposed to be haunted house. 7:01 P.M., get a surprise to see the eyes of a child looking back at me. Caused me to half-jokingly remark, "Hey, you scared me. This house is supposed to be haunted."

By month's end, he returned to New York City, still without a gun. Because he had not obtained a weapon he believed to be appropriate to carry out his plan, the anniversary date of January 24 passed, leaving him disappointed and increasingly anxious that he had not yet confronted Saldana. Without possessing the weapon of his choice, he decided nevertheless that it was time to face his intended victim. He knocked on the door of her New York apartment, but no one answered and he left.

Using hotel-lobby pay phones, which he liked because of the "privacy" they provided him, or sometimes calling from public telephones in the two Manhattan train stations, Grand Central and Pennsylvania Station, he began contacting people associated with Saldana. Through these calls he managed to learn in early February that Saldana was not then living at the Chelsea address he had found under her name in the Manhattan telephone book. He made a call to the apartment, where the telephone number had not been changed, and spoke to the tenant living there. The apartment was being sublet to a friend of Saldana's husband.

Then he attempted to contact Saldana's New York theatrical agent, Selma Rubin, whose office was in Forest Hills, Queens. In a rare slip of his concentration he made a mistake, a moment in which chance might have brought a different future for him and others. Jackson had just spoken by telephone to Rubin's secretary, who had told him to call back in an hour when the agent would be free to speak to him. The incident that followed is another illustration of the fixed nature of his obsessions:

Upon hanging up, approx. 11.08 A.M., I suffered a shock when I discovered my document bag was not beside me (to lose it would be equivalent to losing my soul and losing my mind simultaneously—the worst disaster ever, since it contains all my sentimental-sacred papers pertaining to Theresa Saldana and other loved ones in my life, including my hopes and dreams of meeting them again in Heaven). Imagine my relief when I found it sitting on the ledge of a phone midway down the row of phones where I had accidentally left it behind to move to another phone. Fortunately, a good-natured and wise middle-aged New York gentleman had been keeping an eye on it (unknowingly) acting as a "guardian angel" against whatever evil power that had caused me to become absent-minded by standing watch over it while he was talking on the phone.

The prospect of the loss had "stunned me with dismay," Jackson wrote later that day in his diary. His reclaiming of the black bag kept him on course.

Through his various research efforts of making telephone calls and consulting references in libraries, he began to receive more information leading him closer to his target. Using a pay phone in Grand Central Station, he called Rubin back as the secretary had suggested. They spoke for eight minutes, Jackson later noted. He pretended to be a radio reporter from Great Britain. He later recounted that he learned in that call that Theresa Saldana lived in Los Angeles most of the year and usually returned to New York City to be with her family at Christmastime. He noted in his diary that the actress would be in California until April.

That evening, he boarded another Greyhound bus using his Ameripass ticket and began a circuitous route to southern California.

Throughout his travels, Jackson budgeted his money well, spending just a few dollars a day on food. After his first night in New York City, he apparently never paid for a night's lodging again. He conducted research to determine where he would get the best rate of exchange for his British currency. He often slept in bus stations. He washed in public rest rooms. He did not buy full meals. His diet consisted of small purchases to stave off the hunger of the moment: orange juice, milk, bananas, cheese, candy bars, cookies, soda, potato chips, apples, peanuts, and occasionally, small portions of sandwich meat.

His first stop after leaving New York this time was Atlantic City, where he visited a casino and strolled on the Boardwalk. Then he was on to Washington, D.C. He took a tour of the White House, then occupied by President Ronald Reagan, who was just beginning his second year in office, fully recovered from the wounds suffered in the assassination attempt by John Hinckley the year before. Out of curiosity, Jackson went to the Watergate complex, site of the famous bungled burglary in 1972 that began the chain of events culminating in the resignation of President Richard Nixon two years later.

From Washington, he continued south to Tennessee, with stops in Chattanooga and Knoxville, both cities where Marvin Hubbard, one of the five convicts who had joined Cretzer in the Alcatraz escape attempt, and one of the two other men killed with him, had once walked. Hubbard had kidnapped a policeman during an armed robbery in Chattanooga in 1942, according to author Clark Howard, whose book *Six Against the Rock* chronicled the uprising. Hubbard was later arrested and then escaped from jail in Knoxville. Clark's book had been published in 1977. Although Jackson makes no mention of it in his diaries, it is possible that he found it in a library and read it.

Jackson attended mass at a Roman Catholic church in Chattanooga and "from a mystical point of view" was moved by the priest's sermon reference to Saint Teresa. He then traveled through Alabama before arriving in Miami on February 10.

From there, he made the ninety-mile trip through the Florida Keys to Key West, returning to Miami two days later. He arrived back in Miami on a Friday afternoon. He was almost out of U.S. currency, and with the end of the banking business day approaching, he began a frantic search to find an institution still open where he could exchange some more British money for American dollars. He walked out of the first bank he came to because he thought the five-dollar commission for the transaction too much to pay.

So I tried the Florida National Bank, 169 East Flagler Street, but learned business ceases at 2 P.M., and when I reached the Bank of Miami, 21 south east 1st Avenue at 3 P.M., the guard—similar to previous bank—told me in the customary curt Spanish manner that here too was closed for business. I began to panic and curse Christ in my torment. I realised tomorrow was Saturday and I was damned if I would stay in Miami until Monday (already behind schedule in my journey to L.A.). . . .

Desperate, he returned to the first bank and paid the commission. After touring downtown and walking along Biscayne Bay he boarded a northbound bus at 11:00 P.M. For the next several days he journeyed back through the Deep South.

Local monuments interested him, and he absorbed more bits of regional history to add to the disparate knowledge of Americana he had obtained during all of his days in the Aberdeen Public Library. He seemed especially intrigued by statues of Confederate General Thomas "Stonewall" Jackson and President Andrew Jackson. Sometimes he felt a closer personal link to the men these monuments honored than was supported by reality.

I'd lent a certain resemblance to Stonewall Jackson. It virtually seemed that I represented a reincarnation of him, except that he was of Scottish-Irish extraction and I was Scottish with some English blood from my father's side, whose grandfather can be traced back to Sheffield, Yorkshire.

He wrote that one odd encounter had struck him as amusing.

. . . half-jokingly asked 2 colored dames next to phones in lobby of Sheraton Inn Hotel, Mobile, Alabama, around 8:35 P.M., if the person singing in section 'C' (loud disco music room) was saying 'oobe-doobee' and if so what does it mean, but they seemed puzzled and didn't answer.

As he headed west he adopted a firmer self-discipline, which he believed would strengthen him and help him accomplish his goal. One change he instituted in Colorado Springs, Colorado.

Decided for sake of mission and Theresa Saldana, to forego seeing "Thief of Bagdad" and "Adventures of Robin Hood" Errol Flynn at Ogden Theater (I told girl I would return at 4.55 P.M.) I must not visit any cinema to indulge in amusement or nostalgia until Theresa Saldana precedes me into eternity first, so that she can be with me in spirit when I watch a film in a cinema. I will only see a film before Theresa's death if Theresa Saldana herself is in it.

From time to time, and in several cities, Jackson's strange meanderings attracted the attention of police. One such encounter took place in Colorado Springs, where he had returned after going to Denver. He later wrote in his diary that he had encountered "serious trouble" about 10:25 one night as he stood outside the entrance to a courthouse making notes of the evening's activities.

A security guard from the county office building across the street, suspicious of my motives for being there, came over and questioned me. I explained and showed him my passport when he asked for I.D. Obliged to accompany him to office across street where I sat down at 10:30 P.M. while he then put a call through to the Colorado Springs Police Department to check me out. Security guard something of a rat. He said things over the phone which weren't true, such as that I had been sketching details of the judicial building, later claiming I had been sitting down as I did this (I was standing). The police arrived about 10:45 P.M. Total of two squad cars and I had to stretch out hands onto side of patrol car with legs apart while I was searched for weapons. Satisfied with my more or less genuine explanation that I was on a freelance assignment, making out a time table report on my whereabouts and places visited and experiences during my travels, they let me go at about 10:50 P.M.

Jackson's passport, of course, was valid, and the police had no legitimate cause to hold him. He was told to stay in the bus station until morning, when he could freely roam near the municipal buildings to continue his "survey." Instead, Jackson left Colorado Springs and on February 22 arrived in Pueblo, Colorado, a location spiritually important to him. This was the birthplace and childhood home of Joseph Cretzer.

He went to the local library and read accounts of the 1946 prison escape attempt on microfilmed copies of the *Pueblo Chieftain*. Then he embarked on a pilgrimage. He later recorded that "Finally, at 9:23 P.M.," he arrived at what he believed to have been Cretzer's boyhood home. He was uncertain of the street number, which he had obtained from a "faded photo copy of his old school records," a document apparently published in the newspaper accounts of the Alcatraz incident.

He went to the door and spoke to the current resident, "a young man of Mexican extraction," lying that relatives of his had lived there sixty years ago and he wanted to verify the address. He stayed at the door only a short time. He was having misgivings about which house had been Cretzer's. He crossed the street and knocked on the window of another house, but received no reply. He finally decided that the first house he had gone to was the right one. Then he went to the school Cretzer had attended, Columbian Elementary.

... spoke to two caretakers of school through glass door ... (shit-faced reality making a mockery of the nostalgic, sacred occasion) ... police car which unknown to me had been searching for me, after cynical, older caretaker had phoned cops behind my back, caught up with me. I was asked for identity and I showed them passport. Once again I explained like I did to the cops last night in Colorado Springs. Older cop advised me to avoid area east of where we stood and to put my passport on my person rather than in black document bag. Said a lot of burglaries and damage to schools happened in Pueblo.

The next day Jackson was traveling by bus again. In Kingman, Arizona, the birthplace of the cowboy actor Andy Devine, whom Jackson somehow linked to his mission, he signed a church guestbook. He identified himself as "The Man in the Iron Mask," because he thought that aptly described his tormented life.

It is like having been more than 30 years locked up in a prison in an iron mask shutting out all the warmth of human contact tantamount to a dog's muzzle, without justification, no kissing, no conversation with women, an iron shell covering the expressive personality; a cocoon of Virgo style symbiosis isolation and loss of identity or cold, paranoid, uncommunicative withdrawal imposed upon me by the oppressive regime of cold fate combined with social taboos, sophisticated customs and bourgeois system of laws and regulations.

One of his most frequently purchased candy snacks was deeply symbolic for Jackson. Often when he put coins into a vending machine, his choice was a Three Musketeers bar. The author of the swashbuckling historical romance novel *The Three Musketeers* was Alexandre Dumas, who also wrote *The Man in the Iron Mask*. Dumas was a writer no doubt brought to Jackson's attention by his schoolteachers; he later read Dumas' books at the library and mentioned his name in his diaries.

His expressions of self-pity were common. He became convinced that people looked at him differently after he masturbated than at other times, that somehow the activity affected the "physical characteristics of my ill-favored facial features."

On February 26, Jackson's bus crossed into California. Once in Los Angeles, he spent a great deal of time at the Greyhound bus station downtown, where he kept his belongings, mostly clothes, in a locker. He napped in hotel lobbies and spent the nights in the back hallways of apartment buildings.

He began to scour public records to obtain Saldana's address. He went to the Los Angeles County Hall of Records to check names in the property tax rolls. Saldana, who was renting an apartment with her husband, was not listed there. Jackson went to a Southern California Gas Company office where he asked a clerk named Eva Walters to help him locate his "long-lost relatives," displaying his British passport for identification. The woman did not provide any information to Jackson, but she would remember him because he had displayed great irritation at having to wait to talk to her.

On March 4 he went to the "Mr. Keane" investigative agency and paid a one-hundred-dollar search fee. One investigator, Lloyd Shulman, would later say that Jackson "had a lot of information he wanted us to verify. He had like a whole book which he showed the investigator." That same day Jackson noted in his diary that he had obtained Saldana's current address, 1263 North Hayworth Avenue in West Hollywood. He did not, however, reveal the source of this information.

He had learned that Saldana was married but the news did not make him feel more distant from her. He merely viewed Saldana's husband as irrelevant to the relationship he imagined he had with the actress.

Saldana herself would later recount that people close to her, innocently and unwittingly, had given her stalker valuable information. On March 8, for example, Saldana's mother called excitedly from New York to report that she had just received a telephone call from an assistant to movie director Martin Scorsese, who supposedly was in London and needed to contact Theresa immediately. The caller had insisted on an address in case it was necessary to send a telegram.

Initially, there had been no reason to doubt the veracity of the caller. Saldana's parents' telephone number was unlisted and Saldana had worked for the director in *Raging Bull*. The actress later wrote that for a half hour after her mother's call, "I was hopping around the apartment singing and dancing, sure that Scorsese had another film role for me."

The euphoria was soon shattered by a call from Selma Rubin, who according to Saldana said, "Theresa—there's a nut looking for you. I'm very worried." By now, Rubin had received at least four telephone calls, which she recognized to be from the same man.

Each time the caller identified himself differently and Rubin refused to provide him with any information.

In one exchange, the caller had said he was "Mr. Thomas" of the William Morris Agency and he asked for the actress's address and telephone number because he had a "million dollar" publicity deal to offer her. To confirm her suspicion about the unfamiliar name, Rubin called the agency for verification. She was not surprised to learn that there was no such person employed there.

Soon enough, Saldana made a chilling observation. One of the names the caller had used with Rubin matched that used by the man who had called her mother claiming to be Martin Scorsese's "assistant." Rubin advised Saldana to get out of the apartment immediately. Saldana later would write that she also called the West Hollywood Division of the Los Angeles County Sheriff's Department but was told that there was nothing police could do unless she was actually being harassed.

Finally, according to a report Saldana's husband would later give to police, "Mr. Thomas" called Saldana herself and said he had a plan that would provide a great deal of publicity. The actress replied that she wasn't interested. The caller then asked if she would be interested in making some pornographic films. She emphatically said she was not interested and hung up. Afterward Theresa Saldana reported the telephone incident to police.

Jackson, of course, had made all of these troubling telephone calls. This ploy of Jackson's is an example of how shrewd powers of intelligence can coexist with a major mental disorder, combining to make a schizophrenic like Jackson an especially dangerous man.

By March 10, Jackson still had not obtained a gun. He was becoming more frantic in the grip of his obsession, feelings which were intensified when he passed a movie theater where *Raging Bull* was showing.

The pangs of love-sick emotion jar my nerves
in electric waves of poignant anguish, which
cause me to shake my head with convulsive
"shell-shock" twists, whenever vivid images of
Theresa enter my imagination.

In the midst of all this, the convolutions of Jackson's
wide-ranging concerns sometimes allowed small matters to seem unusually important. He was disappointed,
for example, after visiting a Goodwill store because he
had not been able to find a "suitable sport jacket."

Having been stopped and questioned by policemen
in other cities, he was now increasingly vigilant not to
attract attention that might lead to his arrest on minor
matters, perhaps resulting in the discovery of past troubles and leading to his deportation before he could complete his mission.

Rested at bus stop seat . . . so drowsy my head
kept nodding (falling forward), but I would always jerk my head up to give the impression to
passing motorists, after lapsing into fleeting unconsciousness, in order to avoid making it seem
I was a bum or a drunk, especially as I was afraid
a passing patrol car would see me asleep.

He finally obtained a weapon, but it was not a gun.
He bought a Korean-made, five-inch, wooden-handled
steak knife for five dollars, displeased that it was
cheaply manufactured. Then, he obtained a hammer. He
carried both items around with him in his document
bag, planning to use one or the other to kill a lone
policeman from whom he would steal a gun to use to
shoot Saldana. As had happened in other cities, he
waited outside several Los Angeles police substations,
but never saw an opportunity to surprise and overwhelm
a lone officer walking by.

On Thursday, March 11, he expressed moments of depression.

> I continued cursing my frustration and futility. . . . I was definitely at the lowest ebb in spirit, and this wretched, depressing, pessimistic feeling of soul-destroying doom continued to "dog me" today . . . convinced that I was literally in hell—and everyone else only existed as creatures who added to my suffering in hell—they being immune to complex psychological torture that I am undergoing (Their minds being at peace while mine is disturbed).

After wandering through West Hollywood, he went to downtown Los Angeles and worked on his diary in the lobby of the Westin Bonaventure Hotel. There, he decided that his inner voice had become a hindrance to his mission. He vowed to stop talking to himself negatively in order that he might press on with his task. On Friday, March 12, he concluded that he should eat more "properly," as an additional preparation for "D-day."

> But if strategically necessary I could limit my food to just 3 Musketeers chocolate bars, make my cash spin out for a special purpose (short delay in mission).

Passing a construction site he saw a crowbar lying on the ground, picked it up and put it in his document bag. He thought he might use it to pry open a window at Saldana's apartment. Later in the day he made his first visit to the building in which the apartment was located. He walked up the stairs and passed by the door, but did not stop or knock.

He was still following his initial conviction that he could only carry out the killing of Saldana with a gun.

His inability to obtain one left him wondering, temporarily, about his next step.

> Maybe I will just give this whole thing up in
> defeat and go back to Great Britain. I am down
> to my last $9.

On Sunday, March 14, he returned to the sprawling, fountain-filled lobby of the Westin Bonaventure Hotel in downtown Los Angeles. He was now assuming that he would be completely out of funds by Tuesday, March 16. Broke, he would surrender at the British consulate in Beverly Hills, declare himself a pauper, and be flown back to London at government expense. He began a new letter to Saldana which he intended to mail upon his return to England:

> I acknowledge with the deepest regret that I
> am a total stranger to you. . . . Strategically, my
> mission has been a disaster. In the process of
> endeavoring to get in touch with you, a collateral
> vision, if there was ever, I have used all of my
> savings which took years to accumulate. . . .

He would not, however, go to the British consulate or ever mail the letter. The truth is, Arthur Jackson was a man without options. His all-encompassing goal would not allow a return to Great Britain. He was powerless to control his overwhelming obsession.

In the afternoon, he left the Bonaventure and went to the lobby of the Hollywood Roosevelt Hotel, where he continued writing the letter to Saldana. Shortly before 9:00 P.M. a security guard ushered him out of the building. He secluded himself in the hallway of an apartment building not far from the Roosevelt and resumed his writing. He began to recount an experience he had had in a Hollywood church a few weeks before. In the quiet place of worship he had started to repeat

to himself that Saldana was his "salvation" and his
"Jesus Christ." Midway through the sentence describing this scene, Jackson stopped writing. He placed the
unfinished letter in his black bag with his other belongings, including the cheap, wood-handled knife.

He had to walk only a few blocks to reach Hayworth
Avenue where Saldana lived. He waited outside her
apartment building for several hours, hoping to see her.
When that did not happen, he left, sneaking into the
laundry room of a nearby apartment building. It was
late. He spent the night sleeping on sheets of cardboard.

CHAPTER FIVE

❘❙❘❙❙❘❘

The Attack

I never achieved anything worthwhile in this life.

—ARTHUR JACKSON, 1981

On Monday, March 15, 1982, at 7:10 A.M., Arthur Jackson resumed his vigil on Hayworth Avenue outside Theresa Saldana's apartment building.

Shortly after 8:00 A.M., Mary Greenspan, a resident of the neighborhood, opened a window in her apartment and noticed a bearded, scruffy-looking man pacing back and forth on the sidewalk. He was a stranger to her and she noticed that he carried a black satchel. He was wearing brown trousers and a blue, zippered jacket. Greenspan thought that the man appeared to be "a little different" from those who usually pass by. Over the next two hours, Greenspan noticed several times that the man was continuing to pace the sidewalk.

As he walked, Jackson thought he was successfully pretending to be "casually waiting" for someone to pick him up in a car.

At 9:30, Jeffrey Fenn, a twenty-eight-year-old delivery man for the Sparklett's Water Company, was sitting in his truck and reading the morning newspaper while parked near an intersection on Hayworth Avenue. He didn't notice Jackson, who was farther up the block.

Jackson waited for his first sight of Saldana, in person, in his life. He was prepared to do only one thing when she finally appeared. Previous to this day, Jackson had expressed a hope that he might be able to engender a normal relationship with the actress, rather than carry out the plan described in his death sentence petition:

> ... a miracle such as Theresa suddenly, in a mutual affinity, love at first sight, experience, show some geniality, an interest, were I to speak to her and ask her for a date, instead of launching into a homicidal attack without delay.

The dream of this nonviolent alternative was just that, another of his fantasies. This one had long since disappeared from his thoughts.

> However, I have to be realistic, as far as I am concerned, miracles of that kind only happen in Heaven and not on earth.

At 10:00 A.M., Theresa Saldana, twenty-seven years old, said goodbye to her husband, Fred Feliciano, who worked for Behavioral Health Services in Hollywood. Saldana would later say that up until the moment that she walked out the door of her apartment to attend a piano class at Los Angeles City College, this time of her life had been an idyllic period for her. "I was leading a happy and fulfilling life. My career as an actress was on the rise, I enjoyed attending college part-time, and my handsome husband and I lived in a lovely apartment in trendy West Hollywood. Fred and I were close to our families, had plenty of good friends, and were active socially."

The fear that had set in the week before because of the strange phone calls had dissipated. "None of us had seen anyone suspicious," she later said. Some of the extra precautions that had been quickly instituted had already been put aside.

Saldana walked away from her apartment building and turned left toward her automobile, which was parked in front of an apartment house adjacent to hers. She leaned forward slightly to unlock her car door. Jackson silently came up quite close and stood over her left shoulder. She did not know he was there until he spoke. Enunciating his words with extreme slowness, he asked, "Are you Theresa Saldana?"

The young woman quickly turned and stared into Jackson's face for a second or two, long enough for fear to register. Her reaction was quick, the result of pure instinct alerting her that she faced danger. She tried to run, but Jackson stopped her movement by grabbing her shoulder roughly with his right hand. Then he tightly wrapped his left arm around her waist in a grip she would later describe as "viselike." She struggled fiercely to get away as he pulled the cheap steak knife from his satchel with his now-free right hand. In an instant, he was stabbing her repeatedly in the chest.

A "blood cry for help" from Saldana startled telephone company worker Sandra Pond, who was four hundred feet away and placing safety cones around her parked truck. She looked up to see Jackson striking Saldana "as hard as somebody could possibly hit another person."

Fenn, the water delivery man, who was by now at a nearby building unloading a customer's order, also was startled by Saldana's screams one hundred feet away. When he looked up, he saw Jackson dragging Saldana backward. From this distance, Fenn thought that the attacker was beating the woman with a clenched fist, pounding hard into her body. He couldn't understand the young woman's words at first. The screams reached him only as a high-pitched shriek, obviously a cry of distress, and Fenn immediately ran to help, moving uphill along Hayworth Avenue to get there. Once closer, he could understand Saldana's pleas and the words "Help me! Help me!"

Saldana was vainly trying to block the pummeling knife thrusts with her arms. Once she was able to grab the knife with her left hand, but she was severely slashed doing so.

Fenn finally saw the knife in Jackson's hand as Saldana fell to the ground, bleeding profusely and screaming, "He is killing me, he is killing me. I can't breathe. I can't breathe. I'm going to die. I'm going to die." Jackson was moving backward toward the curb, dragging Saldana, who was kicking and flailing.

The attack had lasted for nearly two minutes before Saldana finally felt Jackson being lifted off of her by Fenn. She would later write of this moment: "Just as I felt the last of my strength slip away, I looked up and saw an angel. There behind the assailant was a tall, beautiful blond man. As if in slow motion, I saw him pull the attacker away from me."

Fenn had grabbed Jackson's knife-wielding right hand and wrapped his left arm around the assailant's neck. He pulled Jackson's arm back as far as he could, forcing Jackson to drop the knife to the street. The weapon's blade had been bent from striking bone. Jackson continued to struggle ferociously for half a minute before Fenn, five feet eleven inches tall and weighing 165 pounds, just a bit larger than Jackson, disabled him with sharp kicks to the backs of his knees.

Fenn sat on top of Jackson, holding his face to the pavement and bending the assailant's arms up and behind his body so he couldn't move. The police, called just a few minutes earlier by Saldana's neighbors, had not yet arrived. A crowd of onlookers grew larger, encircling the two men in the street. Fenn, who had dreams of becoming a policeman, didn't know whether Jackson carried any other weapons and wasn't taking any chances by loosening his grip.

Jackson spoke coherently. Fenn understood every word his prisoner said.

"How long has it been since I stabbed her? Has five minutes been up yet?" Jackson asked in a curiously methodical tone of voice. No one answered him. Jackson assumed that he had killed Saldana. His compulsion now was to determine the precise time in order later to memorialize the moment in his diary. He repeated his question concerning the time.

Jackson complained that he had a heart condition and told Fenn that he didn't have to be so rough. He said that he couldn't breathe because Fenn was sitting on him, pressing his body into the pavement. "You can let me go. There are fifty people here. I cannot do anything." Fenn continued to hold on tightly.

A man named Eddie Karas, who had been driving by when he saw Fenn running to the rescue, had stopped his car and now approached the two men. Karas looked down at Jackson, who was firmly pinned down by Fenn. "You must be some kind of lunatic," Karas said.

"Maybe I am. Maybe I am. I have my reasons," Jackson replied. "But it will come out in the end. It's all in the briefcase."

All this took place very quickly. Saldana, meanwhile, no doubt in shock, was trying to get back to her apartment. Karas had heard her screaming, "I can't breathe. I can't breathe. I'm going to die. I'm going to die." Feliciano had heard the screams but at first did not know they were from his wife when he ran out of the apartment to see what was happening. Then he saw her, seriously injured and bloody, moving toward him. He later told police that she was screaming, "He found me. He stabbed me."

He carried her into their apartment and called police and the fire department. Joseph Viterelli, who lived in a nearby apartment building, aided Feliciano. The neighbor listened to Saldana talk about being "stalked" by someone during the past week, saying she thought it might be related to her role in *Raging Bull*, or a part she had had at a small theater in Hollywood six weeks before.

By this time, about four minutes after Fenn's rescue, a Los Angeles County Fire Department ambulance was already there and Los Angeles County Sheriff's deputies were arriving, responding to a report of a "disturbance in the street." Deputy Eddie Jones approached Fenn, who announced, "This is the guy and there's the knife."

Jones picked up the document-filled black bag and Jackson volunteered the information that it belonged to him.

Another deputy was given directions to Saldana's apartment, but he needed only to follow a trail of blood that led from the street and up the building's stairs. The paramedics were already administering first aid to Saldana, in preparation for a fast drive to Cedars-Sinai Medical Center, one of the region's major hospitals, just a short distance away.

At the hospital, Dr. Alexander Stein, a cardiac-thoracic surgeon, was alerted that an emergency case was due momentarily. He was waiting in a sixth-floor operating room when Saldana was rushed in on a stretcher. Her body was wrapped in a pressure suit designed to prevent bleeding. The device had done little good because of the locations and seriousness of her wounds. Her pulse was now barely palpable and the anesthesiologist who had accompanied her from the first-floor emergency room had not been able to record any blood pressure.

In medical terminology, Saldana had exsanguinated. Almost all of the blood circulating in her veins and arteries had exited through the knife wounds, much of it pooling in her chest cavity, and was no longer available to be pumped by her heart to the vital organs of her body.

Dr. Stein recognized immediately that her condition could not be more critical. Without immediate treatment she would live just a few more minutes. For the next four and a half hours, Dr. Stein and others on the medical team repaired the most serious injuries. In the process they pumped twenty-six pints of replacement blood back into her body. Having been presented with an almost hopeless case, the medical team brought its emergency patient back from the edge of death.

Meanwhile, Jackson was in custody at the sheriff's West Hollywood substation, just a few blocks from the hospital. Five witnesses to the attack had also been transported there to be interviewed by detectives. As the booking procedure began, Jackson asked for a comb and said he wanted to wash up. First, though, detectives took pictures of his bloodstained hands, photographs later to be offered as evidence.

An investigator documented the collection of items in Jackson's black bag. Some were mysterious and others mundane. They included the seven-page "Solemn Petition for Execution" inside a large brown envelope; a 1982 Youth Hostels Association membership card in the name of Arthur Richard Jackson, whose address was listed as the Belvedere Hotel in the Paddington section of London; toilet articles; a large screwdriver; two "Consent to Search" forms written and signed by Jackson; a red 1982 pocket diary with the inscription "C/O The Office of Michael The Archangel and Vice-President of Heaven"; a two-page hand-printed document titled "Declaration of Attestation"; several pages of seemingly random notes; a British passport number 216891D; a business card from "Mr. Keane—Tracer of Missing Persons"; a one-hundred-dollar receipt signed by Mr. Keane and dated "3-4-82"; a Los Angeles city map; and shoe polish. Finally, there was a piece of paper bearing the address "1263 N. Hayworth Ave., Apt. #3 L.A. C.A. 90046" and a corresponding telephone number, "650-0767."

Detective Sergeant Fred Kalas, the case investigator, and another detective began their interview of Jackson. Throughout, Kalas thought that Jackson communicated well although he thought the prisoner was "pretty weird." Jackson told him that he had stabbed Saldana in the chest "because it would be ungentlemanly to stab a woman in the back."

Jackson willingly provided background information about himself as well as making incriminating statements. He said that he had used the alias Arthur John Jackson in 1965, was unmarried, had no permanent address, and had served in the U.S. Army. His last job in the United States had been many years before as a warehouse worker at a business whose name he did not remember, one of his rare lapses of memory about details of his past.

The Scotsman reported that he had been arrested by Los Angeles police on February 23, 1959, for possession of a concealed weapon, a knife; was convicted, and had served a ninety-day jail sentence. This was quickly confirmed by a check of county records.

His statements were not always accurate, although it is possible he was not deliberately lying. He may have come to believe that the incorrect information he was providing actually was true. He said he had been deported in 1961 because his visa had expired, telling the detectives nothing about his letter to the White House. Additionally, he said that before his departure from the United States that time he had been examined by psychiatrists at Patton State Hospital in San Bernardino County.

Kalas interrupted Jackson to say that he did not want to continue the conversation without first reading his prisoner his constitutional rights. Jackson interrupted Kalas to ask about Saldana's condition. When the detective said that doctors were optimistic about her recovery, Jackson became upset, complaining that all of his planning had been in vain.

The detective told his prisoner that he was surprised by his reaction, that he would have thought Jackson would be relieved at the news that Saldana would probably recover from her injuries, thus eliminating the possibility of a murder conviction. "You don't understand," Jackson replied. "It's all in my papers, it's in the papers in my black bag. Why don't you look in my papers? It will tell you everything you want to know."

First, though, Kalas wanted to finish informing Jackson of his rights as a criminal suspect. At the end of the recital, he asked Jackson if he understood. "Yes," Jackson said. The suspect's answer was certainly sufficient to comply with the law that required all arrestees to be so informed, although in time Kalas would come to see that Jackson's sense of understanding was unusual, to say the least.

Although a penniless resident of the United Kingdom, Jackson was protected in the United States by the constitutional rights granted equally to all criminal defendants, whether they are U.S. citizens or not. Told that he had the right to be represented by an attorney before answering investigators' questions, Jackson replied, "Well, we should follow the form. If the rules say I should have an attorney present, I think we should." Jackson was told that a public defender would be appointed and the questioning was terminated for the time being.

The investigators then completed lengthy police reports, including compilations of witness statements. In those documents, Jackson was identified as an unemployed transient. That night he was held in a "special handling" area of the county jail, although he was not isolated from other prisoners also being held there.

The next morning, the attack on Saldana was in the news around the world. Her attachment to Hollywood granted her new and immediate celebrity status. In Aberdeen, a librarian who, unlike her colleagues, had always harbored a fearful, uneasy feeling about Jackson, heard a radio news account of the incident. The assailant was not named but was said to be an Aberdeen native. Instinctively, the librarian immediately realized that the attacker had to be Arthur Jackson.

Jackson seemed not to have taken to heart Detective Kalas's report the day before that Saldana, although seriously wounded, had survived the attack. When an armed robber named Dennis Day Gibeau began a conversation with Jackson, the Scotsman announced that he was in custody because he had *killed* an actress named Saldana.

"No," said Gibeau, who had read newspaper articles Jackson had not seen. "I just read she is in stable condition." Other prisoners confirmed Gibeau's news and Jackson, as had happened with Kalas, again became upset and angry.

Jackson read the newspaper himself. He bristled because the article mentioned that he had tried to contact Saldana's mother. He insisted to his fellow prisoners that the call had been made by a private detective he had hired. The thought that his mission had failed overwhelmed him.

"Well, you are lucky she is alive, you know," Gibeau said to Jackson. "It's stiffer on a guy when someone dies. Don't you wish she was alive?"

"Why do you think I tried to kill her? Not so she could be alive," Jackson said disappointedly.

"Did she see you coming?" Gibeau asked.

"No."

"How come she didn't see you?"

"Because I came from behind."

"Is it too bad the man came along when he did?"

"Yeah, I would have got her and maybe him, too, and they wouldn't even know who to look for."

"Was he bigger than you?"

"Yes."

Jackson talked freely with Gibeau for five hours or more. He described the knife he had used as "one of those cheap jobs," explaining that he hadn't had enough money to buy a gun. He described his six-week search for Saldana. He told Gibeau that killing Saldana was a "mission" and that he had other "targets." Gibeau assumed that Jackson was referring to other women, although no further explanation was offered.

Jackson said he had chosen Saldana as his target because she was "so innocent, an angel." Gibeau asked Jackson why he had not simply called the actress directly, to tell her that he loved her. Jackson responded that he knew Saldana would never have spoken to him, and besides, he complained, she was surrounded by "Hollywood types."

Later that morning Jackson told a jail guard that he wanted to speak to Detective Kalas. Escorted by guards to the investigator's office, Jackson offered cooperation in return for some concessions. He wanted certain toilet articles available to him in jail and the promise that he could shave at least every second day. He wanted the opportunity to complete his notes, particularly for the 14th and 15th of March. And he wanted his execution petition to be delivered to the United States Supreme Court.

In return, Jackson offered to solve "a murder and two armed robberies in Europe," but at this time offered no additional details about when or where those alleged crimes had taken place. Local detectives apparently did not pursue just how much Jackson did know about crimes elsewhere. The notion that Jackson would offer vague promises to solve other unspecified crimes must have seemed like just so much more craziness spewing out of their prisoner.

The suspect never looked into the detective's eyes during the interviews. During these interrogation sessions, Jackson just stared blankly, either down at the floor or straight ahead.

Kalas told Jackson that he had not yet been able to read the documents investigators had found in the black satchel the day before. They had found a locker key, however. Jackson gave police his consent to search locker number 905 at the Greyhound bus station in downtown Los Angeles without first obtaining a warrant. Jackson said he kept toilet articles, a bag of clothing, and a few other items there, one of which he wanted brought to him. He asked Kalas to retrieve an astrology book, *Linda Goodman's Sun Signs*.

The next day, two days after the attack, Kalas started reading Jackson's diaries and other documents. The detective began to decipher the maze of references to Jackson's mission and Saldana.

Looking for clues to the motive behind the attack, Kalas noted one entry in which Jackson remarked that the knife he had purchased was a "Galaxy" and that he hated the thought of stabbing Theresa Saldana to death with a knife made in Japan. Another entry made the same day referred to Jackson's pacing in front of Saldana's West Twenty-fifth Street apartment in New York looking for anyone resembling the actress.

The meticulousness of Jackson's search was documented with diary entries such as that on March 3, in which he revealed that he had looked for Saldana's name in local college enrollment records and had considered going to Sacramento, the state capital, some four hundred miles north of Los Angeles, to check Department of Motor Vehicles records.

Upon inquiry from the Los Angeles County Sheriff's Department, other agencies began to learn that past encounters with Arthur Jackson were buried deep in their files, and this information was passed on to the sheriff's investigators.

The Immigration and Naturalization Service searched its records and confirmed the previous deportations. Those records had certainly been unavailable to government workers at John F. Kennedy International Airport the previous New Year's Day.

Patton State Hospital records showed that Jackson

had been a patient for a short time in 1961 after voluntarily committing himself. Los Angeles Police Department records showed that Jackson had been booked on February 25, 1959, on the concealed weapon charge and had been released from the county jail on April 30, 1959.

Kalas was also getting information from Saldana. The day after the attack, doctors allowed the detective to talk to her as she lay in the intensive care unit of the hospital. She told Kalas that as soon as Jackson asked her if she was Theresa Saldana, she knew that this was the man who had been calling, an intuition that led to a "terror" gripping her. She remembered that she had not answered Jackson but had tried to "shy away from him."

She had never seen him before, she said, but now she would never forget his face. Her attacker's features were indelibly locked in her memory.

Her worry about being stalked had begun about a month before the attack, when she learned that someone identifying himself as "Andrew or Arthur Jackson" had called her New York apartment seeking to locate her. After that and other calls she began to take precautions. She asked officials at Los Angeles Community College to withdraw her records from the files, so that they could not be easily located. Her husband often escorted her to her car.

During the hospital interview, the detective showed Saldana some samples of Jackson's strange writings. She later wrote, "I could bring myself to read only a few words. The handwriting was abnormally tiny, and my gaze was so unsteady that the print seemed to dance before my eyes. Besides, I was horrified to see the written, tangible proof of this gruesome plot against me. I turned my head away, repulsed."

Detective Kalas did not overstay his welcome at the hospital. He was convinced that Saldana would be a helpful and sympathetic witness.

With a great deal of evidentiary material already in hand, Kalas began to retrace Jackson's steps in the weeks preceding the attack. He went to the Mr. Keane Detective Agency on Beverly Boulevard and talked to Gary Tarin, an investigator for the agency. He showed Tarin the receipt found in Jackson's black satchel. Tarin said he remembered Jackson and pulled out a file folder with Jackson's name. The file included a photocopy of Jackson's British passport, identifying the bearer's occupation as "writer." The file revealed that Jackson had come to the office on March 4 with a request that Saldana be located.

According to Tarin, Jackson had said that he was a screenwriter who had submitted scripts to Saldana's theatrical agent and that they had not been returned to him. Now he wanted to locate the actress himself to get his material back.

Jackson had provided the private detective with no local address. He said that he would check back periodically. He returned a few days later and asked about progress in his case. Tarin said that he provided Jackson with the name and telephone number of Saldana's Los Angeles agent, Talent Management. Tarin recalled that Jackson seemed to react to the information dispassionately. He used the office telephone and then typed some notes for a few minutes before leaving.

Tarin said that Jackson had in his possession a long list of New York addresses. Jackson also told Tarin that he had come to Los Angeles because he had "gotten nowhere in New York."

Kalas pieced together Jackson's cross-country efforts to locate Saldana. The detective called Scott Beal, a friend of Fred Feliciano, who was subletting Saldana's New York City apartment. Beal said that in mid-February a man identifying himself as Arthur Jackson, and claiming that he was an employee of a British radio station, called and said that he wanted to contact Saldana to arrange an interview. The caller did not sound convincing. He was apologetic, unprofessional, and refused to give further information about himself. In turn, Beal offered nothing to the caller. Feliciano then instructed Beal to give the man the name of Saldana's New York agent if he called back.

The investigative documentation mounted and was coupled with the incontrovertible evidence from the crime scene. There were eyewitnesses, Jackson's confession, the bloodstains, the assault weapon, and the revealing contents of the black bag.

That Jackson had committed the act of brutally attacking Saldana was irrefutable. Less clear was how psychiatry and the law would define this violent act in terms of its criminality. That determination would affect any future confinement of Jackson. Soon, the doctors would provide their diagnosis, but the lawyers and the judges would control the debate.

CHAPTER SIX

❘❙❘❙❙❘❙❘

Psychiatry and the Law

Fifteen days after the attack, Saldana was still suffering greatly from her wounds, just at the beginning of a recovery that would take years. The previous Friday she had undergone surgery again, this time to repair the tendons and nerves in the palm of her hand, cut when she defensively grabbed the knife Jackson had been wielding.

She had not yet been released as a patient from Cedars-Sinai Medical Center. However, doctors did allow a brief journey during which she would be confined to a wheelchair. On this Tuesday morning, two weeks after the confrontation on Hayworth Avenue, she was on her way to testify at Jackson's preliminary hearing in Beverly Hills Municipal Court a few blocks away from the hospital.

As she would later movingly recount in her book, *Beyond Survival*, Saldana was encountering deep psychological pain along with her excruciating physical hurt. There was an omnipresent fear of more danger lurking in every shadow. As she entered the courthouse, where "so many strangers" stared at her, "I was terrified on many different levels.... The prospect of seeing and identifying the assailant turned my blood to ice water. I could hardly breathe."

Presided over by Municipal Court Judge Jill Jakes, the hearing on March 30 was a necessary prelude to a criminal trial, intended to offer evidence to the judge as to whether the state's criminal case was sufficient, according to constitutional standards, to prosecute before a jury. Deputy District Attorneys Philip H. Wynn and Vivian Somoza represented the People of the State of California and Deputy Public Defender Fred Manaster represented Arthur Jackson.

The only evidence offered during the short hearing was oral testimony.

Concerned for Saldana's obvious pain, the judge told the victim that it wouldn't be necessary for her to raise her right hand as she took an oath to tell the truth. Saldana interrupted the judge, declaring that she would raise her hand. She was a sympathetic presence, and her recounting of the attack was compelling.

"I was fighting him and fighting him for what seemed like a long time, but probably wasn't, and after receiving the deep gash, I began to become very faint and I didn't feel I could fight anymore, and then . . ."

Her voice trailed off. Emotion had overcome her. There was little surprise that this retelling would be traumatic for her, especially since it was coupled with the inevitable tension of being in the same room with Jackson, facing her assailant for the first time since the attack. She was physically safe from Jackson now. He sat at the defense table with court deputies nearby ready to restrain him if necessary. There was, however, absolutely no way to protect her from the emotional terror that she must have felt.

"Just take your time," the prosecutor said in an attempt to soothe his witness.

"Can we do anything to make you more comfortable?" Judge Jakes asked.

"No, I'm okay. I can continue," Saldana replied. She resumed her chronology of that awful morning.

"Then, suddenly, a man came, and he took the man who was stabbing me away, and I saw the man's face and it just imprinted on my brain."

"Do you see the man who grabbed you and stabbed you in court here today?"

"Yes, I do."

"Would you point that person out?"

"You don't want me to say what happened after that point?"

"No. Do you see the person who stabbed you here today?"

"Yes. He is the man in the blue shirt at the end of the table there," Saldana said, pointing to Arthur Jackson.

The simple question-and-answer format hid the swirling complexities of the relationship between these two people, one obsessively sought at all costs by Jackson and so completely unwanted by Saldana. He saw her as his salvation, while she was totally repulsed by this stranger, with whom she was now unavoidably entwined. She had but one thought looking again at her attacker, she would later write: "that he personified evil. An aura of malice and derangement seemed to emanate from his being. The sight of him made me feel sickened and deeply, unutterably depressed."

When the prosecuter ended his brief series of questions to her, defense attorney Manaster solicitously asked Saldana if it was comfortable for her to be facing in his direction. Normally, he stood at the defense table to conduct his examinations. Perhaps he was referring only to the discomfort of moving her body a bit to look at him from her location in the witness area. His usual position would cause Jackson to be in Saldana's line of sight when she looked at the defense lawyer.

"I would rather face this way," she replied, motioning in a direction that would not force her to see her attacker. Manaster complied with her wishes and stepped away from his client.

The defense had little to offer; there was no doubt that this matter was moving forward to trial. Manaster asked Saldana about her previous confirmation that Arthur Jackson was, without question, the man who had attacked her.

While her identification of Jackson was irrefutable, the violence of the episode had blurred her memory of peripheral details. "I think he was wrinkled. I remember him having something on that was very wrinkled," she said.

She recalled that nothing on the morning of the attack signaled a clue to her that things were amiss in her neighborhood. "It seemed to be a normal day on Hayworth, which is—there is not much activity, but it's basically a lot of elderly people live there and people are about, gardeners and things. It's not busy, but it's a safe feeling. It's not deserted."

She did not believe that she had ever seen Jackson before the morning of the attack. "There is also a chance that at times—when I perform, fans do come up to me after a performance or movie and ask for an autograph or something like that. It's possible he could have done that and I wouldn't remember the face, because there have been many of those people over the years."

Manaster finished his cross-examination quickly, not challenging with arguments of his own the inevitable decision from the judge that Jackson would be bound over for trial. He concluded by saying, "No affirmative defense at this time, your honor." The only viable affirmative defense he could have offered was a plea by Jackson that he was not guilty by reason of insanity. That, however, was a position Jackson would consistently refuse to take.

"Stand up please, Mr. Jackson," Judge Jakes ordered. The defendant stood up and looked at the judge.

"Mr. Jackson, it appears to me, based on the testimony of the witness we have heard this morning, that the crime of attempted murder did take place on the date of March 15th and there is sufficient cause to believe you are guilty of having committed it."

Jackson would be tried on two felony charges: attempted murder in the first degree and assault with a deadly weapon. Bail was continued at ten thousand dollars, an impossibly high figure for the penniless defendant, ensuring his continued confinement in jail until the trial. He would be formally arraigned on the charges on April 13 in Superior Court in Santa Monica, Judge Jakes ordered.

That done, Manaster asked for a sidebar conference, a session in which the lawyers and judge talk out of the hearing range of courtroom observers and the defendant. Manaster told the judge that he was concerned about Jackson's mental state. "He has indicated some statements which to me are suicidal. I did call the infirmary and the jail nurse, and they did have him secluded for a while. I think being in a regular [jail] module could be dangerous, so one request I have to the court is to have the jail medical staff evaluate him for the possibility of being put in the infirmary, secluded from other prisoners."

Manaster also asked that some toilet articles seized by police, particularly a special shampoo Jackson used for a scalp condition, be returned to him for use in jail. "I don't think he is going to get that," Judge Jakes responded, now cautious because of the defense attorney's concerns about suicide. "How do we know it isn't poison?" she asked. The judge ordered a psychiatric evaluation of Jackson, which took place the next evening in the medical clinic at the Los Angeles County Jail.

Sheriff's Deputy Charles Mitchell escorted Jackson to the evaluation and listened as Jackson answered a nurse's questions. The prisoner declared that he did not have thoughts of suicide. He explained that expressing such thoughts would be a sign of mental instability, which he believed would hamper his case. He told the nurse that he would not be convicted of a crime. He seemed to presume that his religious-based mission would be seen by others as justification enough for his actions.

Unaware of the effect his candor here could have on his trial, Jackson told the nurse that if he had had a revolver, he would have done a "professional job." He said he knew that by using a knife he had had only a fifty-fifty chance to accomplish his mission and kill Saldana.

At one point during this session, Jackson asked to be returned to the jail's high-security section, where he had left a Bible.

"They always get religion after the fact," a guard joked.

"I have done this before," Jackson quickly replied without elaboration. To those who heard him, he left the clear impression that he was referring to killing.

When the nurse's interview was concluded, the sheriff's deputy wrote in his report that "The suspect was subsequently transferred to 7000 Hospital for closer observation."

At Jackson's arraignment two weeks later, a "not guilty" plea was entered on his behalf. Deputy Public Defender Steven Moyer was appointed as his trial lawyer. From the outset, Moyer knew that he would be utilizing to some degree Arthur Jackson's psychiatric condition to explain and defend the actions of his client. For centuries, in cases involving acts committed by people suffering from severe mental illness, the law has provided for the reduction or elimination of criminal responsibility. Moyer, after his initial interview of Jackson, had no doubt that his client merited such consideration.

Moyer would need to look at the psychological issue from several vantage points. He required sound psychiatric consultation to confirm as strongly as possible the parameters of Jackson's mental deterioration. He also had to consider how others in the legal system, including prosecutors, judges, and jurors, would react to his presentation of a psychiatric defense in this matter, which was receiving a great deal of publicity.

Most important to developing his trial strategy, Moyer had to consider that he faced a distrusting and vengeful public attitude toward psychiatric defenses. This public opinion surely would be reflected in what the press wrote about the case, and that could also affect opinion in the jury pool.

As the prosecution of Arthur Jackson moved forward, there was a rising tide of public outrage over the results of two other criminal trials involving defendants who had raised psychiatric issues to explain their actions. Those two cases, one in California and one in Washington, D.C., involved men who had committed acts of violence and, after testimony concerning their mental illnesses, saw their criminal responsibility either reduced or eliminated in court proceedings. Each case had dominated public attention for a time. The majority of Americans were not happy with the outcome of either, according to polls that revealed widespread distrust of psychiatric defenses in general. These misgivings, so widely held in society, were spawned to a large degree by a misunderstanding of the psychiatrist's role in the criminal justice system.

Both incidents involved gun attacks on elected officials. The defendants in the two cases, Dan White and John Hinckley, had come to represent for many Americans the failure of the criminal judicial system. Many people were uncomfortable with a legal process that seemed to them to sweep aside the notion of responsible behavior and instead focus on abstract concepts, such as "state of mind." To many, psychiatric defenses amounted to nothing more than illegitimate courtroom ploys, rather than proper use of medical knowledge about the effects of mental illness on a person.

In California, particularly, because it had happened close to home, there was continuing controversy about two killings that had taken place four years earlier. San Francisco mayor George Moscone and city supervisor Harvey Milk had been shot to death by Dan White, a former city supervisor. White, in a much-criticized trial, was convicted of killing the two men, but the jurors, to the consternation of the prosecutor and others, accepted the defense's psychiatric testimony and reduced the severity of the charges the state had brought against White.

White, although imprisoned, was still the focus of a continuing debate because he was to be paroled early in 1984. The actions he and his lawyer took at the trial had led the California legislature in 1981 to change the state law and limit some psychiatric defenses, alterations that affected Jackson's trial.

Dan White was thirty-two years old at the time of the shootings. A high school dropout who became an army paratrooper, White then returned to San Francisco where he first held a job as a fireman before joining the city police force. He quit his police department job once, rejoined the force, and then left again in 1977 when he ran for one of several supervisor positions, winning on a platform of law-and-order conservatism.

His salary as a supervisor, a post equivalent to that of alderman or council member in other municipalities, was half what he had earned as a policeman. True to his history of moodiness and change-of-heart actions, and expressing reluctance and ambivalence about his decision, he resigned from the political office on November 10, 1978, claiming that he couldn't stay on because of personal financial pressures.

Within hours of his precipitous resignation he said he wanted to be reinstated to the Board of Supervisors. His request by itself, however, because he had formally resigned, could not return him to office. His supervisor's seat was now legally vacant. The city charter gave authority to Mayor Moscone to choose to reappoint White, or to name anyone else he wanted as a successor to the seat. Moscone struggled with the decision, and there was much accompanying debate in the city. Harvey Milk, an openly avowed homosexual representing a liberal constituency, lobbied against the conservative White's reinstatement.

White had made his reinstatement request on November 17. Nine days later, on November 26, Moscone announced his decision. He would not return Dan White to the Board of Supervisors. White first heard about his rejection from a news reporter calling him for comment.

The next day, carrying a concealed handgun, White surreptitiously entered San Francisco City Hall through a basement window, avoiding the building's proper entrances where electronic security devices would have detected his weapon. Obviously unaware of the danger White presented, Moscone readily admitted the former supervisor to his office, presumably expecting only to be engaged in debate about the action he had taken. Others nearby heard the sounds of a brief argument before White pulled out his gun and shot Moscone. Within two minutes, White had moved on to Milk's office, where he also shot and killed the supervisor. He left City Hall without being apprehended. Within a few minutes, he surrendered at a nearby police station. He turned over his .38-caliber pistol and nine empty bullet cartridges.

The city was, naturally, in shock over the deaths. Tensions were further aggravated because the shootings had a tinge of antihomosexual bias attached to them, fueling simmering resentment in the highly vocal and politically active homosexual community of San Francisco, particularly against the police department. Then-Supervisor Diane Feinstein, close to both Moscone and Milk, first came into national prominence when she announced the homicides to a distraught crowd at City Hall. As a result, she furthered her political career by maintaining order, helping to calm a troubled citizenry. She later became mayor, lost the California governor's office to former U.S. Senator Pete Wilson by a slim margin in 1990, and went on to win a seat in the United States Senate in 1992.

The case against Dan White attracted its greatest controversy when White's defense lawyer, Douglas Schmidt, presented substantial psychiatric testimony at trial that a depression-associated diet of junk food had altered White's body chemistry and, therefore, had negatively affected White's thought process at the time he shot his victims. White's mental ability to control and conform his conduct had been diminished by depression and the associated effects of the sugar-laden diet, the lawyer argued.

California law then allowed this defense of "diminished capacity," meaning that a defendant could attempt to prove that his mental process had been impaired to the extent that he was incapable of achieving the mental states necessary to be convicted of criminal charges. In the case of murder in the first degree, California law required that the defendant, at the time of the crime, had to be able to deliberate and premeditate with "malice aforethought" and possess the "intent to kill."

White's explanation for his actions became derisively known as the "Twinkie Defense," for the brand name of one of the snack foods with which the normally athletic and health-conscious man had allegedly been gorging himself prior to the shootings. "Mental illness cracked this man," White's lawyer told the jurors at the opening of the trial.

Whatever ridicule the argument was receiving in some quarters outside the courtroom, the jurors were persuaded that White had been psychologically impaired at the time of the shootings. Some jurors were observed crying during the dramatic playing of a tape recording of White's twenty-five-minute oral confession to police. Babbling and crying during the entire discussion with investigators, he said that when he confronted

Milk, "it was like my head was going to burst." He claimed that Milk "started kind of smirking. He smirked at me and said 'Too bad.' I got all flushed up and hot and shot him. . . . I've been under an awful lot of pressure. I couldn't take it anymore."

The jury convicted White on two counts of manslaughter, lesser crimes than the first-degree murder charges sought by the prosecution. Specifically, the jury had concluded that White had been mentally incapable of forming "malice aforethought," as the law required. The phrase can be difficult for laypeople to understand because its legal definition does not follow what one might expect from the two words themselves. California law then defined malice, in part, as the ability to control and conform one's conduct to the requirements of the law.

The prosecution was criticized for an inadequate presentation. Among the defects, the critics said, was a lack of proper stress on White's conservative, antihomosexual stance as a possible motive for acting out against Moscone and Milk, both strong proponents of codifying homosexual rights, a policy to which White was adamantly opposed.

The judge levied the maximum sentence possible, seven years and eight months, which meant that White could be paroled from prison within four years, which seemed to many to be a disappointingly short time of incarceration for what White had done. The night of the sentencing hearing, San Francisco was routed by destructive protest demonstrations.

The California Court of Appeal later upheld the conviction and sentence as appropriate under the law, but also offered some sympathy for the viewpoints of those who believed White had gotten away with something. "The facts and circumstances of this case virtually mandate the imposition of the maximum penalty allowed by law," the court said in response to White's lawyer's arguments seeking a further reduction. Then the appeals court noted that an argument could be made that the evidence "fully supported a conviction for the crimes of murder in the first degree." Appeals court judges, however, are not empowered to increase punishments with which they disagree, only reduce them where appropriate. Additionally, the appeals court must accept all of the trial's findings of fact and deal only with issues of misapplied law.

Responding to the public outcry that the state's laws were faulty in the area of psychiatric defenses, the California legislature acted by adopting revisions. In 1981, Governor Edmund G. Brown, Jr., signed into law a bill to ban "diminished capacity" as a defense in a state criminal trial. The bill had been overwhelmingly adopted by both houses of the legislature. The law went into effect on New Year's Day 1982, the day Arthur Jackson landed at John F. Kennedy International Airport in New York City. Although applicable to Jackson's trial, the new statute would not have the full limitations against certain psychiatric testimony that the legislation's promoters had intended.

In abolishing the psychiatric defense of diminished capacity, the state's lawmakers argued that California had gone far beyond what other states in the country allowed. Senate President Pro Tem David A. Roberti, a Democrat from Los Angeles, had sponsored the bill. After one successful legislative vote he told the *Los Angeles Times*, "Dropping the so-called diminished capacity defense from the state jurisprudence system is an important step toward making our courts what they were intended to be—places for determining guilt or innocence. [Diminished capacity] permits the jury to use relatively unobjective [*sic*] criteria to determine guilt. Diminished capacity relies heavily on psychiatry, which makes its determinations without hard evidence."

The second case that brought public focus on psychiatric defenses was the assassination attempt against

President Ronald Reagan on March 30, 1981, only two months after his inauguration. The videotape of the shooting outside the Washington Hilton Hotel, where the President had just delivered a speech, was shown over and over again on television news programs, imprinting its senseless violence on the American consciousness. There were horrifyingly dramatic pictures of Secret Service agents with weapons drawn and quickly apprehending would-be assassin John Hinckley as the President was being protectively pushed into his limousine and others lay bleeding and wounded on the sidewalk just a few yards away. The pain on the face of one Secret Service agent, falling backward and clutching his abdomen, was visible. There was no doubt where the shots had come from as other Secret Service agents, some brandishing automatic weapons, piled on Hinckley. Television news showed exactly what Hinckley had done, in contrast to the lingering controversy over the John F. Kennedy assassination by Lee Harvey Oswald, which many have questioned in the decades since.

Public upset arose from a widely perceived disparity between Hinckley's undeniable physical act that afternoon—aiming and firing his gun and wounding four people—and the eventual jury verdict.

Unquestionably, John Hinckley was a deeply disturbed young man when he shot the President, a policeman, a Secret Service agent, and White House Press Secretary James Brady, who suffered the most serious wounds in the incident. Brady, who will never fully recover, was later joined by his wife in becoming a forceful proponent of gun control, inspiring federal legislation called the "Brady Bill," which requires a five-day waiting period to purchase a handgun.

Hinckley's goal had been to impress the actress Jodie Foster, on whom he vainly showered affection through telephone calls and letters to her at Yale University where she was an undergraduate. She wisely rejected all the advances made by this obviously disturbed fan.

John Hinckley had a long history of mental illness with which his affluent Colorado family had tried to contend through psychiatric care. The trial evidence demonstrated that Hinckley's psychiatric problems had produced a debilitated mental state at the time of the shooting. The jury accepted the defense plea and found Hinckley "not guilty by reason of insanity." The verdict was a bitterly unsatisfying solution for many Americans. Across the country, people could not understand or accept the concept that although Hinckley, unquestionably, had pulled the trigger again and again, he could still be found "not guilty" of a crime. The test used then in the District of Columbia jurisdiction to legally determine that a defendant had been insane at the time of the event had been formulated by the American Law Institute. The criteria included the identical definition California law stipulated for finding malice aforethought: that the defendant had to have the capacity to conform his conduct to the requirements of the law.

The combination of law and psychiatry can result in debate over murky issues. English law has historically defined a crime as a combination of a physical act and a simultaneous state of mind. Popular opinion mistakenly assumes that physical acts alone define crime. Psychiatric testimony has become increasingly important in criminal trials during the past fifty years, presented to explain and identify the complicated mental states inherent in crimes. Such evidence is intended to help juries determine the level of criminality reached by a defendant's actions.

While safeguards in the law to protect the mentally impaired date back hundreds of years, psychiatry as a medical specialty is a relatively new development of this century, combining the arts of medicine and psychology. Only in the past few decades has psychiatry been refined as a forensic science for courtroom use.

Psychiatric defenses can take several forms when offered in a trial. Entering a plea of "not guilty by reason of insanity" is a legal option available only to the defendant and is called an "affirmative defense." The purpose of the plea is to eliminate all criminal responsibility of the person charged. However, a successful insanity plea is not equal to a verdict of "not guilty," after which a defendant is free to go. When found not guilty by reason of insanity, a person is not automatically released from custody. Most often the person is confined in a secure psychiatric treatment facility, in many cases for a longer period of time than if imprisoned following a guilty verdict in a criminal trial.

John Hinckley, for example, remains in custody thirteen years after the assassination attempt, much longer than most people convicted of shooting but not killing others, even considering that the attempted murder of a president or other federal official is a crime viewed more seriously than the attempted murder of an average citizen. The high visibility of this case virtually ensures that Hinckley will not be released from confinement in a mental institution in the near future.

The principle that we do not incarcerate people in jails or prisons to punish them for actions over which they have no control reflects our humanity as a society. Psychiatric defenses rest on hundreds of years of legal precedent, confirming a compassionate recognition in the law of the intellectual and emotional limitations of the mentally ill.

Still, public sympathy for psychiatric defenses has never been broad-based or strong. Public sentiment favors holding mentally ill people like John Hinckley and Arthur Jackson not only responsible but punishable for their conduct.

There is also the wide belief, based on many dismaying examples, that too often the violent mentally ill are released from confinement far too soon. Particularly in state hospitals, where doctors are routinely overworked and underpaid, a wide range of psychiatric competence sometimes results in cases of stunningly poor judgment, further eroding public trust in the profession. Many times the physicians making such diagnoses are "acting psychiatrists" who actually are general practitioners or retirees from other specialties.

Examples of this unfortunate process are plentiful. In California a man complained that his neighbor was purposely transmitting constipation-inducing "radio waves." The "victim" pleaded with his neighbor to stop the "assault." Nothing changed, of course. The problems were a creation of a disturbed imagination in the delusional "victim," who then purchased a shotgun and killed his next-door "tormenter."

The defendant was diagnosed as a paranoid schizophrenic and adjudicated "not guilty by reason of insanity." He was sent to a state mental health facility where his psychiatric condition was periodically reviewed, as required by law, to determine whether he had improved enough psychologically to justify release from custody.

In a hospital interview by a staff psychiatrist five years after the shooting, the man was asked, "Can you guarantee us that you will never harm anybody else?"

"Absolutely," he replied.

"How can we be sure?" the psychiatrist asked.

"Because the guy who was constipating me is now dead," the patient replied.

That response, demonstrating that the man was still in the grip of the delusion that had caused him to act so irrationally in the first place, should have ensured the inmate's continued confinement. The psychiatrist, however, recommended release, declaring that the patient was no longer a danger to society because he expressed no threats against anyone else. In a remarkably inept decision by the judge reviewing the recommendation, the man was set free. The judge's deliberation was faulty because it focused not on whether the man was still mentally ill and required further psychiatric treatment, but solely on the imperfect assessment of whether the man was likely to harm anyone again. The man disappeared into society with no government-agency supervision or follow-up, free to go wherever he wished. No state employs a tracking system capable of readily determining whether the man ever again acted out on his delusions. His incomplete story stands as a disturbing example of countless episodes in which mentally ill and dangerous people, unpredictable "emotional volcanoes" who have the capacity to erupt with violence at any time, are released by a legal system that could and should maintain some supervisory link but does not.

To demonstrate that someone's sanity has been restored, courts are supposed to require testimony from the examining psychiatrist indicating that the person no longer constitutes a danger to the health and safety of others as a result of his or her mental condition. A significant problem with the review of mentally ill people in custody, apart from intrinsically incompetent diagnosis, is that even skilled psychiatric evaluation in a protective hospital setting offers little indication of how a person will react once returned to the stresses of daily life. In addition, the patient-inmate is likely to be taking prescribed medication, which further ameliorates symptoms. Most individuals who are dangerous because of mental illness are not active threats 95 percent of the time, but the potential is always there. Public mistrust is fed by case after case of mentally ill people being prematurely released from confinement, sometimes to commit more horrible acts.

History seems to emphasize that only in high-profile cases, such as that of John Hinckley, is there always sufficient oversight to eliminate or minimize mistakes. In high-visibility cases, the nature of the crime and public response to it sometimes dictate highly conservative responses from psychiatrists unwilling to take a chance with their reputations by confirming that someone's sanity has been restored.

On the basis of pure statistics, releasing an individual who has killed another human and been found not guilty by reason of insanity offers a lesser risk to society than releasing a person who has been criminally convicted of crimes and imprisoned. The recidivism rate for the first group is relatively low, about 15 percent, as opposed to 62 percent for released convicts.

A psychiatrist would always be on safe ground in determining that sanity has not been restored to someone who suffers from schizophrenia and has been found not guilty by reason of insanity. Because the mental disorder is incurable and can only be controlled through medication and therapy, there is always possible a viable argument that the individual continues to represent a danger to the health and safety of others, just because his disease caused him to act out aggressively in the past.

At the other end of the scale, in insanity plea cases that have received no publicity, there is a tendency to release people in a shorter period of time than they would have spent in custody if they had been convicted of a crime and sent to prison.

The ability of the state to confine mentally ill people against their will, no matter how beneficial that may be to an individual in need of treatment or a society in need of protection, has become a daunting task because of changing social policy and a pattern of judicial review since the 1950s. In the socially turbulent era of the sixties, civil libertarians began to argue that there is no fundamental difference between a locked hospital ward and a jail cell. Their legal challenges led to court decisions that characterized mental hospitals as "sterile prisons."

To equate the two types of institutions is a mistake, however. They are similar only in their function of physically confining and controlling a group of people. A fundamental difference between the two is found in the training of the staffs. There is a vast dissimilarity between the workplace attitudes and job duties of hospital nursing personnel and those of prison guards.

The atmosphere created by those confined in each type of place is also qualitatively different. Eighty-five percent of our prison population can be labeled *psychopaths*, a term synonymous with *sociopath* or *antisocial personality*. The phrase defines an individual prone to come into conflict with society who does not, or cannot, learn from experience. Medically labeled a "character disorder," this condition's prevalence in the prison system creates a tremendous problem of control for prison officials. Alternately, 85 percent of the residents of a state hospital are *psychotic*, a generic term for a variety of mental illnesses involving disturbances in thinking or emotions. Because these diseases are affected by neurotransmitters in the brain, reliable mood-altering drugs are available to blunt the psychotic symptoms, thus creating a largely benign population that is more easily controlled than a group of prison inmates.

As Jackson's trial date approached, Dan White was serving his sentence and the issues emanating from his case were still much discussed in the press. (White committed suicide shortly after being released from prison in 1984.) In an additional exhibition of public reaction, beyond the legislative revision of California statutes, a "Victim's Bill of Rights" was passed by the voters in a highly politicized initiative. One element of the measure went even further than the state statute in limiting psychiatric defenses.

Steven Moyer knew that his defense of Arthur Jackson would involve a battle against public misconceptions and stereotypes about mental illness. Before he could concentrate on that, however, the defense lawyer encountered a dilemma evolving from Jackson's prolific writing. On April 2, eighteen days after his arrest, Jackson wrote a letter to Terry Willows, a Los Angeles–based British journalist working for the London newspaper the

Star. The newspaper account that followed concentrated on Jackson's offer of restitution to his victim. Moyer obtained a copy of the letter from Willows. The document read in part:

> I have already mentioned the plan to the Public defender twice in Beverly Hills Municipal Court, March 17 and March 30. On that latter date, Theresa sat only a few yards from me giving evidence in a wheelchair. We must try and help her now that she didn't die and survived. . . . However, if my special request [to die by state-administered execution], which is an extremely reasonable one considering how generous my offer is in exchange for it, is rejected, then we all lose. No one wins . . . by endeavoring to win my special request, I am not only out to vindicate myself, of course, but to provide a strategic and convenient means of paying—of raising funds to pay for Theresa Saldana's medical expenses and to award her criminal compensation, substantial damages, as well as to disclose intelligence on unsolved major crimes, including murder committed in the United Kingdom, in exchange for the granting of my special request.

The section that seemed most important to Moyer was Jackson's oblique references to other crimes that he would solve in return for his proposed concessions. Jackson had made the same offer to Moyer, although he had been more specific about the crimes to which he was referring. Moyer's instinct was that Jackson was mentioning other crimes as a ploy, that he had not actually committed them but was just using his phenomenal memory of detail by reciting from news stories he had read in Great Britain about unsolved crimes. On April 28, Moyer sent a letter to Robert Craig, a London barrister, soliciting his help in legal research.

"As you might expect," Moyer wrote, "I am preparing an insanity defense with respect to the Saldana attempted murder case. . . . It would obviously be helpful in presenting the insanity defense to establish that Mr. Jackson's claim of 'bank raids,' and 'murder' in the United Kingdom are false. However, should such claims be true, it is imperative that all inquiries and results thereof be kept completely confidential." Moyer asked Craig to provide newspaper clippings and the physical descriptions of the suspects in unsolved cases to which Jackson might be referring.

The defense lawyer was concerned that Jackson might start talking in greater detail to law enforcement investigators or reporters about these matters. From a tactical standpoint as a defense lawyer, whether Jackson's claims were true or not was almost irrelevant to Moyer. He believed that anything Jackson said could provide ammunition for the prosecutor and thereby complicate his job of defending his client. Moyer obtained a court order requiring any law enforcement agency wishing to interview Jackson to contact the defense lawyer first. In addition, Moyer advised Jackson not to discuss with anyone, especially news reporters, his claims of knowledge about other crimes.

Moyer was right that the district attorney's office would pursue any lead. Investigators there, too, had obtained a copy of Jackson's letter to Willows and made an effort to determine if Jackson had been involved in other crimes before attacking Saldana. Inquiries were made of Interpol, the international police agency, as well as law enforcement authorities at Scotland Yard in London. The prosecutor, Michael Knight, had a hunch that Jackson was telling the truth about having committed crimes before.

Jackson, district attorney investigators quickly determined, had no criminal record in the United Kingdom. In response to their request, no records of unsolved crimes that could even remotely be traced to Jackson's claims were produced. This matter quietly receded into the background and was not even mentioned again during the remainder of the prosecution. Everyone involved in the case in Los Angeles turned their attention to the facts and circumstances of the attack on Saldana.

From the beginning, Moyer believed his client was insane, and his trial preparation emphasized a compatible strategy. His first, small hurdle was the federal government bureaucracy. The General Services Administration's National Personnel Records Center denied Moyer's request for hospital reports emanating from Jackson's previous deportations. The government said that Moyer, a lawyer, could not receive the records directly because "they contain information that can be interpreted and explained properly only by a physician." Moyer then submitted the name and address of one of his consulting psychiatrists, a person who could receive the documents under federal guidelines.

Moyer's task was to determine with as much persuasive psychiatric data as possible the boundaries of Jackson's thought process and whether he possessed any control over his violent behavior.

First, he needed to determine whether Jackson was so mentally ill that he would be judged incompetent to stand trial at all. The analysis of that question would, in any case, provide psychological data to later support whatever defense Moyer might eventually choose to employ. The prevailing standard in California in 1982 for determining mental competency required a threefold test. To be categorized competent to stand trial, the defendant was required to understand the nature and purposes of the legal proceedings, have the ability to cooperate with a lawyer in presenting a defense, and understand his or her relationship to the pending criminal charges.

Moyer already knew that Jackson could cooperate in his defense in accordance with the legal definition. The Scotsman was spending hours answering questions fully, even adding extraneous details and facts the defense attorney didn't need.

Two forensic psychiatrists, Ronald Markman, M.D., the coauthor of this book, and John M. Stahlberg, M.D., both frequently called by prosecutors and defense attorneys in southern California as expert witnesses, were hired by Moyer to examine Jackson.

When he was being evaluated by Dr. Markman, Jackson attempted to set up the ground rules. He was as much a questioner as an answerer, asking details of the psychiatrist's background and trying to control the interview. When the subjects of mental illness and psychiatric defenses to the crimes were raised by the doctor, Jackson digressed, asking a question about an unrelated subject. He was unwilling to accept or acknowledge that there was something psychologically wrong with him.

The interview employed a standard format of clinical psychiatric questions designed to test whether Jackson's behavior matched a pattern associated with schizophrenia. First, Dr. Markman concluded that Jackson's mental illness was not the product of organic damage, which would have revealed itself in impaired answers to questions requiring certain types of memory.

In his hours with Dr. Markman, there was no intensity in Jackson's voice when he spoke of Theresa Saldana, although she was a woman with whom he had been obsessed for more than a year. He had tried to kill her, and yet his tone of voice when he spoke of her registered as if she were a complete stranger to him, someone whom he had not met or ever heard of. Jackson seemed to deal with the interview as a trifling intellectual exercise, raising barriers against any emotionalism, a reaction typical of his condition.

The defendant explained that he had acted "on behalf of the Order of the Knights of St. Michael and the Kingdom of Heaven." He was, he said quite seriously, the only member of this organization. As an incentive, though, he offered to admit people from his defense team to the order as a reward for arranging his execution at Alcatraz.

Jackson's behavioral history was an important guide to determining his current psychiatric diagnosis. His condition had been documented for thirty years and was classically consistent with schizophrenia. There wasn't one aspect of Jackson's life in which he hadn't expressed some abnormality of thought or behavior.

The suspect's diary and other writings consistently demonstrated his skewed outlook on life and were a reflection of his mental illness. Those documents that Jackson carried with him, and which he treated as though they were incalculably valuable religious artifacts, were full of unnecessary and irrelevant detail, always jumping from topic to topic. The special intensity of the writing reflected an obsessive-compulsive nature. Arthur Jackson was an individual who, simply, was incapable of normal thought.

Insistent that he had no interest in inflicting pain on Saldana, Jackson repeated that he only wanted "to fulfill my mission," seeming not to recognize that to do so would obviously cause pain to Saldana, however brief, even if he had killed her with the first knife thrust. And certainly, he did not consider that her death or injury would inflict sorrow on others. He was aware that human laws did not give him the right to attack Saldana, but he believed that secular rules did not apply to him. He was acting under the moral guidance of a greater force, one which he called the "laws of Heaven and spiritual conscience." If he could try again, he said, he would be more "efficient, so there would be no disfigurement."

Despite the extremely serious criminal charges, and the horror of the event itself, Jackson concerned himself with minutiae, finding vital importance in irrelevance. He once pointedly corrected Dr. Markman during the examination after the psychiatrist mistakenly missed the precise date, by two days, on which Jackson had seen *Defiance*.

He did not agree with the assessment of his mental illness made by either doctor. "And I think to try and make something more complicated of [my condition] is really barking up the wrong tree," Jackson told Dr. Markman. He described himself to Dr. Stahlberg as a "philosophic misanthrope."

There was no doubt, though, that his mental illness was chronic and had never responded positively to treatment. There were no psychological strengths to be found in Arthur Jackson, unless credit were to be given for his ability to survive in a withdrawn state without real need for other human contact on any regular basis.

Neither psychiatrist considered Jackson a suicide risk. He had had many opportunities to kill himself, and the only documented attempt had been almost twenty-six years before in New York City when he had taken the overdose of sleeping pills. Jackson was determined to die by being shot in the head by state-hired executioners, the way Cretzer had been killed at the hands of prison guards. This was a form of suicide, perhaps, but not in Jackson's view.

The two psychiatrists independently arrived at the same diagnosis. They concluded that Jackson suffered from a chronic paranoid schizophrenia, and this condition had been the primary, underlying cause of the compulsive, focused, violent attack against Saldana. As crazy as Jackson was, though, the doctors agreed that according to California law, he was competent to stand trial as a criminal defendant.

This seeming paradox, that a defendant could be "crazy" and "competent" at the same time, results from a conflict between medical diagnosis and legal definition.

Central to examining the dynamics between psychiatry and the law is understanding the purpose for which psychiatrists were initially brought into the legal system: to explain the actions of defendants in a way that would relieve those defendants of criminal responsibility for their acts. When psychiatrists were first called upon to testify as experts they dealt solely with the issue of insanity, the extreme condition that relieves someone completely of criminal responsibility.

There is a common public perception, as noted before, that the insanity defense is overused and abused. In practice, however, such pleas are rarely employed by defense attorneys, and in even fewer instances are they successful.

The legal foundation for the insanity plea used today comes from a nineteenth-century British case. Daniel McNaughton, a Scotsman driven by deeply passionate political delusions, attempted to assassinate the British prime minister, Sir Robert Peel, on January 20, 1843. (Attacks against the well-known by mentally disturbed people are not a modern phenomenon of the television age. Queen Victoria, among others, was the target of an attempted assassination.)

In his attack on Peel, McNaughton fired a gun and missed his target, killing instead the prime minister's private secretary, who was walking alongside. McNaughton was immediately arrested and put on trial at the Old Bailey in London two months later.

The prosecution argued that, as a general principle, mentally ill people should face legal responsibility if they can intellectually distinguish between right and wrong, without consideration of whether they were capable of controlling their behavior or rationally understood their act. The defense responded that those who suffered from a severe mental illness that abnormally prescribed their thoughts and behavior, as McNaughton allegedly did, should not be held criminally responsible for their actions. That meant that they should not be punished for what they did as a result of a psychological malady.

The court agreed with the defense. The *Times* of London published a critical editorial lamenting that "the judge in his treatment of the madman yields to the decision of the physician, and the physician in his treatment becomes the judge." The newspaper editorialists, like many people, believed that the only relevant point to consider was whether someone physically committed an act.

Although McNaughton had been found not guilty by reason of insanity, he did not escape action by the state. He was confined to a lunatic asylum where he died twenty-two years later at age fifty.

Not surprisingly, the McNaughton decision elicited a public outcry, and in response the House of Lords appointed a fifteen-judge panel which established a standard for determining legal insanity. The result of their work, the "McNaughton Rule" as it came to be known, in essence defined insanity as the inability to distinguish right from wrong, or to understand the nature and quality of one's act. The rules in the McNaughton opinion have shaped legal thought for the 150 years since they were written.

In many instances, defense lawyers advise their clients against an insanity plea, even when it would unquestionably be accepted by the prosecution and the court. Often, if a simple guilty plea is entered, a defendant will be exposed to a shorter time of confinement in a jail than if he were to be confined in a mental institution after an insanity plea. Usually not taken into consideration is whether a defendant could benefit from treatment in a hospital.

Constitutional interpretations have come to prevent prosecutors from introducing the insanity issue, no matter how beneficial to the government's interests of protecting society. One inherent problem is practical. Under the law, a person is presumed sane until proven insane. The prosecution cannot prove insanity without the cooperation of the defendant, and criminal defendants have an absolute constitutional right not to talk to or cooperate with government investigators.

Furthermore, allowing prosecutors to raise the insanity question as a means of seeking the longest confinement of the defendant possible, even in a hospital, conflicts with long-established concepts of judicial fairness and justice. Once an insanity plea is accepted, the defendant's involuntary confinement to a hospital can last as long as psychiatrists continue to determine that the mental illness is producing dangerousness, for the lifetime of the individual in some cases.

Central to public suspicion of insanity pleas is that the confinement that follows such a plea is indeterminate. There always is the possibility that a hospital confinement might also be far shorter, sometimes shockingly more brief, than the potential prison term that otherwise could have been imposed upon criminal conviction. If psychiatrists conclude that the person's debilitating mental condition no longer exists and, therefore, that the person no longer constitutes a danger, there are no grounds for further confinement of the person. Within this precept lies the crux of public discomfort with the process, particularly when sensational cases reveal that inadequate medical decisions have resulted in the release of a dangerous patient, sometimes within days of the plea.

Many people suspect that a large number of defendants feign insanity in order to avoid punishment. Notorious cases feed the public imagination, such as the well-publicized courtroom claims of U.S. Department of Justice prosecutors that Mafia members Anthony Acceturo and Vincent "The Chin" Gigante long used mental illness as a ploy to avoid prosecution. In practice, however, such efforts rarely succeed. In almost all instances, if an examination of a defendant is conducted by a trained, experienced forensic psychiatrist, such malingering can easily be discovered and exposed to the court.

Recent court decisions have refined the procedures by which someone may be kept confined after a not guilty by reason of insanity plea. Presently, an individual cannot be confined for a period longer than the maximum sentence resulting from a regular guilty verdict, unless subsequent legal proceedings determine that the person continues to constitute an imminent danger to others, a difficult process under the law.

Over the years since the insanity plea was first employed, the time spent in confinement by people who successfully use the plea has, in general, diminished. Well into the nineteenth century people found not guilty by reason of insanity invariably faced lifelong confinement in a mental institution. In common law these individuals were viewed as ''mad dogs'' or ''inculcated with the devil.'' The McNaughton Rule itself was evidence of a growing perplexity within the judiciary, befuddled in its attempt to effectively deal with mentally disturbed people and their criminallike behavior.

Now, 150 years later, the judiciary is still grappling with the same complex issues. Some states, Michigan among them, have been experimenting with an alternative verdict of ''guilty, but mentally disordered.'' The problem with this approach is that an argument can be made that everybody who commits a crime is mentally disturbed. This raises a number of troubling questions for the courts. Among them is whether certain psychiatric diagnoses can be excluded from this verdict. For example, an antisocial personality, common among many criminals, is evidence of emotional disturbance. Whether that condition then relieves someone of criminal responsibility has been intensely debated.

In practice, as courts, like other government entities, have become restrained by dwindling budgets, the best psychiatric information is not always provided. Sometimes judges authorize payment for only the briefest psychiatric examination in order to fulfill statutory requirements. While such examinations may be legally sufficient, they can be medically incomplete and cursory.

Today, when medicine and law clash, medicine loses. The United States is a country dominated by lawyers and legal thinking. Every forensic psychiatrist has examined people whom he or she found to be terribly ill and in need of treatment, but later watched the same people walk freely out the courtroom door, untreated and not knowing where their next step was going to take them.

In one stunning coincidental hallway meeting of two men awaiting court hearings, a man who thought he was Jesus met a man who thought he was God. As ludicrous as it sounds, the two embraced, respecting in all seriousness each other's self-identification. Perhaps even more outrageous, a few hours later one of them was released by a judge because he didn't fulfill the civil criteria for involuntary hospitalization. In order to qualify, a person must be judged gravely disabled and unable to provide for food, clothing, or shelter. In this case, the judge determined that the man seemed to exist well enough on his own with a Social Security check, even though he lived on a park bench and foraged for food in Dumpsters.

As a society we consistently release dangerous or helpless people from confinement because, under the law, personal freedom has been placed on a higher plane than the need to treat illness. Using the same logic, courts have determined that individuals who are confined have the right to refuse treatment and remain sick.

Into this debate came the case of Arthur Richard Jackson. The defendant himself did not allow the insanity question to surface in court, but he could not avoid another curious mixture of law and psychiatry. The same psychiatrists who had diagnosed Jackson's deep, obsessive, thought-altering mental illness nonetheless necessarily found him mentally competent to stand trial, according to the definitions of state statute.

The difference between insanity and competency, in legal terms, is that insanity deals with the mental condition in the past, and only in connection with issues of criminal responsibility for a past act. Competency deals with the defendant's current psychiatric condition and his capacity to proceed with the trial. The standards for determining each state of mind are different.

The legal conclusion that Jackson could cooperate "rationally" with his lawyer may seem a bewildering one. There is logic in the formula, however. However "crazy" Jackson's reason for trying to kill Saldana may have been, the fact is, he offered his attorney an explanation of his actual motivation, which allowed the defense attorney to choose appropriate defense tactics. Jackson was able to articulate *his* reality of why events occurred as they did; the *behavior* may be crazy, but the *narration* of events is rational. Jackson's verbalization is an accurate reflection of why he acted as he did.

Steven Moyer, Jackson's defense attorney, didn't think that the competency standard made sense. He believed that the courts created a fiction in deeming Jackson and people like him "competent" for any purpose. The defense lawyer was not convinced that Jackson was capable of making "knowing and intelligent decisions" about how to proceed at trial. He was also bothered by a procedure that attempted to hold mentally ill people like Arthur Jackson criminally responsible for their conduct.

The truth was that while Jackson may have cognitively understood his act on some level, he lacked the capacity to conform and control his conduct. He knew that society defined what he did as criminal. But similarly to the civil disobedient, Jackson *believed* his purpose was higher than the law and he was, therefore, *compelled* to act according to that calling despite "earthly" consequences.

Had Jackson been viewed incompetent to stand trial, the result would have only postponed court action, not precluded it forever. A defendant is usually determined to be incompetent only when blatantly and actively psychotic to the point where a rational question-answer conversation with his attorney is impossible. Then, the person is confined to a hospital where attempts are made to reverse the condition. If treatment succeeds, competency is deemed to have been restored and the trial goes forward.

Being adjudged competent to stand trial, Jackson was able to control his trial strategy, a right of all defendants. Moyer was ethically bound to comply with Jackson's instructions, even if he knew they were decisions emanating from madness and inimical to the best interests of his client or society.

Moyer suggested that he seek a continuance of the trial, to give time for the White and Hinckley controversies to cool. He believed that the White verdict, a conviction on a lesser charge because of diminished capacity, had been "absolutely correct," but he also recognized that both cases had created a strong backlash of public sentiment against psychiatric defenses, which would surely be reflected by jurors empaneled at Jackson's trial. Moyer tried to explain that dilemma to his client.

Jackson, though, insisted on moving forward to trial, eager to continue his "divine mission."

"I think with what we've got we should go to the district attorney, and we should talk about entering a plea of not guilty by reason of insanity," Moyer said to his client.

"I don't want to make a psychiatric defense because I'm not crazy," Jackson answered.

"Ethically, I have to tell you the consequences of this if we win the insanity plea trial," Moyer said to Jackson.

"What's that?"

"They'll put you in a mental hospital."

"That's wonderful, that's wonderful. Because I'm not ill and they'll let me go. So I should do it."

"I wanted to stop at this point," Moyer later told the authors, "as a human being and as a citizen, and say to him, 'Great, let's enter the plea and I'll fight like crazy to get it.' Because that's what I felt he needed, society needed, and Saldana needed. It would just be over." Moyer, though, had ethical and legal obligations particular to a defense attorney. He had to present his client with his best judgment of the effects of the available options.

"Well, Dr. Markman and Dr. Stahlberg both say otherwise. They say that they think you're mentally ill, you need treatment, and in their opinion you will never get out."

Jackson, without anger, said, "If that's what they say, they're wrong. But I can't take the chance. I don't want to do it. I want to get out. I have an agenda. Well then, why don't we just have a trial?"

In his execution petition, Jackson had considered the possibility that he would be found insane and thus not subject to the death penalty, a scenario he wished to avoid.

Remember, not only am I desperate to get out of this world, but also the angels in heaven are anxious to get me out. I interpret this as viewed in a hypothetical sense rather than in a schizophrenic way of thinking because I am damned if I want to weaken or prejudice my own case for death by execution on the pretext of a cynical psychiatrist or of a vindictive prosecutor who may claim that my religious or romantic sentiments are evidence of insanity—delusions of grandeur/megalomania.—and recommends opposing the death penalty either before or after the deal between the U.S. authorities and myself has been approved. No one wins, we all lose if this type of "snake in the grass" game is to be reckoned with, and to sabotage the whole works.

If his petition were to be granted by the government, Jackson certainly didn't want "outside forces" tampering with his plans.

Nor would I tolerate a situation in which placard carrying liberal pressure groups and so-called "do-gooders," together with death penalty abolitionists, began demonstrating for the shortsighted, misguided and mundane purpose of preventing me from fulfilling my sacred mission. And that goes for "Bible-Thumping" Christian Fundamentalists who think they are right, and everyone else with different religious ideals (e.g., myself) are wrong.

The district attorney's office, through prosecutor Michael Knight, made a crucial pretrial strategy decision. Their stance, combined with Jackson's adamance about an insanity plea, would have unsettling reverberations in the years to come. The prosecution's pretrial position was a significant factor in forcing Moyer to limit his defense strategy options.

While the two men remember their exchanges somewhat differently, both Moyer and Knight agree that the defense attorney was put on notice that the district attorney's office would strenuously object to an insanity plea.

"I just can't accept [the plea]," Moyer recalled Knight saying.

Moyer believed that Knight was working on orders from superiors whose decision was politically motivated because of the extensive publicity Saldana could generate. In the end, he couldn't continue to try to convince his client to plead insanity if the prosecution was going to fight it. Because the California legislature had technically eliminated the trial use of "diminished capacity," Moyer planned to argue a similar variation on the theme, that Jackson had "diminished intent."

The legislature had acted because of growing public opinion that too many defendants had used diminished capacity pleas to inappropriately reduce their level of responsibility, particularly in homicide cases. Additionally, the definition of diminished capacity used by California courts was significantly more liberal than that used in other jurisdictions. Once certain normal states of mind were no longer attributable to a defendant in a homicide case, the severest criminal charge for which the person could be held responsible was manslaughter. That, in turn, meant a tremendous decrease in the potential prison time faced by a defendant, from a life sentence for first-degree murder to, in some cases, less than six years for manslaughter. One 1970s case involving a man who raped and strangled his victim, but on the basis of psychiatric testimony was later found guilty of only involuntary manslaughter, brought comments of outrage from both the judge and prosecutor and helped focus public opinion against diminished capacity defenses.

The true effect of the new laws, however, was that psychiatric testimony remained essentially unchanged. The "diminished intent" argument Moyer planned to make was virtually identical to a "diminished capacity" defense. The switching of words was a means of getting around the rigorous controls placed upon the courts by the legislature and the electorate. A political analogy would be a legislative body that is prohibited by the electorate from raising taxes and instead institutes certain "fees," which are nothing more than new taxes.

In California, court cases addressed to what extent psychiatrists could explain the previous actions of defendants. So-called ultimate issues of fact are the province of the jury, including whether the defendant did, in fact, premeditate, one of the conditions for a first-degree murder conviction. Court rulings prohibited psychiatrists from being asked on the witness stand, "Could the defendant premeditate?" The same court rulings, however, allowed the psychiatrist to be asked the question "Could the defendant plan ahead?"

A turbulent political climate surrounded the issues in the Jackson case. Proposition 8, the "Victim's Bill of Rights," although already approved by voters, would not become law until the following year. Still, the mood of the electorate had to be of concern to politicians.

Los Angeles County District Attorney Robert Philibosian was in a reelection campaign, and there was the perception among some in the office that the district attorney would appear weak to the voters if he "rolled over" and did not challenge an insanity plea in the Jackson case. The DA's office wanted Jackson prosecuted, convicted, and imprisoned on criminal charges. Among the high-profile lobbying groups pressing for such action was an organization formed by Saldana called "Victims for Victims."

Moyer knew that in almost every case in which a defendant was obviously suffering from severe mental illness, an insanity plea was an outcome agreeable to both prosecution and defense. The duplicity of the position maintained by the district attorney's office in the Jackson case is found in the numerous low-visibility cases where prosecutors routinely, and appropriately, accepted such pleas without challenge.

Moyer believed that Knight was an ethical and talented lawyer. Knight had been a deputy district attorney for twelve years and was part of a special prosecutions unit. The defense lawyer felt, however, that the district attorney's office, by stating its intention to challenge an insanity plea by Jackson, was a political entity making a decision that was in the best interest of neither Saldana nor society. The prosecution, in his view, had options and chose the one most politically advantageous.

A defense attorney's only responsibility is the vigorous defense of a client. The office of district attorney should be concerned with matters beyond the statistics of prosecutorial wins in the courtroom. The publicly elected district attorney has an obligation to see that justice is done by ensuring that cases are prosecuted only to the degree that the facts and the law allow. Sometimes that includes accepting appropriate insanity pleas.

Interestingly, neither of the two lawyers who would face each other in the courtroom seemed to be adopting a position just because their job required a particular stance. Each, by temperament and experience, had developed legal philosophies which, in this matter, clashed.

Moyer felt trapped. He believed that his client's deep-rooted mental illness cried out for use of the insanity plea, but the intransigence of both the district attorney's office and his own client prevented him from pursuing that option. "As a defense attorney you do what your client wants you to do," Moyer said. "If he tells you, 'I want out,' you try to get him out, whether or not you think he's a scumbag, a danger or anything else. . . . This is something courts, lawyers, and legislatures have been grappling with for centuries, and nobody has been able to deal with it effectively. . . . But a prosecutor has a different duty and a higher duty."

Knight, son of an Indiana steelworker and a man who worked his way through law school as a policeman, was professionally comfortable with carrying out office policy in this case. He did not believe the law was being bent injudiciously, and he set out to present a strong prosecution.

He thought that the best prosecutors knew everything there was to be known about a case, and that required reading every available document. In this case, that was a daunting task. Knight brought Jackson's writings home, poring over every sentence to see "if there is some clue, some relevance, some meaning, and whether it will show purpose and intent on the part of a man who has demonstrated capacity for violence. I wanted to understand why he was able to do what he did."

Knight never doubted that Jackson was mentally disordered to some degree. The prosecutor came to view this defendant as a "very intelligent fellow. Not all of his thinking is what you'd consider normal thinking, but in his mind he certainly had purpose and intent."

Initially, Knight wasn't sure about the accuracy of Jackson's diaries. "Until I had read everything. Then I got the picture of a man who not only is, but was extremely honest about his thought process, very forward about what his intentions were. Not in the sense that he could go to other people and relate with other people or communicate with other people ... but he was a very disciplined individual as to what he was doing, what his purpose was.

"He was smart enough to know that Theresa Saldana wasn't going to have anything to do with him. His writings were replete with the fact that he accepted his own position [in life], that he would be rejected by her and he would never have a chance with her in this life. The fuzzy thinking, obviously, was that he could kill her and get the death penalty and then spend eternity with her in some blissful peace."

Knight felt some sympathy for Jackson. "I thought he had a crummy life. He was a pathetic individual. I felt badly that an individual would have to go through everything he's gone through."

The prosecutor was incensed when he read medical records delineating the extent of the shock treatments Jackson had received at Kingseat Hospital. "To put somebody in a coma is bad enough. But secondarily to put him through electroshock treatment while he's in an altered state already, I thought was barbaric." Knight wondered whether the Kingseat treatment had been more damaging than helpful. "It was after that that he began to have marked problems, recurrences, going back in and out. . . . I thought that the psychiatrists had done a number on this guy and had probably damaged him. He probably would have been a lot better off if he had not gone to that clinic in Scotland."

Moyer believed that Jackson's legal best interests were in conflict with his psychiatric best interests. As Jackson's advocate, Moyer was obliged to seek the shortest time of confinement possible. The judicial system did not provide him with the option he thought best, a nonadversarial procedure by which medical documentation and testimony confirms a defendant's mental illness and results in hospitalization rather than a criminal trial.

Guiding Knight was his conclusion that Jackson was a dangerous man. "So I was intent on doing everything I could to see that he got a successful prosecution for what I believe was a vicious attack and attempt to kill, and that he would get the maximum time in light of the fact that he still possessed the intent to kill this woman. And it was a terrible crime."

With the trial about to begin, both lawyers and the judge who would preside were briefly distracted by a television producer's offers, which they found distasteful. Hollywood ethics were threatening to taint the proceedings.

Saldana was to portray herself in a television movie chronicling her physical and psychological recovery from the attack. Some of the proceeds reportedly would benefit Victims for Victims. The project was a noble enough effort in itself. Undeniably, Saldana was a completely innocent victim. Unfortunately, Hollywood's penchant to follow its own production agenda, without regard for the rules of conduct or sense of propriety elsewhere in society, resulted in unseemly overtures to some who should not have been approached at all.

Both Moyer and Knight say independent of each other that they were offered large sums of money to portray themselves in the movie and, apparently, in each instance claims were made that others had already agreed to participate.

"The person who contacted me represented himself to be Theresa Saldana's agent in some capacity, and he was contacting me on behalf of Theresa Saldana. So I was, in effect, being contacted by the victim," Moyer said. "[This] at least can be construed as an attempt to buy me, to get me to compromise my client's case for money. I don't believe that was their intent at all. I think what we were dealing with was 'the biz,' and that people involved in television and motion picture making in general have their own agendas and that is to get the movie made. And they don't understand the nuances of legal technicalities. Their feeling is that everybody is receptive to money and fame and fortune and 'what's wrong with that?' But an attorney or judge has to avoid even the appearance of impropriety."

Moyer said he was even shown a proposed contract by which Arthur Jackson would sign over the rights to his story. He later said he was told by the producer that both Knight and the trial judge, Laurence J. Rittenband, had already agreed to participate in the project and, because of that, the defense lawyer asked for a meeting with the judge and the prosecutor.

"First of all, nobody has discussed this with me and had they done so I would have either held them in contempt or, at minimum, thrown them out of here," Moyer quotes Rittenband as saying. The judge made it clear he would not tolerate any such agreements by any of the legal officers of the court participating in the trial.

When the movie eventually aired, actors played the parts of prosecutor, defense attorney, and judge.

The defense attorney and the prosecutor agreed on one issue. Because no one denied that Jackson had committed the attack, there would be no harsh cross-examination of Saldana. The defense lawyer suggested that the actress might be put more at ease if they were to meet prior to trial. Knight agreed and arranged a conference. Moyer left the brief session fully convinced of Saldana's unsurprising and unyielding determination to see Jackson imprisoned forever.

Arthur Jackson's last Aberdeen home
Photo by Dr. Ronald Markman

A page from Arthur Jackson's diary after arriving in
New York to begin his search for Theresa Saldana
L.A. County District Attorney Evidence Document

Notes Jackson made to himself while tracking Theresa Saldana

L.A. County District Attorn
Evidence Docum

Arthur Jackson during the 1982 trial
AP/Wide World Photos

Theresa Saldana
AP/Wide World Photos

Los Angeles County Assistant District Attorney Michael Knight, the prosecutor in 1982
Photo by Ron LaBrecque

Los Angeles County Superior Court Judge Laurence J. Rittenband who presided over the 1982 trial   *Court photo*

Steven Moyer, Jackson's 1982 trial defense attorney
Photo by Dr. Ronald Markman

The two "demand notes" Jackson used in the 1967 armed robberies in London   *L.A. County District Attorney Evidence Document*

Anthony Fletcher and his ten-year-old son Martin several months before his death　　　　　　　　*Courtesy Valerie Fletcher Howard*

Valerie Fletcher Howard and her three children shortly after the death of her husband Anthony Fletcher

Courtesy Valerie Fletcher Howard

Detective Chief Inspector Douglas Harrison of Scotland Yard
Photo by Dr. Ronald Markman

Scotland Yard's murder arrest warrant for Arthur Jackson

Los Angeles County Assistant District Attorney William Hodgman
Photo by Ron LaBrecque

Reiner, Los Angeles Coun-
District Attorney, who
ered the local prosecution
1990

District Attorney's Office;
Official photo by
Portraits by Merrett

Susan Gruber, the prosecutor
in the 1990 trial
Photo by Ron LaBrecque

man Kava, Arthur Jackson's
ense attorney in 1990
Photo by Ron LaBrecque

Theresa Saldana during the filming of *Victims for Victims*
AP/Wide World Photos

CHAPTER SEVEN

❙❙❙❙❙

The First Trial

The Santa Monica branch of Los Angeles County
Superior Court is burdened each day with the per-
plexing tensions of crime in a sprawling urban region.
The building's pretty location, fronted by an expanse
of green lawn over which ocean breezes flow from the
Pacific a quarter mile away, is in contrast to the brutality dealt with inside. Arthur Jackson's trial on charges
of first-degree attempted murder began there on September 30, 1982, before Judge Laurence J. Rittenband.

Rittenband, born on Christmas day in 1905, was 76
when the trial began, and was the oldest jurist in the
Los Angeles County Superior Court, respected for his
knowledge of law and known as a congenial but essentially private man. He was unmarried and followed an
unvarying daily routine of lunch at the Hillcrest Country Club in West Los Angeles, a golf course popular
with some stars of the "old Hollywood" and not far
from the Twentieth Century–Fox movie studios. Defense lawyers considered Rittenband tough, stern, and
essentially a fair man.

The first matter discussed in the proceeding was a
request from defense counsel Steven Moyer for permission to bring clothes for Jackson to change into each
morning before court. The defendant's blue jumpsuit,
provided by the county jail and carrying lettering identifying him as a prisoner, would be inappropriate during

the trial because the inmate's uniform could provide a constant, prejudicial suggestion to jurors about the defendant's guilt. Jackson's own clothes, bloodstained during the attack on Saldana, were being held as evidence. Rittenband quickly granted the request. For the remainder of the trial Jackson wore an inexpensive suit and tie that Moyer himself had purchased for his client.

The extensive media coverage of the trial worried Moyer. Television and newspaper stories properly created a sympathetic victim in Saldana. She undoubtedly was that, but Moyer wondered whether too many people among those in Los Angeles County who would constitute the jury pool had already reached a conclusion that Jackson was, in contrast, an evil person and guilty of a criminal act. Forming such predeterminations could leave the panel members closed-minded to the admittedly subtle, psychiatric arguments he planned to present to them. He was especially wary because the reporting about the Jackson-Saldana case included "much speculation and theory" comparing Jackson to John Hinckley, about whom there was intense negative opinion. Moyer did not seek to change the venue of the trial, a tactic common in high-publicity cases.

The defense attorney did wonder, though, how the media presence in the courtroom, evidenced by a television camera, newspaper still photographers, and reporters taking notes, would affect Jackson. He worried that their presence might incite in his client some spontaneous outburst that could further lessen any sympathy the jurors might feel for his mental condition. The defense lawyer told Judge Rittenband, "I have been informed by both my client and by Doctors John Stahlberg and Ronald Markman that, to say the least, Mr. Jackson's emotional state at this time is unstable. I am concerned that with the presence of the camera that we will permit in the court, and members of the press sitting in the court, that it may have an unsettling effect on Mr. Jackson, which could be to the detriment not only of a fair trial to Mr. Jackson but also to the interests of justice in this case and the decorum of the court.''

In asking that no news cameras be allowed in the courtroom, Moyer was on the weak side of this First Amendment argument, but he wanted his position recorded in the trial record, just in case the question became a relevant issue in a later appeal. He already knew the court's position. In a pretrial conference with the lawyers, the judge had joked to Moyer, ''You better buy three or four good suits because we're going to have cameras in there.''

Judge Rittenband was media-wise and experienced in high-publicity cases. He had presided in the statutory rape case against movie director Roman Polanski, who had fled the country rather than face trial. For the Jackson trial, Judge Rittenband, as is standard practice, allowed one television camera in the courtroom, with all television affiliates having equal access to the transmissions. ''I will do as I have done in other matters, which have had much wider publicity than this case. All of the media are to pool their resources so far as coverage is concerned so [activity in the courtroom] is kept at an absolute minimum. In past cases there has been nothing which in any way prejudiced any of the defendants and I will see that this defendant is not prejudiced either.''

Media coverage, not surprisingly, seemed to be welcomed by the district attorney's office. ''As far as the People are concerned it doesn't make any difference to us whether there are cameras or not any cameras or newspeople,'' Knight told Judge Rittenband. As a personal reaction, though, the prosecutor found the impromptu, jostling press conferences outside the courtroom distasteful. There was worldwide press representation. A daily, somewhat chaotic congregation of television videotape cameras, lights, and microphones accompanied sometimes shouted questions from the reporters who greeted the lawyers and witnesses each time they entered and exited the courtroom.

Knight and Moyer took several days to question prospective jurors about their backgrounds and biases. The panel the lawyers finally selected was sworn in on Thursday afternoon, October 7. The next morning, the two lawyers made their opening statements.

At the core of the prosecution's case was the depiction of the defendant as an unquestionably disturbed man who was, nonetheless, still capable of rationally devising and carrying out plans with criminal intent. Knight stood before the jurors and said, "It is our intention to prove that that was a premeditated and deliberated first-degree attempted murder." Knight would use Jackson's own writings to support that contention:

> It was important that I be very careful to concentrate on the vital organ, synonymous with Cupid shooting an arrow to the heart, and to avoid other areas of the body if I could, even to the extent of subconsciously avoiding the breast region, I mean, not having been entirely on target, but at least I tried.

The prosecutor sought to identify comprehensible logic in Jackson's thoughts and actions. "There was a motive, a reason behind her death. The writings are evidence that he thought about his own life, how miserable it had been for him, how he had never really accomplished much in life. All of his love affairs were doomed. He anguished over the loss of his mother two years ago. Suicide filled him with a sense of dread and it had a stigma of dishonor. And he thought about suicide as not the thing he would want to do and that a better way, perhaps, would be to commit some kind of crime, a capital offense or capital offenses, kill somebody else and then have the state do it, have the state execute him for murders."

Knight did not expect that winning a jury verdict of attempted murder in the first degree would be easy. That result would require the jury to conclude that Jackson's mental illness did not inhibit his capability to form certain states of mind required by the law. Jackson was obviously a mentally disturbed man, and Knight knew that there would be ample defense testimony jurors might use to conclude that Jackson's actions were a product of his mental illness, requiring by law a conviction on a lesser charge. "You never know what a jury is going to do," he explained afterward. "You have twelve minds. In a biblical sense Jesus Christ had twelve apostles and lost one along the way. For a prosecutor to keep twelve jurors together is a difficult thing, to have them all on the same wavelength. This case wasn't an issue of 'Did he do it?', it was 'What did it constitute under the law? What type of crime was it?' "

Knight's opening statement was fact-driven. He described the upcoming testimony of his witnesses, all of whom, except one, would discuss only actual events without offering opinion concerning Jackson's state of mind. He discussed the details of Jackson's cross-country search to find Saldana and to obtain a gun with which to kill her. The prosecutor described those travels as a goal-accomplishing expedition, driven by Jackson's concentrated and well-thought-out preplanning. Knight avoided phrasing his argument in a way that would emphasize to the jury the bizarre aspects of Jackson's life.

In sum, according to the assistant district attorney, Jackson committed the act of violence against Saldana using reasoned thought. Therefore, the defendant was responsible for his deeds, guilty of the crime in the first degree, and subject to punishment.

The prosecutor qualified some comments, acknowledging that Jackson did suffer from a defective thought process. He implied, though, that the defendant possessed the ability of normal self-control. In relation to his violence on Hayworth Avenue the previous March, Knight offered, Jackson had simply chosen not to exercise that ability to curb destructive behavior. "He recognized that this was not normal," Knight said of Jackson's thoughts about killing Saldana, further suggesting that the defendant could have stopped himself from acting out on those thoughts.

Steven Moyer offered the jurors an argument centering on subtle psychological and legal dynamics. He took into account the suffering of the victim but offered the notion that her pain did not automatically translate into criminal blame against the attacker. Moyer knew from the outset that this would be a difficult concept for the jurors to accept. Saldana, Moyer said, "is the innocent object of a major religious, grandiose delusion which is definitive of the mental disease known as schizophrenia, in this case, paranoid type."

Now, for the first time, the jury heard about the strangest contortions of Jackson's mind. "He believes . . . that he is here on a divine mission from God. He wants to be executed in Alcatraz—D Block, because a man named Joseph Cretzer was killed in the riot of Alcatraz in 1946 and that Joseph Cretzer was Mr. Jackson's soul mate and that he is in Purgatory and that his soul cannot be released until Mr. Jackson is likewise executed." Moyer also recounted Jackson's psychological history dating back to his voluntary admission to Kingseat Hospital in Aberdeen when he was a seventeen-year-old.

Moyer's statement was relatively brief, and he soon arrived at the crux of his presentation. Somehow, he had to convince jurors that Jackson's state of mind at the time of the attack was so abnormally altered that his diminished mental condition should relieve him of either partial or total criminal responsibility. This necessitated the use of legal definitions easily misunderstood by the average person. "The evidence is being offered to you ladies and gentlemen on the issue of whether or not Mr. Jackson actually formed malice aforethought and it is the position of the defense that after you listen to all of this evidence, you will come to the conclusion that there is at least a reasonable doubt as to whether or not Mr. Jackson formed malice aforethought. And you will, I believe, come to the conclusion that Mr. Jackson actually believes that he is here as a representative of God on his mission.''

With that, Moyer ended. Judge Rittenband recessed the court for lunch. In mid-afternoon, when the trial resumed, Michael Knight stood and announced his first witness.

''The People call Theresa Saldana,'' the prosecutor said.

Less than seven months had passed since the attack. The actress was taking the stand against her attacker sooner than many crime victims see prosecution take place, evidence of the priority placed on the matter by the district attorney's office. In the overcrowded courts of Los Angeles County, comparable, but less publicized criminal cases might be delayed for one, two, or even more years. Defendants in felony cases have a constitutional right to be brought to trial speedily. By California statute the time limit facing prosecutors is sixty days from the moment charges are filed against a defendant. The reality is that procedural delays, often instituted initially by the defense, but also by the prosecution and sometimes the court itself, mean most trials take place, at the earliest, many months after the charges have been filed. As a celebrity garnering a great deal of media coverage, Theresa Saldana had a certain leverage to insist that prosecution was moved forward swiftly. This wish would not necessarily have to have been presented forcibly to the district attorney's office, a place attuned to public opinion and in most cases eager to pursue high-profile matters. Most victims do not have any say in how a criminal case proceeds or is prosecuted, an anxiety-producing situation in which Saldana would take an interest later. In this case, though, the wishes of the victim and prosecutorial strategy coincided.

Saldana, a slight woman whose sad expression could radiate the pain and fear she continued to feel, was a compelling sight as she sat in the witness chair. There was common recognition that her clothing hid horrible scars. She wore an orthotic, a bracelike device from her collarbone to her waist which put pressure on the chest-surgery incision to promote its healing.

With a firmness in her voice, she took the oath to tell the truth. But when she sat down and was asked by the court clerk to state her name, the emotion of this moment, when she was once again facing her attacker, overtook her. It was not the first time she had faced him in a courtroom. Her previous confrontation with Jackson at the preliminary hearing, however, did not seem to make this third encounter of her life with him any easier. Saldana reacted as though seeing him was a shockingly fresh reminder of the attack. She began to cry. Judge Rittenband asked his bailiff to bring a glass of water to her.

Then, composing herself, she calmly answered some preliminary biographical questions, informing the jury that she was a twenty-eight-year-old "actress, singer, dancer" who, on March 15 of that year, had lived at 1263 North Hayworth Avenue in West Hollywood with her husband, Fred Feliciano.

Michael Knight led up to a recounting of the attack by asking her to discuss the strange phone calls her family and business colleagues had received in the weeks prior to March 15. The prosecutor knew that his witness's memories of Jackson's assault would support a heartfelt and compelling courtroom presentation. Her retelling was a chilling chronicle. The facts of that March 15 morning were not in dispute; Moyer would not challenge her recitations of any detail of what had happened to her.

On the morning of the attack Saldana had awakened

about 8:00 A.M., she told the jury. About 10:00 A.M., she had been walking toward her car, carrying her handbag and her college books. She had tried to run when first confronted by Jackson, "But the person grabbed me and pulled out a knife and repeatedly stabbed me." Her injuries had kept her in the hospital for three and a half months, she told a stilled courtroom.

Just the sight of this young woman, still recovering from her horrible physical wounds and in emotional distress, might have seemed testimony enough without her having spoken a word.

"Would you point [the assailant] out for the jury?" Knight asked his witness.

"I just remember that he appeared very wrinkled and disheveled. He is the man sitting right there behind the table," Saldana said, pointing to Arthur Jackson. No one, of course, had the slightest doubt about her identification of Jackson as the attacker.

Knight introduced into evidence ten photographs of Saldana's wounds, gruesome pictures taken during her first days in the hospital. He then displayed for the jury "a kitchen-type utility knife with a wooden handle."

"That is the knife the defendant had," Saldana confirmed.

Moyer knew that jurors would be fully sympathetic to Saldana, so this was not a time for the defense to question her ability to positively identify the weapon which she probably never focused on, either when Jackson was stabbing her or afterward when she was making her escape from him. Besides, despite the terror of the moment, Saldana had been able to correctly recall other details. Forcing Knight to prove, by another method, that the knife he now displayed to the jury truly was the weapon that Jackson had used would be wasted effort.

Knight had previously placed Jackson's black attaché bag on the table before him. Now he asked Saldana,

"Does that appear to be the bag that the defendant wa
carrying at the time that you first saw him?''

"That's the bag the defendant was carrying," sh
replied.

"Was it in about the same condition it is in now?"

"Approximately."

"You don't see anything different about it now tha
occurred at that time, do you?''

"Not particularly, but I saw it for only a flash of
second before the attack began.''

"I have no further questions."

Knight's questioning of Saldana had been relativel
brief. Moyer's cross-examination was decidedly shorte
taking up only forty-three lines of type in the cou
reporter's transcript. The defense lawyer's intention wa
to demonstrate that Jackson's obsession with Saldan
could only be viewed as crazy because of the strang
intensity of his focus on her, a woman he knew onl
from watching three of her movie performances. Th
exchange between the defense attorney and the witnes
was actually longer than Moyer had anticipated becaus
of Saldana's apparent bristling at the portion of hi
examination which focused on the extent of he
movie appearances.

"As far as you know, you have never had any per
sonal contact with Arthur Jackson; is that right?'
Moyer asked.

"As far as I remember, yes, but—I am not tha
sure," Saldana replied.

"As far as you know?''

"But I am not that sure."

"You said that you were in a movie called *Defianc*
and you were in the *Raging Bull*?''

"Yes."

"*Defiance* preceded *Raging Bull*?''

"Yes."

"Would it be accurate to say that *Raging Bull* wa

the motion picture with the most box office play that
you have been in?''

"Yes."

"And this is not designed to be anything demeaning
or anything, but you did not star in *Raging Bull* or
anything, did you?''

"No."

"You were in that movie for about five minutes?"

"I have no idea what my on-screen time was. I
worked for six weeks on the picture."

"You had one line in that movie?"

"I had other lines as well. It is very improvisational
in those films."

"You never saw the final cut?"

"I saw one. I saw it once."

"And in that final cut, you had one line; isn't that
true?''

"If I have only seen a movie once, generally I am
not concentrating on how many lines I have or don't
have. I am just watching the movie."

"Do you recall the line 'Leave her alone. She didn't
mean anything by it'?''

"Yes."

"That was your line, wasn't it?"

"I guess it was."

"Okay, nothing further."

The prosecution followed with testimony designed to
bolster the state's position that the savage attack had
been a well-planned and single-minded effort. Knight
wanted to demonstrate that Jackson was not ambiguous
about wanting to kill Saldana, that the preparation was
extensive and the cruelty of the final moments could
have no other meaning than to reveal a murderous
intent.

The rescuer, Jeffrey Fenn, recounted the ferocity he
encountered when he had to struggle so hard with Jackson to pull him away from Saldana. Other witnesses on
Hayworth Avenue on that March morning told the ju-

rors what they had seen. They included Sandra Pone
the Bell Telephone repair technician; and the neighbor
Sam Lefohn, George Camara, Mary Greenspan, An
thony Maiuro, and Eddie Karas. Several police officer
talked about their involvement, including Deputy Eddi
Jones, Jr., who discussed his arrest of Jackson durin
which he observed blood on the suspect's hands. Alon
with the knife, jurors examined Jackson's bloodstaine
clothes, which had been confiscated after his arrest.

This was the easy part of his case, Knight knew
proving that Jackson had physically committed the ac
of attacking Saldana.

The potential volatility of the trial, both lawyers be
lieved, rested in the psychiatric testimony which woul
guide jurors in determining the level of Jackson's crimi
nal responsibility. The prosecutor was not fully confi
dent that he could convince the jury that Jackson's stat
of mind, or *mens rea*, an important legal element fo
the commission of a crime, was sound enough to hol
the defendant legally responsible and, therefore, guilt
of first-degree attempted murder. Similarly, Moyer wa
not convinced he could persuade the jury to believ
that Jackson's mental illness was so encompassing tha
it relieved him of some level of criminal responsibility

Knight interspersed his presentation with excerpt
from Jackson's writings that illustrated the defendant'
unyielding determination. He offered a string of wit
nesses who demonstrated that the defendant ha
planned his attack and conducted his search for Saldan
with logical premeditation. The tone of this approac
was that Jackson's thought process and ability to carry
out his plans were not so impaired as to clear him o
blame for his deeds.

Among others who told jurors about their encounter
with Jackson in the weeks prior to the attack were Ev
Walters, the Southern California Gas Company em
ployee, and two investigators from the private detectiv
agency Jackson had hired. Their testimony was use

by Knight to support his contention that Jackson had conducted an intelligent and skillful hunt to track down his victim.

Dennis Day Gibeau, the county jail prisoner with whom Jackson had conversed just after the attack, provided a bit of comic relief in an otherwise serious proceeding. Gibeau's purpose was to recount Jackson's reaction of disgust to the news that Saldana had survived the attack, an indication that Jackson held no remorse afterward for what he had done.

Cross-examined by Moyer about his motive to testify, Gibeau unwittingly presented himself as a parody of the classic jailhouse informant, not recognizing that others there found humorous his discussion of right and wrong. Moyer stood up, held Gibeau's computerized "rap sheet" at forehead level and let one end drop. The document stretched to the floor. He had come forward, Gibeau said, because "a feeling of senseless murder took place inside of me, if you want to know the truth. There is some things I don't like myself and I am a criminal. They say that criminals got codes, too. It is not just a sense of duty. It is a sense of what is senseless and what is not."

Gibeau was one of Knight's last witnesses. The prosecutor knew that his most crucial parrying with the defense would come later in the trial, through his cross-examination of Moyer's psychiatric witnesses. In debate, with the jury absent from the courtroom, he tried to make sure beforehand that Moyer's psychiatrist witnesses would not transcend the limit of medical opinion prescribed by the new laws enacted in reaction to other controversial cases.

"It is the People's position that the law has changed quite radically in terms of what is to be allowed in way of psychiatric testimony," he said to Judge Rittenband. "In any event, as to the ultimate issue of whether or not a person could reach a mental state [at the time the alleged crime was committed], that has now become an issue for the jury and not to be opinioned by some doctor.'' Knight correctly sensed that the "mood of the people" expressed a decided lack of public sympathy for psychiatric defenses. The whole intent of changing the law, he said, "is based on the knowledge and understanding now that psychiatrists can only give a guess as to what was in the mind of someone so many months before.''

In the case of Arthur Jackson, though, the medical history and exhibition of classic schizophrenic symptoms was bountiful enough to lead any number of psychiatrists to the same conclusion as that of Doctors Markman and Stahlberg. Later, Dr. Markman testified, "I think if you got a hundred psychiatrists examining Mr. Jackson, I doubt you would get any more than one or two of them disagreeing with that diagnosis.''

Nonetheless, Knight suggested that such psychiatric diagnosis was all guesswork, that opinions were sometimes guided by which side of the case was paying the bill for the psychiatrist's time. "There are so many cases that it is even legion ... where we had seven or eight psychiatrists and we have run the gamut, we have run the entire spectrum from insane to sane and everything in between, all the doctors disagreeing as to exactly what has taken place.''

In the end, Knight was not successful in his effort to limit extensively what opinion the doctors would be allowed to offer. Judge Rittenband did not restrict the jury in any significant way from hearing most of the psychiatric testimony proposed by Moyer.

This debate over the limitations of psychiatric testimony revolved around two sections of the California Penal Code that had been enacted because of public dismay over some sensational cases, including those of Dan White and John Hinckley. Although these statutes specifically banned the use of "diminished capacity" medical-opinion testimony, there remained a great deal of room for psychiatric opinion to be imparted to the "trier of fact," in this case, the jury. The leeway was apparently much wider than intended by the California lawmakers.

The penal code sections by which Moyer, Knight, and Judge Rittenband were guided were creations of finespun distinctions, easily circumvented in court merely by altering the form of the question to the psychiatrist testifying in the witness chair. The statutes said:

California Penal Code Section 28: "(a) Evidence of mental disease, mental defect, or mental disorder shall not be admitted to negate the capacity to form any mental state, including, but not limited to, purpose, intent, knowledge, or malice aforethought, with which the accused committed the act. Evidence of mental disease, mental defect, or mental disorder is admissible on the issue as to whether the criminal defendant actually formed any such mental state. (b) As a matter of public policy there shall be no defense of diminished capacity, diminished responsibility, or irresistible impulse in a criminal action. (c) This section shall not be applicable to any insanity hearing. . . ."

California Penal Code Section 29: "In the guilt phase of a criminal action, any expert testifying about a defendant's mental illness, mental disorder, or mental defect shall not testify as to whether the defendant had or did not have the required mental states, which include, but are not limited to, purpose, intent, knowledge, malice aforethought, for the crimes charged. The question as to whether the defendant had or did not have the required mental states shall be decided by the trier of fact."

As he prepared to present his side of the case, Moy
er's concerns about Jackson's courtroom demeanor had
long since vanished. Jackson seemed to pay no attention
to what was happening in the spectators' sections of
the courtroom, much less reacting visibly in any un
usual way toward the people or television equipment
there. Instead, Jackson concentrated on his writing. It
was common practice for Moyer to provide his clients
with pads and pencils and tell them to write whatever
they wanted during trial. For Jackson, an obsessed dia
rist, this was ideal. He wrote comments about testi
mony, passed written questions to Moyer, and generally
demonstrated that he was carefully observing the pro
ceedings, even if his mental perspective was unique
among all those in the courtroom.

Moyer called only two witnesses, psychiatrists Mark
man and Stahlberg. Dr. Markman took the stand first.
After some preliminary exchanges, Moyer introduced
the most important point of his case.

"Doctor, what is your opinion with regard to Mr
Jackson's actual mental condition?"

"I think that he was suffering from a major mental
disorder," Dr. Markman replied. "It is a psychosis. It
is what I would label a chronic paranoid schizophrenia
and, with most people, we call it being crazy."

"Was his conduct a product of his disease?"

"Oh, absolutely. His entire waking existence is a
product of his disease. . . . His actions were a manifesta
tion of his crazy thinking. He is obsessed with a thought
process, meaning that he is totally preoccupied and
thinks about a specific behavior pattern throughout his
entire waking period. This goes back to 1952."

The jurors, it seemed, were attempting to understand
the medical testimony. Judge Rittenband interrupted Dr
Markman's testimony after one panelist wrote a note
asking for a definition of "paranoid schizophrenia."

On the judge's instruction, Dr. Markman responded
to the query: "The problem is one of a thinking disor-

der, meaning that the individual's ability to think in logical terms, and to think in the way that adults abstract, their thought processes are totally disturbed and impaired. . . . It is very primitive and infantile . . . the paranoid aspect of schizophrenia is simply a descriptive term . . . a paranoid can be described as either a person who feels that he is being persecuted by others or being chased by international agencies such as the Communists, or the FBI, or a person who thinks that he is a messenger of God, not necessarily persecuted but exalted, and that is part and parcel of the illogical thinking process.''

Later, Dr. Stahlberg agreed with his medical colleague, explaining that the attack was "the product of a psychotic compulsion as a result of [Jackson's] chronic, paranoid schizophrenia and Mr. Jackson believed he was on a divine mission to kill Miss Saldana, to join her in the hereafter or 'the other side' . . . this belief is a grand delusion.''

A compulsion, Dr. Stahlberg told the jurors, "is an act that an individual is driven or forced to carry out by inner psychological mechanisms and an act over which the individual has little or no control, [a] nearly involuntary act." Later he added that "the delusion is the thought that causes the compulsive behavior. . . . His goal is to complete the compulsive act, period. He will do what he can to do that.''

Jackson, who frequently stared into space, may not have appeared to be concentrating all of the time, but he was actually paying sharp attention. His notes and questions and random comments to his lawyer and others demonstrated his immersion in the testimony, even if he attached a skewed sense of importance to its elements. During a recess, the defendant talked to Dr. Markman and angrily insisted that the psychiatrist had wrongly concluded that he was delusional. "These are just ideas that I have," Jackson said. He also corrected Dr. Stahlberg after the psychiatrist testified that on the morning of the attack Jackson arrived on Hayworth Avenue at 7:50 A.M. Jackson handed Dr. Stahlberg a note that read: "March 15, arrived 7:10 A.M., not 7:50."

Moyer thought he might be making headway with the jury through the psychiatric testimony, which he believed was being offered with a tone of reasonableness and authority.

Then, in an apparent fluke of scheduling, Judge Rittenband interrupted Dr. Markman's testimony for the presentation of a prosecution witness who, Knight said, had been unable to appear in court before this moment. Dr. Alexander Stein, the cardiac-thoracic surgeon at Cedars-Sinai Medical Center who had headed the hospital emergency team responsible for resuscitating Saldana, took the witness stand.

The swift, decisive action required by the dramatic moments in the operating room, ultimately successful, was the centerpiece of Dr. Stein's testimony. The surgeon's recounting of events at the hospital, in some respects, offered an even more frightening version of the attack than Saldana's memories of what had happened on Hayworth Avenue. Dr. Stein brought Jackson's true danger into focus as he talked about the barely living patient rushed to him on March 15. "There is no situation which would be more critical. Had nothing been done very promptly within a matter of a few minutes there is no question in my mind that she would not be alive today."

None of the lawyers could know it then, but further testimony and argument before this jury was, probably, a wasted effort. With the precision of his words recreating the drama in the hospital surgical suite, the physician had told a sobering tale that placed full emphasis on the plight of the victim. It was a presentation powerful enough, Moyer later concluded, to affect jurors so deeply that they probably were unable to turn their attention, or sympathy, back to the more esoteric discussion of the psychiatrists.

In Dr. Stein's reconstruction of the emergency surgery there was as well an unspoken and likely unintended comparison being made. Implied was the distinction between his branch of medicine, with its science, certainty, and proof of results, and psychiatry—sound enough when competently practiced, but necessarily more theoretical. Knight made much of this contrast, not mentioning that the discipline of psychiatry begins with a medical doctor's training.

In Knight's cross-examinations of both psychiatrists, the prosecutor worked diligently to show that Jackson exhibited a range of normal emotions, although neither doctor agreed with the interpretations of Jackson's words and actions as the prosecutor was prompting them to.

Knight pointed out that, for example, Jackson had once written, "I do feel sympathy and sadness for unfortunate people."

"Did you see any sympathy [in Jackson] towards other people?" Knight then asked Dr. Markman.

"I wouldn't label it as sympathy, simply because I don't think that his condition allows for that emotion. I would label it as sensitivity, but sensitivity that was of a detached nature."

There are instances in the diaries where Jackson implies that something that has happened seems funny to him, but the psychiatrists would not concede to Knight that this was a normal expression of humor. "I frankly did not interpret any of his writings as either being humorous or an attempt at humor. . . . These writings are really devoid of humor," Dr. Markman said.

In an aside, Judge Rittenband reinforced the notion that "The matter of humor is very subjective . . . like Bob Hope, I find nothing funny in what he says. Ever."

The psychiatrist agreed that Jackson can express forms of love and hate, but not of a normal nature. "I'm not suggesting that Mr. Jackson cannot hate. I think he can," Dr. Markman responded. "I think the quality of that hatred is totally intertwined with the disturbance that he suffers from ... [and] it is a disturbed love. When your manifestation of love is to destroy someone, I would label that as disturbance.''

Likewise, Jackson's sense of guilt, Dr. Markman testified, ''would be foreign to the average person ... it's an internalized punishment of one's self.... Not that he didn't mean to kill her, he's not [feeling] guilty because of that, he's guilty because he didn't succeed and because he hurt her.... He would not have felt guilty if he would have succeeded and he would have killed her immediately. The pain mechanism is what introduced, or imposed guilt upon him.''

Knight asked Dr. Stahlberg what beliefs might have supported Jackson's mission.

''Do you think he believes in an afterlife?''

''Yes, I know he does.''

''Does he believe in God?''

''Yes.''

''The spirit world?''

''Yes.''

Knight's strategy was not so much to attack the specific diagnosis Doctors Markman and Stahlberg had reached concerning Jackson's schizophrenia. He was questioning, instead, the general reliability and credibility of psychiatric diagnosis and opinion to soundly determine the nature of past events. He wondered how psychiatrists could go back in time and know that Jackson's schizophrenia had been debilitating enough to make him incapable of conforming his conduct to the requirements of the law on the morning of March 15, 1982, a time when, obviously, neither doctor had yet examined Jackson.

The prosecutor attempted to introduce the controversial Dan White case with a question about the much-derided ''Twinkie Defense.'' This brought a quick objection from Moyer that the comparison was irrelevant to the issues in this trial, a point sustained by Judge Rittenband.

For decades, the bible of psychiatric diagnosis has been the *Diagnostic and Statistical Manual of Mental Disorders,* produced by the American Psychiatric Association. In its third revision by 1982, and commonly referred to as DSM-III, the book was first published in 1952. Knight ridiculed the manual for periodically changing its definitions. He argued that such revision proved that psychiatrists were not uniform or consistent in matters of diagnosis. He asked Dr. Stahlberg whether the current edition of the manual showed "chaos and confusion about what [schizophrenia] really is?" "I disagree," the psychiatrist replied. "I think DSM-III has reduced what might have been chaos and confusion. I think the issue really is not what label you put to Mr. Jackson, whether it's schizophrenic or manic depressive. The fact is, the man is crazy."

While Knight's adversarial tactic was effective in this courtroom, it contradicted positions taken by his office in other cases in which both Doctors Markman and Stahlberg were hired to testify as experts for the prosecution. The challenge of their competence to make judgments about Jackson's mental illness and how it affected his behavior in this matter belied the reliance the district attorney's office put on these same sorts of judgments, from these same two men, in other trials. The offensive, though, was good trial strategy here since the jurors would not be told about the work previously performed for the district attorney's office by the psychiatrists. Courtroom lawyers consistently attempt to exploit common prejudices believed to be held by jurors. Policemen, it is assumed, for example, tend to be believed more by juries than non–law enforcement witnesses. The same thinking presumes that the credibility of some categories of witness, psychiatrists among them, is more easily discredited in the eyes of average jurors.

As a rebuttal witness, Knight used a Los Angeles psychologist, Jay Ziskin, who made his living primarily by advising lawyers on how to discredit psychiatric testimony. He had written a trial guidebook titled *Coping with Psychiatric and Psychological Testimony.*

Judge Rittenband, in an aside unusually caustic for a presiding judge, and one that was not heard by the jurors, told Knight he didn't think much of this portion of the prosecutor's strategy, nor did the judge seem to have much respect for Ziskin's profession. "As I understand it, [Ziskin's] testimony is going to be limited to rapping another discipline, he is going to rap psychiatry? . . . A psychologist is nothing. It is just a guy with a Ph.D. in psychology. But they are a dime a dozen in the market."

Ziskin did have strong credentials in his field, serving on professional committees and editing professional journals. He had not examined Jackson, though, and therefore could not testify at all about the defendant's mental condition. His role here was solely to condemn psychiatric diagnosis in general. Even that task had a necessarily limited impact on the statements of the two psychiatrists who had already testified. Under cross-examination, Ziskin had to concede that "I can't tell you that any individual psychiatrist is not a good diagnostician." Thus, he was unable to specifically criticize either Dr. Markman or Dr. Stahlberg.

He was certainly blunt in his overall assessment of the discipline, however. "The current status of psychiatric diagnosis is that it's a huge mess," he told the jury. "They lack an adequate classification system, they keep struggling to arrive at one." Ziskin called DSM-III an "experimental classification system . . . they get together and vote on what is or is not a mental disorder."

When Moyer cross-examined him, Ziskin was firm in his dubious assessment of the value of clinical observation.

"Then their experience is worthless?" the defense attorney asked.

"That is essentially correct," Ziskin replied.

Moyer knew where he was heading in this line of questioning. He hoped to set a trap for Ziskin, whose wife was a clinical psychologist treating patients in hospitals. The tactic appeared to work. Ziskin apparently hadn't anticipated that Moyer would turn the questioning to his own wife's work.

"And I take it you think she's full of baloney?" Moyer asked.

"No, nothing I say here today has anything to do with treatment. She does treat them. I do know she does not diagnose."

"She treats them without diagnosing?"

"That's the way most people in the field work. Except where they have to make a diagnosis for institutional purposes."

Later, Moyer called Ziskin's testimony "intellectually dishonest" because it was a "pitch" exploiting the fact that "juries don't like psychiatrists, psychiatry, or psychiatric defenses in a court of law. And if you give them a reason to reject it, even though you and they are winking at each other, they will ignore the law. I think this was as cynical a prosecution theory as you could get." Moyer held no personal animosity toward Ziskin, though. Apart from this trial, Moyer said he thought that, personally, Ziskin was "a good guy," and believed his book to be "excellent." A few years before he had hired Ziskin as a consultant in a case.

The final plea to the jury by Moyer, and the judge's explanation of the law to the panel before its deliberations, was a complicated presentation containing subtleties of law that, understandably, were not easily understood by laypeople.

In his closing argument, prosecutor Knight asked the jurors not to probe the depths of Jackson's troubled mind but to accept the incontrovertible facts of the case as the foundation for a decision he deemed to be a simple one to reach.

"I'm asking you to use your common sense," he said. "The only way this system can ever work is that people keep in the back of their minds that when things look like a duck, and walk like a duck and quack like a duck, they are probably a duck."

Therefore, Knight implied, if Arthur Jackson acted like a man attempting murder, he had to be guilty of attempted murder.

"There is no legal excuse for his actions. This is not the result of an unavoidable accident of misfortune, so it was an unlawful attempt on his part. . . . He tried to kill Theresa Saldana, there is no question about that.

"I don't think there is any question in his writings that you are going to find that he premeditated this murder. . . . There is no question that this man has mental problems, that he has some disorder. We never questioned that. We questioned whether or not those people who sit on that stand as experts can tell you what went on in the mind of the individual at the time he committed a crime. That is what we question."

To emphasize his point about the difficulty of accurate psychiatric diagnosis, Knight read from Herman Melville's *Billy Budd*: "Who in the rainbow can draw the line where the violet tint ends and where the orange tint begins? Distinctly, we see the difference of the color, but where exactly does the first one visibly enter into the other." Then, to make his connection between that literary conundrum and this trial, he added, "So with sanity and insanity.

"I don't know whether he may be schizophrenic or not," the prosecutor said. "It doesn't make any difference in this case. Schizophrenia is not a defense to murder. . . . The idea is this; you are responsible for the acts that you understand you are doing and you understand that you shouldn't be doing, and if you do them anyway, you are responsible."

Moyer, whose defense options were limited by his client before trial because Jackson had refused to plead not guilty by reason of insanity, had a difficult task. There was probably little he could do to dissuade the jurors from issuing a verdict that would ensure that Jackson was incarcerated for as long as the law would allow. Technically, jurors in criminal trials are mandated to deal only with matters of guilt, not the form or length of punishment, except in death penalty cases where their response is specifically directed by the judge. As a practical exercise, though, Moyer knew that the jurors would be hard-pressed not to think about how their verdict would affect the length of confinement Jackson would face.

Moyer wanted the panel to find some middle ground, admittedly an unlikely prospect in this case. "I am not asking you to acquit Arthur Jackson. I am not asking you to find him not guilty. I am asking you to find Arthur Jackson guilty of attempted voluntary manslaughter ... the intentional and unlawful attempted killing of a human being without malice aforethought ... murder requires malice while manslaughter does not. ... He clearly intended to kill Theresa. ... We all know that he premeditated." The defense attorney's primary argument was that Arthur Jackson could not have stopped himself because he was acting on an uncontrollable compulsion, which was the product of a psychiatrically diagnosed mental illness.

Intellectually, Moyer believed that he had made sound legal arguments. His instincts, however, pointed to the reality. Jackson's writings showed that he had premeditated. To argue that he had not deliberated according to the legal standard was "a distinction without a difference. I can understand that nobody was going to buy it. The guy was clearly dangerous and people are just not going to feel sympathy for him and they're going to want to put him away as long as possible."

Tactically, at least in terms of what he had been

allowed to present, the trial had gone reasonably well for Moyer. In fact, he had been surprised by how often his objections to comments or proposed testimony from the prosecution had been sustained by Judge Rittenband. Moyer's colleagues in the public defender's office even joked about it. Moyer assumed that Judge Rittenband's rulings were not exclusively largesse, but examples of unusual caution to limit the possibility of being overruled by an appeals court. Everyone was certainly aware that this case was the first test of the new state law prohibiting diminished capacity defenses.

Important in the instructions given by Judge Rittenband to the jurors was the direction that "You must take all of the evidence into consideration and determine if at the time when the crime allegedly was committed, the defendant was suffering from some abnormal or physical condition which caused him not to form the intent or the mental state essential to commit the crime of attempted murder. You must give the defendant the benefit of the doubt."

The explanation of a sophisticated legal concept, malice aforethought, was an important part of the instructions. The judge read from a document previously hammered out in conferences with the two lawyers, although Moyer had unsuccessfully objected to several passages: "Malice is implied when the attempted killing results from an intentional act involving a high degree of probability that it will result in death, which act is done for a base, antisocial purpose and with a wanton disregard for human life. The mental state constituting malice aforethought does not necessarily require any ill will or hatred of the person attempted to be killed."

Just what juries do listen to and what they accept or reject is a mystery to many lawyers. These jurors, it seems, were moved neither by the subtleties of the law nor by the psychiatric testimony. Their deliberation was short and uncontentious. They returned with a unanimous verdict late on Monday afternoon, October 25. They found Jackson guilty of both counts, first-degree attempted murder and assault with a deadly weapon.

"There was no question that he did it and no question that he was crazy," juror Geraldine Wolf, the mother of a well-known Los Angeles lawyer and mother-in-law to a psychiatrist, later told the authors. "He must have been crazy because she was stabbed so many times. I felt sorry for Theresa Saldana. [Jackson] looked like a crazy person. The eyes were kind of going back and forth. I think people should be accountable for their actions regardless of whether they are crazy or not. I wasn't concentrating on the real law. I had no sympathy for the man at all."

A well-presented psychiatric defense, the trial demonstrated, can have unintended results. "The better you are at it, the more effective you are at portraying a guy as being dangerous," Moyer observed.

Jurors find it easier to render a severe verdict against a person with whom they cannot identify than against someone with whom they may empathize. The more disturbed and nonhuman the testimony depicts a defendant as being, the more the jurors can divorce themselves from any positive feeling for the person. This reaction is similar to wartime, when enemies assume greater individual evil in stereotype, as though one is making judgments about nonhumans.

Applying strict legal definitions, the jury verdict finding Jackson guilty was incorrect, although acceptable by appeals courts because jurors can disregard what they choose to disregard. The psychiatric evidence had negated or, at the very least, raised sufficient reasonable doubt about the presence of "malice" in Jackson, one of the elements required to prove murder and attempted murder.

In this regard, Jackson has a singly important psychiatric attribute that should have been a determining factor in this case. His obsessive, paranoid drive made it impossible for him to conform his conduct to society's standards. Nothing of the moral fiber that inhibits, or should inhibit, a normal person from improper acts is present in Arthur Jackson to restrain him. For example, it is reasonable to speculate that he would have attacked Saldana had a policeman been standing nearby on the sidewalk, ensuring his immediate arrest. The threat of punishment, a possibility considered by most wrongdoers, has no constraining meaning for Jackson. In Arthur Jackson's mind, the ultimate punishment, the death penalty, was actually an incentive to act.

Jackson's schizophrenia did not give him the opportunity to weigh the question of *whether* he should kill, but only how he should do it. He was compelled to act. Because psychiatric diagnosis showed that his mental condition made him incapable of harnessing the impulse to act, he could not harbor "malice aforethought" as it is legally defined. The phrase is a legalistic "work of art" having little to do with the dictionary definitions of either *malice* or *aforethought*. The phrase deals with intention, and the California Penal Code regarding this concept reads in part:

> . . . malice may be expressed or implied. It is expressed when there is manifested a deliberate intention unlawfully to take away the life of a fellow creature. It is implied when no considerable provocation appears or when the circumstances attending the killing show an abandoned and malignant heart. . . .

Interestingly enough, the California statute's use of some archaic language remaining from English law, in its reference to "an abandoned and malignant heart," emphasizes the point that for centuries lawmakers have been largely unsuccessful in clearly quantifying the complicated issue of how mental illness affects criminal responsibility.

Taking a broader psychiatric view, the attack on Saldana in Los Angeles in March of 1982, because of its connection to Jackson's fantasies about Joseph Cretzer, is directly linked to the early 1950s in Aberdeen when Jackson was first identified as having a mental disorder. The ineffective treatment he received, at the outset and afterward, did not deter him from his increasingly dangerous path.

If the complicated process of a criminal trial involved only strict interpretations by legal technicians, rather than the subjective vagaries of the jury system, Jackson would have been found guilty of attempted manslaughter. Undeniably, while that verdict would have conformed to the words of the statutes, the result would not have well served the innocent victim or society.

The best solution would have been for the justice system to have initially accepted Jackson's insanity and confined him in a high-security mental hospital, probably for the rest of his life. Instead, Jackson now faced the punitive prison system, where a finite sentence for confinement would not coincide with any diminution of his mental illness. Thus, Saldana and society faced the potential of seeing this still-dangerous man released from prison someday.

In preparation for Jackson's sentencing by Judge Rittenband, the county probation office prepared a report, unusual because its subject was requesting punishment far stronger than what the law allowed the judge to impose. Jackson wanted the judge to review his death petition. In an interview with the probation officer, Jackson recounted the decades of events leading to his attack on Saldana, including his affection for an army colleague whom he felt Saldana represented, and which he now laid down as his primary motivation in seeking out the actress: "I returned to the United States to look for [his] female [counterpart]. . . . It was something sacred. A revival of 25 years ago . . . I think my special request should be granted because of spiritual values

and principles at stake. I have no fear or regret. There
was a moral and spiritual reason for my acts."

Jackson offered no character references to the probation officer. He had given his lawyer the names of several relatives, none of whom had responded to Moyer's
requests for information about Jackson. Moyer was
quoted in an Aberdeen newspaper expressing his dismay that no acquaintances or relatives of Jackson's had
offered to help.

Aberdeen, in fact, had moved to cut its links to Jackson. The welfare apartment he had shared with his
mother and continued to live in after her death,
which Aberdeen housing officials did not know he had
abandoned until they learned of his arrest, had now
been cleared of all his belongings and furniture. City
officials had written to Jackson after learning of his
impending trial in Los Angeles, seeking instructions for
disposal of his property. They did not receive a reply
from Jackson or anyone else. The items Jackson had
left behind in the building were either donated to char-
ity or thrown away, and the apartment was soon taken
over by new tenants.

The probation report considered how much of a
threat Jackson would pose when his sentence was completed. Sheriff's investigator Kalas was quoted, charac-
terizing Jackson as being "dangerous as hell."

Noting that the Immigration and Naturalization Service had already placed a "hold" on Jackson, meaning
that he would be subject to deportation upon his release
from state custody, the probation officer was not optimistic about the future: "Unfortunately, the court has
little option as to how the defendant can be sentenced,
only as to how long. The sad fact is that at the end of
the defendant's prescribed sentence he will be free to
wander about despite his obvious potential for violence.
Even if defendant is deported, there are no official arrangements made with receiving country regarding ongoing supervision. Despite two prior deportations,

defendant has returned to this country, and, he is cunning enough and motivated enough to try again. Probation officer agrees with the investigating officer that, at least, during the time that defendant is in custody in the United States that he be placed in a high security facility during his stay at the Department of Corrections.''

The probation officer cited Jackson's psychiatric condition as both aggravating and mitigating factors for determining the length of the sentence. On the aggravating side the officer wrote that "defendant's chronic paranoid schizophrenic condition makes his potential for violence very great." This was followed with a corresponding argument in favor of mitigation because "defendant was suffering from mental illness at the time the offense occurred."

In the final analysis, the probation officer recommended that the judge impose the longest incarceration possible under state sentencing guidelines. "Although the factors in aggravation and mitigation are equal in number, those in aggravation are more significant, and it is recommended that defendant be sentenced to high-base term."

A sentencing hearing was held one month after the trial.

Saldana, under California's new "Victim's Bill of Rights," was allowed to make a statement to Judge Rittenband before he pronounced sentence.

"My body will be scarred forever," she told the court. "I have had extensive surgery and endured a tremendous amount of physical pain and emotional anguish. I'm convinced that if released, Mr. Jackson poses a definite threat to the lives and well-being of myself and other citizens. It's unfortunate that the maximum penalty for the offenses isn't greater, but it is my hope that the court will exercise its discretion to impose the [longest] sentence possible under the law."

Judge Rittenband acknowledged that the testimony

had proven to him that Jackson's mental illness was so entrenched as to make him a continuing danger.

"Now, apart from the dastardly attack on Miss Saldana, and the terrible physical, emotional and psychiatric injuries which were inflicted upon her and which she has just described, my ongoing concern is what will happen after the defendant has been released from state prison. That's Miss Saldana's concern also."

Judge Rittenband emphasized Jackson's proven capabilities to overcome obstacles in executing his plans for violence. "Now, of course, the defendant can be and will be deported after he's released from the state prison, but that doesn't really mean anything because on one or two other occasions he had been deported and then came back again to this country, and he inflicted this harm on an innocent girl and wrecked her career, and it is strongly possible with the mental condition that he has that if he does return again that he's going to possibly inflict similar injury on other innocent victims."

Rittenband suggested that there ought to be a better way to deal with Jackson, to protect Saldana and others, but the laws now left him with little choice.

"Now, the psychiatrists who testified that the defendant suffers from paranoia or schizophrenia and that he has been a schizophrenic for many years; it is very small comfort—and your observations that he's crazy and crazy and crazy—to a little woman like Miss Saldana. It doesn't make any difference that he's crazy or not crazy. What happened to her is terrible, and because he was crazy does not make it any less so, and possibly some other victim might also be a victim of his tortuous and twisted mind.

"My opinion—and I don't know what I can do about it—but this defendant ought to be put away in some secure mental facility where he will be out of harm's way and not injure people the way he has Miss Saldana. For her sake, it is our hope that he can constantly re main in a facility where he can't perpetrate the kind of criminal acts which he perpetrated in this case. And if he's released from prison after some years, he will be at large again, and therefore, if it's at all possible, I think he should be put away for the rest of his life so he cannot commit the kind of act which he is capable of doing because of his mental condition.

"I can't do anything about it. I have no alternative but just to sentence him in this particular case for what he has done, for what the jury has found him guilty [of]."

The judge then ordered Jackson sentenced to the longest prison term the charges allowed: nine years on count one, four years for count two, and an additional three years for "inflicting great bodily injury," a total of sixteen years. Under California's sentencing statutes, however, Jackson would spend far fewer than sixteen years in the prison system for these charges. He was given credit for 253 days already served in county jail and an additional 126 days of credit because the jail incarceration had been "good time," served without incident. State law required that Jackson be eligible for parole when he had completed one half of the term, provided he had served the sentence in "good behavior."

Jackson was taken to prison and the expected legal challenge of his conviction was filed on his behalf. Appeals lawyers in the office of the California Public Defender stated at the outset of their presentation that the major question of the action "requires us to determine whether the legislative provisions ... which limit the scope of psychiatric testimony and abolish the defense of diminished capacity, deprived appellant of a fair trial."

The focus of the appeal, of course, centered on admissibility of psychiatric testimony. The lawyers noted that "The jury apparently rejected the evidence regarding Jackson's mental state and returned a verdict of attempted murder in the first degree." Then the appeal contended that the new sections of state law concerning diminished capacity defenses were unconstitutional because they were a "limit on the due process right to present evidence."

The appeals lawyers also argued that Judge Rittenband, over Steven Moyer's objections, had not given the jury proper instructions concerning segments of the law. They wrote that "The trial court erred in failing to give an instruction relating appellant's psychiatric defense to the mental state issues of malice and premeditation" and also "erred in instructing the jury on attempted first degree murder by lying in wait, as there was no evidence of concealment." As a result, according to the appeal, "The trial court erred in imposing the aggravated term."

On the significant point of whether Jackson was deprived of a right to present a diminished capacity defense, the appeals court judges, in their opinion handed down on March 8, 1984, began with a simple response to the public defenders: "We disagree." The new state statutes, in the first judicial review since their passage, had been upheld.

The appeals court explained that "The restrictions of Penal Code 28 are nothing more than a legislative determination that for reasons of reliability or public policy, 'capacity' evidence is inadmissible." According to the court, the real question about the constitutionality of the law in this case was whether the exclusion of "capacity evidence" by the defendant made the prosecution's burden "to prove every fact necessary to constitute the crime beyond a reasonable doubt" unacceptably easier.

The court did admit the difficulties inherent in trying to answer the question of whether mental disease actually prevented Jackson from forming the mental state required by law at the time of the crime. Appeals Court Judge J. Lui, writing in an opinion concurred with by his two review panel colleagues, P. J. Klein and J. Danielson, went on to say, "Jackson, however, has no cause to complain in the present case because the defense psychiatrists essentially answered the more difficult question of whether his condition prevented him from forming the requisite mental state. The defense psychiatrists testified that on the precise day of the stabbing, Jackson's action was a result of his mental disease and a psychotic compulsion, which was defined as a 'nearly involuntary act.' The jury simply did not believe that the mental disorder interfered with Jackson's ability to form the required mental state."

Jackson's appeals lawyers had argued that the jury could not have reached such a conclusion "without expert guidance on how mental disorder relates to mental states." The appeals court, though, accepted the reasoning of California state legislators who had adopted the law. "Here, the Legislature has determined that judges and lay jurors are capable of deciding whether a defendant's mental illness results in an inability to form the mental state legally required to sustain the charge," the opinion said. "We cannot hold, as a matter of law, that this determination is incorrect. The ultimate issue to be decided is, after all, a legal issue, not a scientific one. . . . It is significant to note that much of the psychiatric testimony was given in terms which could be easily understood by the lay jurors."

Dr. Ziskin, the prosecution's rebuttal witness, was given more credence by the appeals court judges than had been allowed by either Steven Moyer or Judge Rittenband. The appeals court cited Ziskin's view that "psychiatrists and their opinions are useless in reconstructing previous mental states," and then added, "Indeed, some legal scholars would preclude the introduction of all psychiatric testimony on mental state issues on the grounds of its inherent unreliability."

In a somewhat cryptic reference to the quality of the statutes under discussion, the appeals judges concurred that Jackson and his lawyer were not hindered in presenting a psychiatric defense: "Regardless of the wisdom of the Legislature's allocation, it is clear that Jackson was afforded an ample opportunity to present his defense in this case."

Judge Rittenband did not fare as well as the prosecutor in this appeals court opinion. The public defender's contention that the judge's instructions to the jury concerning several issues were inadequate was upheld.

Because of that failure on the part of the judge, the appeals court reduced the conviction from attempted first-degree murder to attempted second-degree murder because the jury had not received instructions relating mental disorder to the ability to premeditate. While academically important, the appeals court decision had no practical effect on Jackson because the charges carry identical punishments.

Judge Rittenband was directed to resentence Jackson on the charge of attempted murder in the second degree. If he chose to again impose the maximum term possible, the judge was further directed to state sufficient factors to justify the imposition of that sentence, which the appeals judges said Rittenband had failed to do at the original sentencing hearing.

A little less than five months after the appeals court ruling was handed down, Arthur Jackson was transported from a prison in the northern part of the state back to Santa Monica. On the last day of July in 1984, the lawyers, Theresa Saldana, who was accompanied by family and friends, and others gathered in Judge Rittenband's courtroom for the resentencing hearing.

Without preliminary discussion, Moyer allowed that there was "no legal cause why sentence should not now be imposed." Before announcing his decision, Judge Rittenband said that "the victim in this case would like to say something."

Michael Knight began the presentation by saying that at the end of the trial or afterward, Jackson had attempted to sell the rights to his life story. "It is hard to conceive that somebody could benefit from the type of conduct he has engaged in but should he benefit, I believe restitution to the victim in some way to compensate her for the loss of earnings, for costs and medical expenses which are enormous, should be ordered by this court as part of the imprisonment factor in this case." Knight noted that initially, when Jackson had made a restitution offer shortly after his arrest, Saldana had said that she would refuse to accept any such payment. "I think at this point in time," Knight said, "it is not a matter of whether or not she wishes to gain anything from Mr. Jackson, it is a matter that he should not benefit from what he has done in this particular case."

Moyer objected to the proposal, but Knight argued that the judge had the authority to order the California Community Release Board to make such payments a condition of Jackson's parole in the future.

Judge Rittenband was not sure if he was so empowered, but said, "If I have the power to do that and it can be enforced, I will make the order." Responding to outrage over criminals who profited from books and movies about their misdeeds after being convicted of heinous crimes, state legislatures across the country were instituting so-called Son of Sam laws prohibiting such profits from being paid to criminals. The first such law was passed in New York because of controversy surrounding David Berkowitz, the convicted "Son of Sam" serial killer.

Saldana's statement to Judge Rittenband was as freshly horrifying as the first time she testified in court. She focused on the continuing pain, both emotional and physical, that she and her family still suffered two years and four months after the attack.

"Our lives were shattered. My husband was devastated that he had to stop working. My sister was forced to miss school and give up a semester of teaching . . .

the toll this gruesome, unprovoked attack took upon my parents was worst of all. My father's hair turned completely gray within two weeks, visible proof of the depth of his suffering. And my mother was consumed by emotional panic, anxiety about my condition and that any human being was capable of doing this to her daughter. She suffered from a lengthy bout of depression and I did not see her smile or laugh for over a year. I might, your honor, some day in the future begin to forgive what has been done to me but I do not believe I will ever forgive what this vicious criminal has done to my parents.''

She emphasized that she was further affected by an unfortunate irony. Having been almost stabbed to death as an innocent victim, she said she continued to pay bills related to the attack. Insurance and a ten-thousand-dollar medical reimbursement from the State of California still left ''thousands of dollars'' in remaining medical bills for which she was responsible. Her most lasting physical disability was with her left hand, slashed when she grabbed the knife blade. ''Although it appears to be normal, the function and use of it are severely limited and it still causes me constant, chronic pain.''

The actress also talked about her continuing fear that Jackson would someday be free again, his obsession with her undiminished. She quoted from a long letter he had written over a period of several months following his arrest in 1982:

I swear on the ashes of my dead mother and on the scars of Theresa Saldana that neither God nor I will rest in peace until this special request in my silent petition has been completed.

Jackson was referring to his plan that he be executed by the state, but his several references to how he might have done a more efficient job of ensuring Saldana's death—by using a gun, for example—could give no one the slightest assurance that he wouldn't try again if he had the opportunity. "It is hard to set aside that he will be free again considering what he has already done to me and what he is still cold-bloodedly planning to do," Saldana said.

Even though years would pass before Jackson could even be eligible for parole, that eventuality was obviously causing great distress to Saldana now. "It is very difficult for me to plan my future when I have clear written proof of his continuing plan to murder me," she said.

Jackson's twisted logic was certainly not seen as an acceptable rationale by Saldana, who decried his written comments that the completion of his mission was "important to the salvation of the whole world" and must be "implemented without unreasonable delay." Saldana referred to one of his psychiatric examinations in which he had been asked what he would do if she were to enter the room. Jackson had responded, "Would I attempt to kill you Theresa? Not without a weapon. If there was a gun, yes."

Saldana, of course, rejected Jackson's religious justifications for his actions, particularly "when biblical law clearly states that if you kill another person you shall not enter heaven." Saldana, to be sure, was an entirely unwilling partner in Jackson's schemes. "I will never join Arthur Jackson in heaven or anywhere else," she declared.

Prior to the hearing, Jackson had told Moyer that he would waive his right to make an oral statement. Instead, he gave his lawyer a five-and-one-half-page letter he had written and addressed to Judge Rittenband and Michael Knight. He wanted both men to read it prior to the sentencing. The letter was a jumble of rambling thought, produced with Jackson's typically tiny handwriting.

"I will read it," Judge Rittenband said, apparently

perturbed at the inconvenience. Then, looking at it more closely, he said to Moyer, "It will take me three hours to read this. Tell me in substance what it contains."

"Mr. Jackson does not wish me to state orally in court what is contained in the letter," Moyer replied. "I believe he has the right to submit a written request to the court and he wishes to do so at this time."

The court reporter then notes in the transcript that a pause was taken in the proceedings, although it is not noted just how long it lasted. The delay was presumably much less than the three hours Rittenband had estimated it would take him to actually read the letter.

"The record will show that the Court has read what is nominated the Petition to the State by the Defendant Arthur Richard Jackson, dated July 29, 1984," Rittenband said after the pause. Jackson's latest missive, not surprisingly, centered on his request to be the subject of a state-sponsored execution. Rittenband promptly disregarded the letter's contents and moved ahead with the hearing.

The judge's new sentence surprised no one.

"Under no circumstances will I consider anything but the high term in this particular case for the acts which have been perpetrated by this defendant and the terrible consequences it had upon the victim in this case. She was fortunate that she survived the attack, otherwise he would probably be going to the gas chamber."

The judge, seeming to have forgotten one of the admonitions of the appeals court until now, finally included his rationale for imposing the maximum term. He said that "the offense was obviously premeditated as evidenced by the persistence the defendant used in attempting to injure this victim. The defendant's chronic, paranoid, schizophrenic petition makes his potential for violence very great."

Afterward, Jackson was returned to prison to continue serving the sentence he had begun in 1982, a term of incarceration that fully satisfied no one. If Moyer had won his case and the required sentence had been even shorter than this one, legal principles would have been upheld but the best interests of society and Saldana would have been decidedly underserved. Unquestionably, a paradox can result when the system works to limit incarceration for a mentally ill defendant who demonstrates a potential for violence. Medically, the defendant, who ought to be hospitalized, loses by not receiving proper therapy. Too often, mentally ill people leave the justice system to return to the streets, untreated and still a risk to others.

The law did not allow the judge to confine Jackson in a mental institution. Arthur Jackson was an inmate of the California Department of Corrections, a system in which he would spend most of his time confined to prison-operated psychiatric units that offered security but virtually no treatment. In these facilities, the driving intensity of his obsessions would not be diminished.

CHAPTER EIGHT

❙❙❙❙❙

Anthony Robin Fletcher

Arthur Jackson, fascinated all of his adult life with the bank robber Joseph Cretzer, had also long harbored a special interest in a highly publicized 1967 London bank robbery whose tragic hero was shot to death. Such violent crime was rare in Great Britain at that time, and this incident had dominated the news for days. This was one of the crimes Jackson had told Steven Moyer about in 1982, when the defense attorney thought Jackson might be relying on his extraordinary memory of newspaper stories in an attempt to fraudulently negotiate a deal with the district attorney's office.

In late May of 1987, while incarcerated at the California prison system's maximum security mental health facility at Atascadero, Jackson wrote another of his typically convoluted letters. This one emphasized a detailed discussion of the London bank robbery. Jackson sent the letter to the British consulate in Los Angeles. Then, because of the familiarity with the subject displayed by Jackson in his writing, the letter was transmitted in early June to detectives at New Scotland Yard in London. The story of the bank robbery, as London newspapers had trumpeted at the time and as Jackson well knew, remained incomplete.

On June 29, 1967, a thirty-three-year-old British contractor named Anthony Robin Fletcher, the father of three young children, was approaching the Province National Bank in the Chelsea section of London, walking on his way to an appointment elsewhere.

It was a Thursday morning and there were several customers inside the bank. Unnoticed by others, a nineteen-year-old bank clerk, Alan Victor Bull, was being confronted at one teller's station by a gunman who leaned over the counter and presented a handwritten note that said, "A loaded gun is in my hand. This is a holdup. If you want to die just go ahead and trick or delay me. You got 10 seconds to fill up as of now."

The gunman provided a plain, brown-paper shopping bag for the teller to fill with money. Bull could see that a small black gun was pointed at him. He surreptitiously tried to get the attention of other employees while he slowly placed about $260 in coins into the bag.

"Hurry up, give me the bag. Come on," the robber said, grabbing the paper container. At the same instant, Bull grasped the robber's wrist. The man broke free and in the struggle the bag ripped open, its contents scattering on the bank floor. The gunman pulled the trigger, but the weapon did not fire, apparently because the mechanism jammed. Not stopping to pick up any of the money now spread across the floor, the robber ran out of the bank onto Pont Street, still carrying his gun in his hand and passing Fletcher as he ran. Four bank employees taking chase followed through the doorway a few seconds afterward. From his quick glance at the gun, Fletcher assumed that it was harmless and he yelled to the others, "Let's go and get him, he's got a starter's pistol."

John Morriss, six feet three inches tall and a "second-row forward" in a rugby club, led the pack and quickly reached within "tackling distance" of the gunman, whose weapon, unfortunately for the pursuers, was real. Whatever the cause of the misfiring in the bank, the problem had corrected itself. The robber turned and fired a shot. The bullet passed through Morriss's shoulder and continued on to graze Derek Baker's neck. Both men fell to the ground, wounded. Three of the five, Fletcher, Terrence Martin-Young, and Robert Scott, continued to chase the gunman, who now had turned onto nearby Pavillion Road.

The robber ran into a cul-de-sac fronted by an apartment complex called Cadogan Gardens. Fletcher and Martin–Young, who were faster than Scott, arrived there first and could see that the robber had disappeared into one of the buildings because there was no other exit. Martin-Young left Fletcher, who stayed at the mouth of the cul-de-sac to stand watch, and headed back to the bank to alert police. When Scott reached Fletcher, he took over that watchpost while Fletcher walked further down into the cul-de-sac.

Inside the building, a woman and her daughter were just leaving their ground-floor apartment as the gunman brushed by them, rushing through swinging doors which almost hit the child. His weapon was hidden from their view. The mother yelled out, ''You rude man, can't you look what you're doing?''

As she walked away from her building, obviously still unaware of the danger, the woman saw the ''rude man'' leave her building and approach Fletcher. She saw the man take a ''metal tool object'' from his jacket, but she turned away, continuing to walk with her daughter. A few seconds later she heard a sharp, crackling sound and turned to see Fletcher clutching at his stomach.

''I've been shot, I've been shot,'' Fletcher cried, collapsing to the street. He died almost immediately. Within seconds of firing, the gunman ran out of the cul-de-sac, escaping a massive police search of the neighborhood which had begun just a few minutes after the incident.

A London newspaper reported the next day, ''Police engaged in the murder hunt were not issued firearms, but these were available if needed.'' There was a great deal of publicity about the case throughout Great Britain, particularly because Fletcher, a thirty-three-year-old construction worker with his own small company and the father of three children, was being hailed as a citizen-hero. The *Daily Mirror* headline read, " 'LET'S HAVE A GO' MAN IS SHOT DEAD BY RAIDER,'' using the newly popular "have a go" slogan praising citizen involvement. Fletcher's wife, Valerie, had collapsed when told of her husband's death, according to another newspaper account. Fletcher, one neighbor had told reporters, was "an ideal family man."

The investigators soon matched the demand note used at the bank with a similarly styled note that had been presented in a robbery the day before at Lex Printers, a small stationery and cosmetics business on Garrick Street. Pamela Kavanaugh, the manager, and her assistant Christina Collum, had been alone when a man entered and pointed a small black pistol at them. The man handed the manager a piece of paper and then repeated the note's message: "Hand over what cash you have. My gun is loaded. Give me all the money in the till." The two women stared back and the gunman threatened them saying, "It's no good looking. I'm unstable and I'll let you have it." The manager handed over approximately fifty dollars and the robber left, leaving the two employees unharmed.

Forensic specialists found identical fingerprints on both demand notes, but trying to match them to their owner proved to be a daunting task. Manual searches through tens of thousands of paper records was necessary in that precomputer era. Later, a police report noted, "Extensive search in Fingerprint Branch, New Scotland Yard, failed to yield any identification." The two crude, handwritten documents recovered from two robbery scenes were then sent to the Federal Bureau of Investigation in Washington, D.C. British detectives thought that the robber might have spent time in a U.S. prison because the phrasing of the two demand notes seemed to have an "American" tone. A search of FBI fingerprint files, however, was also fruitless.

Police made television appeals for eyewitnesses or others with helpful information to come forward. An artist's drawing of the gunman composed by using eyewitness descriptions was widely disseminated by police. Curiously, the artist had also utilized suggestions about the man's possible appearance offered by handwriting experts who had studied the demand notes. The sketch depicted a man with dark, Mediterranean features. Because of various eyewitness accounts, investigators assumed that the killer was not a citizen of the United Kingdom.

Because witnesses had described the man as "unkempt" and he had made the comment about being "unstable" to the stationery store clerks, police conducted surveys involving thousands of people at inexpensive hotels, mental health clinics, and drug addiction treatment centers. Detectives assumed that the killer was hiding "underground" in London. Each locker at five London railroad stations was inspected. This intensive effort yielded no new clues.

Each of the bank employees was given a Queen's Commendation medal. By this time Morriss and Baker had recovered from their wounds. Fletcher was posthumously given the George Binney Award, named after a World War II Royal Air Force pilot who, following the war, had died in an act of citizen bravery. The citation, signed by various London officials including commissioners of police, read in part: "Mr. Fletcher showed outstanding courage in joining the pursuit of an armed man who had shot two bank clerks and in gallantly attempting to prevent his escape."

Then, four months after Fletcher's death, on October 25, 1967, an inquest jury at Westminster Coroners Court returned the verdict that the killing was "murder by a person unknown." Detectives continued their work for several more months. Police officers took some two thousand statements from witnesses, potential suspects, and others. A total of sixty detectives from Scotland Yard worked on the case at one time or another. Their physical evidence included the demand note written by the robber and the bullet recovered from Fletcher's body, to be used for ballistics analysis if a suspected murder weapon was ever found. Finally, the active investigation ceased and the case was classified as unsolved, although kept on file on the chance that new information might be brought to police.

There was an additional, sad, residual effect of the bank robbery violence. Robert Scott, one of the bank employees who had joined in the chase, developed an overwhelming fear that the gunman, knowing from newspaper accounts that he was an eyewitness, would come back and kill him. Scott's fellow employees watched his emotional decline as he turned to alcohol and psychiatric counseling to counter the depression his fear caused. On July 24, 1968, a little more than a year after the incident, Scott committed suicide. A London newspaper carried a three-paragraph item, which read in part: "He ended his life in his attic room at a house in Grosvenor Avenue, Carshalton, Surrey. He left an empty pill bottle, an empty sherry bottle and two notes. At the inquest at Sutton yesterday the Coroner, Dr. Mary McHugh, recorded a verdict that Mr. Scott killed himself."

All of these events faded from prominence, in the public consciousness at least, until the late spring of 1987 when Jackson's letter reached Scotland Yard's Chelsea Division. By now, all but a few people in London had long forgotten about the bank robbery and the resulting two deaths. The letter was placed on the desk of Detective Chief Inspector Douglas Harrison almost twenty years to the day after Fletcher had been killed.

Harrison was certainly surprised by the letter's subject because the decades-old Province National Bank incident just happened to be much on his mind then.

Jackson's letter had arrived coincidentally with Scotland Yard's required periodic review of old cases. In these audits, ranking officers decide whether nonessential materials can be discarded to make room in crowded storage areas for materials from newer cases more likely to be solved. Piled before Harrison was the thick docket recording each investigative element of Fletcher's murder case, and nearby were boxes of investigative documents and exhibits, including the victim's bullet-pierced clothing.

Harrison was just about to sign a "docket of retention," to keep on file all of the case materials for another five years, when Jackson's letter was placed on his desk. He was astounded when he noticed the match between the 1967 date Jackson referred to and that on the Scotland Yard Fletcher file in front of him.

Noting that the letter came from a mental institution, Harrison was not surprised that Jackson was confessing to being Fletcher's killer. Over the years police had taken confessions to that crime from "loads of people." The case had generated so much public interest in 1967 that in the months following Fletcher's death police received more than one thousand reports from people all over England saying they had seen the suspect portrayed in the police sketches.

Experienced investigators commonly hear false confessions, all offered for a variety of motives. Usually they are recognizable within seconds. "Once you start getting into the minute details, their stories faded away," Harrison said of the many people who had preceded Jackson in attempting to take blame for Fletcher's death. "They were just glamour seekers. You always get this." The detective, naturally, at first wondered whether Jackson was just gleaning his phenomenal memory for newspaper article details as a ploy to get out of an American prison. Harrison's suspicions about the authenticity of the claims were raised because

Jackson was asking to be extradited "immediately" to England to answer to the charges.

Harrison is a congenial, soft-spoken, bespectacled man who could be mistaken for a banker rather than a homicide detective. Fifty years old when Jackson's letter arrived, he had three grown children. He is the son of a policeman and had grown up wanting no other career for himself. He is a tough, methodical investigator. Jackson's letter intrigued him.

Jackson claimed to be responsible not only for the robbery at the Province National Bank and Fletcher's death, but also the Lex Printers robbery, and an armed robbery at Lloyd's Bank Ltd., Portman Square, London, eighteen months before those two, on December 20, 1965. In that incident, a twenty-two-year-old bank cashier, Kenneth Farquhar, the only teller on duty, told police that a man had entered the bank, placed a demand note on the counter, and threatened to shoot him unless he handed over money. When Farquhar refused, the robber brandished a gun and a knife, vaulted over the counter and grabbed about $360 from the cash drawer before escaping.

Hopeful now that Jackson might be telling the truth, because of the wealth of detail that Jackson had offered, Harrison first contacted officials at Atascadero for some background information about their Scottish inmate. Among other helpful items, Harrison was given enough information to determine that Jackson could have been in London at the times the events took place. Jackson was then sharing an Aberdeen apartment with his mother and occasionally traveling to London. Even so, Harrison thought at first, Jackson still could have just memorized all of the details he had recounted, such as the names of the participants, merely by reading newspaper stories and watching television accounts at the time.

Harrison asked hospital staff to interrogate Jackson further and provided them with some specific questions.

When they relayed Jackson's responses to Scotland
Yard, the detective then knew that Jackson was telling
the truth. The prisoner had confirmed his participation
by relating telling facts that had never been released to
the press, and which could only have been known by
Fletcher's killer. These involved specifics of the gunman's entry into the Cadogan Gardens building and the
encounter with the woman and her daughter, both of
whom witnessed the shooting. Harrison wrote a note
for the files that said, "The communication between
myself and the hospital security staff gave additional
indication that Mr. Jackson could be the man in
question."

To further the case against Jackson, the next step was
to employ the evidence Scotland Yard had collected in
1967, which had been kept in storage ever since. Harrison asked the FBI to send copies of Jackson's fingerprints. Scotland Yard technicians then used those
American records to confirm that "the outstanding
[fingerprints] on both [1967] demand notes were identical to Mr. Jackson's." For Harrison, this was incontrovertible proof that twenty years before Arthur Jackson
had shot and killed Anthony Robin Fletcher.

Harrison plunged into the case with a passion that
grew as the weeks passed. He learned more about the
incidents and the victims. He developed special sympathy for Fletcher's widow, who had since remarried but
had been waiting decades to learn all of the facts of
her husband's death and, perhaps, see justice done to
the killer.

The chief inspector knew that a successful prosecution this long after the crime would require convincing
forensic evidence that would stand on its own without
any reliance on eyewitness testimony, which was sure
to be hazy or nonexistent after all these years. Neither
would the confession, which Jackson could recant upon
his return to London, necessarily be sufficient. Even
with a guilty plea from Jackson, British law would re-

quire a committal hearing at which prosecutors would have to present to a judge convincing evidence of Jackson's guilt as a supplement to his confession, a sound protection against mentally ill people admitting to acts that they did not commit.

Harrison believed that the police officers working on the case in 1967 had done a "thorough, marvelous investigation." The chief investigator at the time, who had spent a year on the matter before finally being forced to relegate it to the files of inactive cases, had since retired to South Africa. Harrison called to congratulate him for his excellent work, which was finally paying off.

After twenty years, news stories about the case were again given prominence. When Jackson sent his letter to British authorities, he had simultaneously sent letters to some London newspapers. His confession resulted in headlines.

Harrison soon learned that the passage of time had not faded the memories of any of the eyewitnesses concerning the action they had seen. One woman repeated verbatim to Harrison what she had told police in her statement in 1967. "I'll never forget a murder. It's been on my mind now twenty-odd years," she told the detective.

Only the features of the gunman were no longer distinct in recall. Of the thirty-five primary witnesses interviewed by detectives in 1967, Harrison and his team found thirty-four of them to requestion in 1987. All remembered what had happened in detail, but not one could identify a photograph of Arthur Jackson as the man they had seen twenty years before. Even the men at Province National Bank who had helped chase the gunman could not now recognize the person in the photograph displayed by detectives. Since Harrison had already determined that a successful prosecution would not require identification of Jackson by witnesses, this did not pose a problem. There was other compelling forensic evidence: fingerprints, palmprints, and handwriting samples. Comparing the 1967 demand notes that police had retained in their files and more recent writing by Jackson, Scotland Yard experts declared they had a match. "The handwriting is quite interesting," Harrison said. "It's so unusual that it's him without a doubt."

Harrison's plan was to seek formal extradition of Jackson, returning him to London to stand trial for murder. Although groundwork for Jackson's deportation from the United States had been laid in 1982 after his arrest, Harrison wanted to take the extra, precautionary step of seeking extradition, a process that would give Jackson, if he were to change his mind about voluntarily returning, no further legal opportunity to delay being taken into the custody of British law enforcement.

In the weeks following Jackson's arrest for the attack on Saldana, the Immigration and Naturalization Service in Los Angeles had prepared a document called a "warrant of arrest and detainer," which was later placed in Jackson's California Department of Corrections file. Upon completion of his prison term, he would be required by the warrant to be brought before a U.S. immigration judge for a hearing at which an order to deport him to the United Kingdom would most likely be issued. Harrison recognized that an extradition procedure would provide stringent guidelines to ensure that Jackson remained in continuous custody of law enforcement officers, first American, then British.

Having obtained enough evidence to satisfy himself of Jackson's guilt, Harrison now wanted to personally interrogate his murder suspect. He coordinated a trip, his first visit to the United States, with FBI Special Agent Dan Payne in the Bureau's Santa Maria, California, field office. In early August, prior to Harrison's arrival, they contacted Dr. Robert Slater, a staff psychiatrist at Atascadero, where Jackson was then confined. Dr. Slater advised the investigators that they would find in Jackson a man who had been a recalcitrant psychiatric patient. He wrote, "Mr. Jackson has steadfastly denied being mentally ill and has declined to participate in any treatment whatsoever for his mental illness. Early in the course of his hospitalization he was treated vigorously with a variety of anti-psychotic agents, but these proved to be ineffective in bringing his psychotic symptomatology into remission, and, as he experienced severe side effects, attempts to treat him with anti-psychotic medications were discontinued. At the present time, the state hospital system [including Department of Corrections hospital facilities] is under the constraints of the so-called Brown decision, and at the present time, he could not be treated with anti-psychotic medication against his will, even if it were indicated, in that he does not meet the criteria for involuntary medication."

Dr. Slater assured the investigators that Jackson's medication consisted only of a mild tranquilizer, Clonazepam, which is similar to Valium, and would not cloud his memory or impede his ability to answer questions. "Mr. Jackson in most situations appears fairly intact, and on casual observation, one might not pick up the fact that he is mentally ill. This is because he is very intelligent and extremely guarded and knows what kind of statements would lead people to suspect him to be mentally ill. However, in certain kinds of focused interactions, his mental illness appears. For example, when I talked to him about his crime, his associations became loose and jumbled, and his delusional system starts becoming apparent. He talks about the fact that his victim in the instant offense has bewitched him and cursed him. He stated that he and his victim were both the victim of 'bad luck' and that there was a 'mutual jinx.' He blames his crime on society, states 'we live in a schizophrenic world,' and maintains the fixed, false belief that his victim had bewitched him."

Dr. Slater gauged Jackson's current state of mind as

troubled and his threat to others quite real. "He is extremely seclusive, suspicious and totally isolated. He will respond when spoken to. He is maximally guarded about revealing what is on his mind. He appears also to be chronically depressed but denies feeling depressed and denies suicidal ideation. This individual is exceedingly dangerous. If released, he would present a substantial danger to the safety of those about him, particularly his most recent victim, Ms. Saldana."

With the preliminary arrangements completed, Harrison boarded a flight from London to the United States and on August 10 he and FBI Special Agent Payne arrived at Atascadero State Hospital, just inland from Morro Bay along California's central coast.

Immediately upon being introduced, Jackson attempted to draw the two into his world of strange logic and bizarre etiquette. He refused to start the interview until Harrison had read a seven-page letter he had prepared for the detective. The chief inspector was patient enough to wait another day for his interview. He agreed to Jackson's condition, took the letter, and left the hospital, returning to his motel.

This letter proposed an elaborate and detailed plan of extradition, all of which Jackson said must be followed or he would not cooperate with authorities once he was returned to England. His first condition was an attempt to ameliorate his feeling that he had been demeaned by being identified as a psychiatric patient and confined in a state facility. He wanted Harrison to arrange his transfer to a federal prison. Another condition was that he "pass through the Golden Gate" during the transfer, an attempt to make an emotional connection to Cretzer.

The next morning the three men were brought together again.

"Can we discuss my letter first?" Jackson asked. Harrison agreed and now the prisoner asked questions of the detective, all concerning the letter's contents.

When the prisoner was convinced that, indeed, Harrison had read the document, Jackson allowed the conversation to move on to other issues. He gave Harrison a new Polaroid picture of himself, because he felt that the hospital photograph "did him a disservice." Fresh fingerprints and palmprints were taken. Agent Payne read Jackson his Miranda rights against self-incrimination and Harrison "cautioned [Jackson] in accordance with English Legislation."

Jackson was wide-ranging and detailed in recounting his past to the two investigators. He talked about his sister, whom he believed was still hospitalized in Scotland but had not seen since 1944 when he was nine years old. He mentioned an aunt who lived in Chicago but he did not know if she was still alive.

Harrison took stock of his suspect, noting first the physical characteristics; he was five feet nine and three-quarter inches tall, weighed 155 pounds, had hazel eyes and deep scars on his right thumb and left calf.

Harrison now realized as he looked into Jackson's face that the composite photo the police artists had produced from witness accounts in 1967 did not depict a person who looked anything like Jackson. The drawing, done when police sketches were still an unperfected innovation, didn't resemble Jackson now or then.

Jackson offered details to bolster his confessions. The investigators, to test the knowledge of their suspect, let Jackson talk without divulging the facts they already knew about. The prisoner began by discussing his purchase of the gun he said he had used to kill Fletcher.

In June of 1967, he said, he traveled on a ferry from England to France and then continued on by land to Italy. In Milan, he purchased a Beretta, a .32-caliber handgun, and a box of ammunition. He had been trained with automatic weapons in the United States military, but still asked the gun store owner to explain the weapon's operation to him. His desire to own a gun was part of his fascination with the United States. He thought it was peculiarly American to have a gun by one's side.

Jackson said that he returned to London late the same month, on the 28th, and spent that night in a hostel on Great Peter Street in Westminster. He told the investigators that he recalled using the name John Arthur Jackson to register at the hotel, one of several variations of his name over the years. Soon after this, he changed it to Joseph Arthur Jackson, taking the bank robber Cretzer's first name as his own for a while.

Jackson recalled that the next morning he went directly from the hostel to the bank, intent on robbery. To later carry his proceeds, he obtained a brown paper bag from a store along the way.

He chose the National Province Bank by happenstance because it was located in a quiet neighborhood where he thought his chances of escaping were excellent. He had noticed that few customers seemed to use the branch at any one time. He had never been inside the institution, but he had "cased" the building the day before. He had no definitive escape plan other than to walk out afterward. As it happened, he ended up going down Pavillion Road into the Chelsea area, with which he was not familiar.

Harrison had the original demand notes with him, but at first did not tell Jackson that he possessed them. When asked about them, Jackson said he couldn't remember the wording, but believed they had been handwritten in normal block printing in which he had made no attempt to disguise his handwriting. He said that more than likely he would have written the National Province Bank note on the back of a deposit slip or some other paper available in the bank. He said that the gun he carried was loaded with a full clip and a bullet in the chamber. He had worn no disguises into the bank and made no effort to conceal his identity. He said he probably had worn a gray woolen sports jacket, no gloves, and black shoes, and was clean-shaven.

He had entered the bank through the west door and saw three or four customers as well as the bank employees in various locations. When he approached the teller, Bull, he rested the gun muzzle on the counter but did not point the weapon directly at the cashier. Jackson told Harrison and Payne that he might have told Bull to hurry as the cashier began to fill the paper bag with coins. It was then that he saw a female cashier, standing twenty feet behind Bull, staring at him. He motioned to her to get down on the floor. When Bull activated the bank alarm and broke the bag of coins on the counter, Jackson felt he had to flee immediately. Turning to run, he attempted to fire the pistol and only then realized that the safety was in the nonfiring position. Once outside, he turned the safety switch off.

As he ran, he turned to see one of the cashiers attempting to stop him with a "rugby-type tackle." He fired once and the man appeared to be hit in the shoulder. Jackson could no longer remember which side of the man's body was wounded. He remembered hoping that the first shot was "deadly," so that a bullet would not be "wasted." This shot at his pursuers was the first time he had fired the weapon since buying it in Milan. He held it in his right hand.

He retraced his escape route along Pavillion Road and into the cul-de-sac. He did not know exactly where he was going, but thought it was in the general direction of Sloane Square.

Once there, and seeing that he might be trapped, he entered an [apartment] house, hoping to find a back door to another street. He found none and then decided to run up the stairs, passing a woman and her daughter who were coming down. When he saw them leave the building he "fell in behind them" to make it appear as if he lived in the house.

Outside, though, he encountered Fletcher, whom he described as "the tall stranger standing alone" and positioned about six or seven yards away. He had a clear view of the man, who he saw was empty-handed. At first, Jackson held his pistol down close to his side.

As Harrison listened, he was impressed with Jackson's "fantastic memory. He was down to the last minute of when the robbery took place. He said, 'No, it was eleven-twenty-three, not eleven-fifteen.' " The detective caught the prisoner in only one factual mistake. Scotland Yard had checked and discovered that *Defiance* had been shown at Aberdeen's Queen's Cinema, not the Odeon Cinema as Jackson had written. During the interview, Harrison mentioned this minor discrepancy to Jackson, an error that "really upset him, to think he made a mistake," the detective later said. The importance of this exchange was to further verify for Harrison that Jackson was recounting the facts of his life truthfully, including his confession to the murder.

Midway through the interrogation, Jackson turned mysterious, not revealing a tidbit of information he viewed as vital and one which he would parcel out only if he were granted his proposed concessions. His "prize" information consisted of Fletcher's last words to Jackson, spoken during the standoff in the cul-de-sac. Jackson said he would not disclose what they were until he was actually back in Great Britain.

However, he was not hesitant to describe the shooting itself. Fletcher "did not make any move" as Jackson walked directly toward him and without hesitation raised his pistol to mid-chest level while standing three feet away. He wanted to be close but not so near that Fletcher might grab his gun. His aim was deliberate because he was afraid of missing if he aimed at Fletcher's head. He said that he recognized full well at the time that his weapon was deadly and knew that if he fired a single shot at someone from this distance he could kill the person. Jackson shot once. Fletcher seemed to groan with "a gasping sound," much like the sound that the wounded bank clerk, Morriss, had made. Jackson said that after firing and watching Fletcher fall to the ground, he "veered off and walked away."

He walked to the South Kensington underground station. He waited several hours at King's Cross Station to board a 4:00 P.M. train out of the city. He spent that night in Newcastle, probably at the Salvation Army Palace for Men. He went on to Aberdeen the next morning. He subsequently learned his victims' names from newspaper stories.

He added a strange embellishment to his tale of escape. He said that while he was making his way to the underground, a man in a white car slowly passed him and said something to the effect of, "You better keep going, pal, if you don't want to be tailed." Jackson said he acknowledged the remark by tapping a rear fender of the car with his right hand.

The shooting was not a cold-blooded act, Jackson insisted, just a necessary consequence of his desperation and desire to escape. He robbed the bank, he said, because he had been upset over an "emotional relationship" that was causing him problems. He would not elaborate.

He told the investigators that he has never felt any remorse over Fletcher's death, although he had briefly felt pity when he pulled the trigger and noticed the look of "impending doom" in Fletcher's eyes. When he learned from press accounts that Fletcher had a wife and family he felt no remorse for them either. He had been consumed, he said, by his own "desperation." The Fletchers were "complete strangers. I didn't know him, therefore, how can I be remorseful. I will tell you his dying words when you bring me back to England. You'll be interested in his dying words." Utilizing the logic of a schizophrenic, Jackson's view was that Fletcher's death had been the man's own fault, for going out of his way to impede Jackson's escape.

The narration completed, Harrison showed Jackson a photocopy of the demand note presented at Province National Bank in 1967. Jackson said it was "very strange to read something after twenty years." The note looked as though "someone else wrote it" and he thought its content was "very dramatic." This was not the way he would write the note today, he told Harrison and Payne.

Told that the robber had been described by witnesses as "unkempt," Jackson said it was possible that he had forgotten to shave that day because of his "unhappiness."

Jackson told his visitors that he had since concealed the weapon in a "safe hiding place," somewhere in England, along with certain documentary evidence that he described as written accounts of his movements and whereabouts at that time. He refused to reveal the hiding place or say when he last saw the pistol.

Jackson said that he had committed the Lex Printers robbery because he was broke, hungry, and thirsty on a warm day in London. He emphasized that he had only wanted to be able to purchase a soft drink, not alcohol, which he does not use. Brandishing the same gun he would use at the Province National Bank the next day, he said he warned the store clerk not to signal for help to workmen repairing a second-story window across the street. He obtained about thirty-five dollars in the robbery, he said. When Harrison finally showed Jackson a copy of the demand note for this robbery, Jackson said he could not recall writing it but that it was possible that he had done so.

The morning passed and the three men stopped their conversation for a lunch break. Afterward, Jackson talked about the 1965 Lloyd's bank robbery, which he said he committed after "casing" the bank for several days. He carried two weapons, he said, including a plastic imitation Colt .45 automatic pistol which shot pellets and a hunting knife with a six-inch blade. He remembered that the customers "disappeared quickly when they realized there was a holdup taking place."

Looking back, Jackson said, the demand note instructions were "silly," something similar to "If I bang the handle of this knife three times on the counter, that means to hurry up.'' When he handed the cashier the note, the man ducked away from the counter and hid behind a partition saying, ''Don't be daft [crazy].'' Jackson said he then leaped over the counter and emptied the cashier's drawer himself, obtaining about five hundred dollars in cash and coins which he scooped up with his hands and stuffed in his jacket pocket. He skinned his shin when he vaulted the counter. The money from that robbery financed his trip to South America and the United States, he told the investigators.

Jackson was adamant that he had committed no other crimes than those to which he was confessing or of which he had previously been convicted, which included only the 1959 concealed weapons charges and the 1982 attack on Saldana. He emphasized again that his actions on the day he killed Fletcher were not the product of a psychiatric problem but the result of a personal relationship that had ''saddened'' him. The long-ago army infatuation was one of the rare instances of affection to which Jackson would admit. He told Harrison and Payne that he had had strong feelings for the military colleague, although he would not admit to any homosexual ''thoughts'' about this other man.

Jackson said that he had waited this long to make the ''revelation of his involvement'' in the 1967 killing because he didn't like being in the Atascadero facility. He had ''tired'' of it. ''I don't want to be here, I'm in the wrong place.'' He disliked the ''leper colony status and stigma of incarceration.'' He wanted a change ''to build my morale,'' something he felt he could accomplish imprisoned within the ''civilization'' of the United Kingdom, where his ''status and environment'' would improve. Imprisonment in a mental health facility was an ''insult,'' he believed. Even though he would still be incarcerated if returned to Great Britain, he felt that being in a ''regular'' prison would give him more dignity.

Jackson believed that if his offer of an exchange of information for transfer out of the United States was accepted, "the law" would get "the better bargain in the long run" because he would be confessing to previously unsolved crimes.

As a matter of investigative procedure, Harrison did not ask about the attack on Saldana and Jackson did not volunteer information about it.

Jackson refused to sign a confession or statement until he was returned to England. Upon further questioning, he repeated his refusal to reveal the location of the murder weapon. Harrison noted that Jackson "reluctantly admitted that he has seen this weapon since 1973." Jackson expressed confidence that the hiding place remained "secure" and that it "has not been disturbed."

Jackson was meticulous about the documentation the investigators used to record the interview. He asked Payne to review his notes and then suggested several minor changes.

Jackson would not be tricked by the adroit questioning of the investigators. Payne told him that much of the information he had provided seemed to come from newspaper accounts. The FBI agent told Jackson that if he revealed the location of the gun, ballistics testing could prove his story. Jackson assured Payne that the weapon was safely stored and could be tested in the future.

Even though Jackson held fast to his vow that he would not reveal the weapon's location, Harrison was pleased with the trip's results. He was certain Jackson was Fletcher's killer. Jackson, however, expressed some disappointment when Harrison discussed a potential timetable coinciding with the end of the sentence he was serving. Jackson said he had thought that he would be extradited within two weeks. That's why he had written to authorities and confessed. He had even waived extradition proceedings, saying, "Take me now and I'll come straightaway." Afterward, he kept in touch with the investigators, worrying about the "security" of his communications to the FBI and the Metropolitan Police in London.

In assessing the interview later, Harrison realized that he had been most surprised by Jackson's lack of remorse: "So calculated. I would have thought that over the years he may have mellowed slightly."

The prisoner had expressed emotion only for his mother, architectural preservation, and animals, including birds he found caught in the fencing at Atascadero. "He was very concerned that [the birds] should be free and fly away," Harrison said later. The detective also developed the impression that Jackson "certainly was very fond of his mother. He was very keen on history and architecture. He was very annoyed that people were destroying buildings and putting up those modern buildings." This almost complete emotional detachment from others displayed by Jackson is another hallmark of schizophrenia; the symptom of autism, or the tendency to turn inward to the exclusion of others.

The Scotland Yard detective left America with every expectation that soon he would be extraditing Jackson to Great Britain. "We've got palmprints, fingerprints. And the handwriting is quite interesting, it's so unusual that it's him without a doubt," the detective told others of his evidence.

Closing the Fletcher case with Jackson's conviction for the murder, Harrison mused, would provide an appropriate end to his own career now that he was close to retirement. The path to Jackson's imprisonment in England now seemed relatively easy, as Jackson himself continued to cooperate. Over time, Harrison would receive more than forty letters from him. Most important, the detective was confident that even without Jackson's self-interested aid, he still could provide prosecutors with everything they needed to be successful in court.

Before long, however, the detective chief inspector would be greatly disappointed. When he returned to London with a sense of triumph, he didn't expect that one of Jackson's own victims would move to block his way.

CHAPTER NINE

|||||||

Fighting Extradition

No one could have been more fearful of Arthur Jackson's release from the California prison system than Theresa Saldana.

By the beginning of 1988, the safety that Jackson's incarceration had provided to her since 1982 was appearing more ephemeral. Various state sentencing and parole guidelines affecting Jackson's imprisonment, including "good behavior" reductions in the maximum twelve-year sentence he had received while imprisoned, meant that he could be eligible for parole later in the year.

She seemed not content to let the judicial system plod forward as she stood silently by. She wanted action by California authorities to ensure that Jackson would remain incarcerated in California. She became a feisty, vocal activist intent on spurring authorities to further action to protect her from Jackson's obsessions.

The actress's understandable emotions led her to be a catalyst in the judicial process, both serving as witness against Jackson at every opportunity and advocating for reform in general. The self-help group she founded, Victims for Victims, offered targets of crime a path to recovery from emotional trauma, a service for which courts and prosecution offices were neither equipped nor designed to provide. The emotional rehabilitation of crime victims, an area largely untended by government, is a worthy project and she was widely praised for this work. Some of Saldana's efforts to see Jackson prosecuted in California, however, were not universally appreciated by some in the legal and law enforcement communities. The legal system is designed to reduce decision-making based on pure emotion. Justice should require a dispassionate view, and some people involved in investigations of Jackson, Harrison among them, came to believe that reason was sometimes being overruled by emotion.

As Jackson's eligibility for parole approached in 1988, this effort against Jackson took an unfortunate turn, the foundation of which had much to do with the visceral reactions of some and the ambition of others. The result did not appear to serve Saldana's best safety interests and at least temporarily delayed the opportunity for prosecutors to follow the proposed British course, which they believed offered the strongest, most far-reaching action to keep Jackson confined. Worrying some people was that this postponement created the possibility, however slight, that Scotland Yard's plan might be permanently derailed.

Publicly closest to Saldana in her efforts to remain protected from Jackson was a Los Angeles security consultant named Gavin de Becker. He had carved out a well-publicized niche in the personal security business, amassing an impressive client list of people in the limelight, mostly Hollywood celebrities and some Washington politicians. De Becker had a reputation for being a skillful buffer between his clients and those on the rough edge of society whose attraction to the famous took dangerous turns. His firm, based in the Studio City section of Los Angeles, provided physical security for his clients and computer technology to assess potential threats against them.

Premiere magazine, a movie-oriented publication, said of de Becker in 1990: "In the history of this town, there has never been a man with such monopolistic control over the safety of its public figures. He has about 120 clients, all media stars.'' The magazine reported that he had started as a ''gofer'' for Elizabeth Taylor and went on from there to build the business that he operates from offices attached to his home. He does not make the address public. Mail and messages are delivered nearby to a storefront commercial mailbox service. In a 1993 article, *People* magazine said that de Becker's ''42-person firm has charged more than $450,000 for year-round protection and other security services.''

De Becker promotes as the cornerstone of his security operation, which had grown to a forty-five person staff by 1993, a computer-aided analytical program designed to weed out the truly dangerous from the merely infatuated. With the aid of forensic psychiatrist Park Dietz, the system was developed to divide into categories of ''dangerousness'' the letters, telephone calls, and other communications to Hollywood celebrities from ''fans.'' According to *Premiere*, out of 5,800 cases under assessment, almost 1,000 people were identified in de Becker's MOSAIC computer program as potential threats to his clients. His ''behavioral assessment system'' was used by law enforcement agencies around the country, the magazine reported. Self-promotional material distributed by de Becker stresses his consulting work for the U.S. Department of Justice, but also emphasizes numerous quotes from newspaper articles about his celebrity security service, the accolades displayed like promotional blurbs in book and movie advertisements.

Saldana met de Becker in 1983 when he was preparing a law enforcement seminar for which she provided videotaped testimony concerning her victim's rights work. Later, she became a pro bono client of his. Together, their publicly stated goal always was that Arthur Jackson should be incarcerated for the longest time possible, not just in prison but in a California prison.

In this case, at least, de Becker was a prolific producer of letters sent to numerous officials. Sometimes the letters were sent directly to the heads of agencies, creating the illusion of an intimidating list of correspondents, even though some of these high-profile letter recipients had little direct connection with the matters at hand. A copy of one de Becker letter concerning Jackson, for example, was sent to FBI Director William Sessions, whose agency had supplied one investigator to assist Harrison. De Becker showed a penchant for boldly stamping some of these letters CONFIDENTIAL. His tone was blunt, putting government officials on notice of their responsibility to protect Saldana, suggesting at least once in this case that the official could be subject to negative publicity if he were deemed to have mishandled the matter.

Shortly after agreeing to help Saldana, de Becker began to warn that Jackson's premature deportation from the United States, under any circumstances, was an unwise course.

In 1984 he wrote to Edward Ylst, the superintendent of the California Medical Facility at Vacaville in northern California, where Jackson was then being held: "While deporting Jackson may represent a somewhat decisive action on the part of the courts or the Department of Corrections, it is likely to have little bearing on the safety issue for Theresa Saldana. I say this because I am aware of travel undertaken by Mr. Jackson to at least 13 countries in addition to scores of cities within the United States. At the time that he undertook his mission to kill Ms. Saldana, for example, he traveled several thousand miles from Scotland to the United States. In short, this individual has shown remarkable mobility for his means and a very high action capability."

By 1988, Jackson had been moved to Atascadero and deportation had a more definitive end result, the proposed trial for the murder of Fletcher. De Becker and

Saldana, however, were treating Douglas Harrison's pending murder charge in London and extradition plans as though they were a burden to overcome rather than a good answer to their difficult problem with Jackson. In April of that year, de Becker both telephoned and wrote to the Atascadero facility's superintendent, Gordon W. Gritter, M.D., alerting him that he and his client were not comfortable with the prospects for Jackson's trial in Great Britain.

De Becker emphasized in his letter to Dr. Gritter that he was speaking on behalf of Saldana: "We are not in favor of Jackson's transfer to the custody of others in England to answer these charges until he has served every possible day here in California, including every possible extension and continuation determined appropriate by psychiatrists and others at Atascadero."

At the core of de Becker's argument was that the British case seemed to him to be weak, leaving open the possibility that if Jackson were not convicted in London he would instantly become eligible for release into society. "Given that the crime in question is 20 years old, we have reason to be concerned about the availability of witnesses, the acceptability of evidence and, consequently, the likelihood that Jackson would be found guilty."

De Becker and Saldana seemed well aware of their special access to media publicity. In his letter to Dr. Gritter, de Becker implied that if state officials did not do as he and his client wished, they would use the media to achieve their goal: "So as to eliminate any questions regarding Theresa Saldana's feelings, she has advised me that she will vocally and publicly resist any release of Jackson to authorities in England prior to his serving every possible day here. Major victim's rights groups have also made inquiries as to the status of the case. We would like to assure them that Theresa Saldana's position is being given ample consideration."

On April 22, Dr. Gritter responded to de Becker in

writing, announcing that state officials had determined that Jackson could be eligible for parole as early as mid-November. There were procedures to be followed, with possible complications, before Jackson would be released from California state custody, however.

Because Jackson was classified as a prisoner who "presents a serious danger of violence to a reasonably foreseeable victim or victims," California law mandated that Saldana be informed ahead of time if California authorities planned to transfer or release him. State officials at this time were required to determine six months before any prospective release date whether a potential parolee could be certified as a "mentally disordered offender." (The law was later ruled unconstitutional by a state court.) If Jackson were so designated, Gritter wrote, the "technical custody" of Jackson would pass from the Department of Corrections to the Board of Prison Terms, "and he will technically be on parole," but he would continue to be confined at Atascadero, one of the prison system's mental health facilities. "This will precipitate a complex series of hearings and reviews if he demands them, as he is certainly likely to do," Dr. Gritter said.

Gritter was right about the unwieldy process. The legal requirements for demonstrating a continuing need to confine and treat an inmate are so stringent that many psychiatrists avoid getting involved in the issue. In some cases involving patients who have requested habeas corpus hearings, seeking release from an institution, the psychiatrists whose recommendations have been challenged have simply failed to show up in court.

"Several imponderables" were connected to Jackson's case, Dr. Gritter noted. "The first of these is the possibility that Mr. Jackson may refuse to accept parole under Penal Code Section 2962. It is his legal right to do so. The effect of that would be that he would continue to serve his prison sentence while continuing to be hospitalized here. Eventually, of course, his term would expire in 1993.''

A second possibility suggested by Dr. Gritter was that Jackson's status as a "technical parolee" could make him more readily subject to deportation. "I cannot evaluate the probability of such a development, but I am sure that you will be interested in exploring it. Your fundamental position, that deportation should be deferred until Mr. Jackson has fully served his California sentence, and any possible extension, certainly seems prudent in the case of this very dangerous man.''

On December 15, 1988, Jackson did reach his mandatory release date and on that day he automatically became a "parolee." The California Board of Prison Terms would have been unable to take any action to prevent his release had Jackson himself not refused to sign a document that listed the conditions to which he had to adhere upon leaving custody. Jackson's reasons were known only to him. The result, though, was that his parole was revoked for six months and his next earliest possible release date was scheduled for June 15, 1989.

In anticipation of that late spring day, Detective Chief Inspector Douglas Harrison intensified his preparations to bring Jackson to trial in London.

When he had returned to London in the summer of 1987 after interviewing Jackson at Atascadero, he had been advised by the London Metropolitan Police legal office to continue his investigation and cement his case. In the two years since his face-to-face meeting with Arthur Jackson, Harrison had learned a great deal about the man.

His first effort after returning had been to supervise a search for the gun Jackson had used in the Fletcher killing. Most likely, Harrison believed, Jackson had left the weapon in London, since he said he had taken it with him from Aberdeen when he left his hometown for the last time in December of 1981. Jackson had expected to smuggle the gun into the United States, where he would use it to kill Saldana. His diaries recount his first trip to the London airport, where he unexpectedly encountered metal detectors. He realized that he would be unable to board the plane without being caught with the gun. He left the airport and returned to the city, where he wandered the streets and passed the time window-shopping, pretending to be a tourist.

Harrison, using Jackson's meticulous diary notes, located the London hotel in which Jackson had stayed just before leaving for the United States on New Year's Day, 1982. He assigned a team of detectives to conduct a search of the building, which had been renovated since Jackson's stay there, limiting the effort. "At a hotel you can't tear *every* floorboard up. We searched his room and [the gun] wasn't there. We really tore it up but we didn't go too far in the building," Harrison said.

Harrison was confident that the murder weapon was to be found secreted somewhere in England. The routes and timing of Jackson's travels in late December of 1981 had provided only limited opportunity for him to find a hiding place for the weapon. Jackson had expressed great confidence that police would not find the gun, which he said he had stored in a "safe place. Nobody will get harmed by it." At the time he hid it, he assumed he would be dying in America, never to return to Great Britain.

Police surveyed bank safe deposit boxes, canvassed gunsmiths in London, and later in Aberdeen, and scoured other possible hiding places Jackson might have believed he could return to later if his mission in the United States failed. No gun was found.

In the process of retracing Jackson's footsteps, Harrison marveled at his suspect's frugality. Jackson, for example, had made the seventeen-mile trip to the London airport on foot to save money. He survived on a package of potato chips or a candy bar a day. He drank only cold water, never tea or coffee.

Harrison went to Aberdeen, where he was aided by Detective Constable David Smith of the city police department. A priority of this phase of the investigation was to determine whether Jackson had given his gun to any of the people he used as references on his passport application in 1981. None of these people was suspected of wrongdoing by Harrison, who thought it possible some acquaintance of Jackson's could have innocently accepted the gun for safekeeping.

Frank LeFevre, the Aberdeen lawyer Jackson had once consulted, told police he knew nothing about the gun. He did want to refute some false statements Jackson had made about him, though, surprised now to learn that Jackson had used him as a reference. LeFevre said that he had never given Jackson permission to use his name on the passport application and told police that he was not a ''business associate'' of Jackson's, as his former client had claimed in the document. LeFevre gave Constable Smith copies of Jackson's writings, which the policeman read, seeking some direct reference to the crimes under investigation. ''Most of them didn't make sense. There was nothing direct,'' Smith said.

Mark Westbrook, Jackson's cousin, told police that he knew very little of his relative and had not seen him for eighteen months prior to the day he had been asked to provide a verifying signature with Jackson's passport picture. Police interviewed another cousin of Jackson's in Aberdeen who said he hadn't seen Jackson in forty years.

When Harrison interviewed Jackson in California, the prisoner had talked about his ''alcoholic'' mother and angrily expressed his belief that certain people in Aberdeen had hastened her death by harassing her. When Harrison checked further, he was surprised to learn that all three people whose names Jackson had given him had died within six months after Jean Jackson's death. Jackson had failed to mention to Harrison that the three people to whom he was referring were dead.

This revelation, of course, led to a new line of inquiry for the investigators. "We wondered whether he had murdered them," Harrison said. Checking the times of the deaths of the three people against entries in Jackson's diary, which had by now proven to be quite an accurate record, investigators concluded that Jackson was apparently occupied elsewhere when each of the people died. Still, detectives wanted to be sure that Jackson had not purposely provided himself with alibis through untrue diary entries. Details of the deaths were further investigated.

One of the deceased was an aunt of Jackson's, his mother's sister, to whom Jackson had referred by mentioning her "bleak suicide note." Aberdeen's medical and death records were conclusive, though, that she had died of natural causes. The document to which Jackson referred merely offered her instructions on disposal of her property. The second death investigated was that of a seventy-six-year-old neighbor of Jackson's who died from cancer on March 10, 1981, another instance in which natural causes were conclusively shown to be the reason. The third death under investigation, another aunt of Jackson's who died on March 14, had suffered a fatal intestinal infection. There wasn't the slightest bit of evidence that suggested homicide was the cause of any of the three deaths. Harrison was relieved to learn that Jackson's penchant for violence had not taken its toll in his hometown. The deaths were simply coincidental to Jackson's irrational anger at the people.

The mystery of how Jackson managed his finances, fascinating to Harrison, was not solved by a canvass of Aberdeen banks. Police found no accounts in Jackson's name. Harrison's time in Aberdeen did produce a surprise for the investigator. "I was so amazed at the total lack of contact between Jackson and anybody else. He was just a total loner.'' This self-isolating behavior was another example of Jackson's schizophrenic autism.

After his 1987 interview of Jackson, Harrison came to recognize that in some ways the case had become his own obsession. "He grates on you," the detective later observed. "He's so meticulous, so exacting. Intense, very intense man. Sad, too. Pathetic.'' Seeing the case through to prosecution had become a compelling goal for the detective, a task he had taken on ''for the benefit of [Fletcher's] family.''

While Harrison was fully sympathetic to Saldana's unwilling and torturous role as a victim of violence, he had also developed a compassion for another of Jackson's victims, the widow of Anthony Robin Fletcher, Valerie. Since remarried and using the last name Howard, she and her three children, as well as others in the family, had endured emotional pain ever since the incident in the cul-de-sac at Cadogan Gardens in 1967.

Valerie Howard had long waited for justice to be served in the death of her first husband. There had been no psychological closure to the deep loss she and her family had suffered. The family's psychological distress following the death of Anthony Fletcher was exacerbated by the mystery of the case. For two decades they could only wonder about the identity of the killer, and presume that he continued to remain free. Fletcher's mother, who had brooded about not knowing who her son's killer was, had died just two months before Harrison received Jackson's letter.

The first news of Jackson's confession reached the murdered man's family through the press. In May of 1987 when Jackson sent his letter to the British consulate in Los Angeles, he simultaneously wrote to the London tabloid *The People*, which published a story about Jackson. On a Sunday morning Valerie Howard's mother telephoned and told her about the newspaper article. Once Mrs. Howard had read it she was still not encouraged that the end to a long ordeal was in sight.

She worried that Jackson might be "just another nut who wants to confess to the murder."

The memories of 1967 had been revived, though. Attempting to get more information, Mrs. Howard called the Chelsea Police Station, the place to which she had been taken twenty years before to perform the necessary task of identifying her dead husband's belongings. Her call was transferred to Detective Harrison, who by this time had already begun investigating whether Jackson's claims could be true. Soon after, the detective visited Mrs. Howard at her home to explain his plan to interview Jackson in the United States. In her presence, he could see that the emotional turmoil she had faced in 1967 "came flooding back to her." The lingering misery of her loss gave Harrison a sense that some additional immediacy was now attached to his work.

Harrison told the woman that he would be forced to wait until Jackson finished his California prison term for the attempted murder of Saldana before he could bring him back to England to stand trial for the murder of her husband. In his conversations with Mrs. Howard, Harrison came to learn more about the ill effects that the murder had wrought on the family. Of Anthony Fletcher's three children, only Martin, the oldest, who was ten in 1967, retained any real memories of their father. A daughter, Tracy, had been two at the time of her father's death and a second son, Jason, had been fourteen months old. "It was terrible," Mrs. Howard said in recalling her recovery. "It was hard to start life over again after eleven years [of marriage]. I never knew any other existence." Before that day, violent death had been a faraway concept for her, something that she had assumed "can't come into your world."

Anthony Fletcher was a construction site demolitions expert whose small company had most recently been involved in the destruction of a bridge over the River Thames which was being salvaged for scrap metal. Before that, his work had involved the compressed-air systems feeding the traffic tunnels that burrowed under the river. He seemed to be in good physical shape and enjoyed "running sports," although he wasn't particularly athletic. At the autopsy, doctors discovered a slight heart defect which they attributed to his work in the abnormal air of the tunnels, although it was unlikely that Fletcher had noticed any problem when he was alive.

Valerie and Anthony Fletcher had met as teenagers. She was fifteen and he was nineteen when they began dating. They were married three years later.

Fletcher had had his own brush with celebrity as a young man while performing three years of military service as a member of the ceremonial Grenadier Guards. At the coronation of Queen Elizabeth in 1952 Fletcher was among the guards posted inside Westminster Abbey for the service. A family heirloom is the Coronation medal he received.

After the murder, his widow displayed the symptoms of a major depression which apparently went untreated for years. Typical of the times, she did not seek psychological counseling. She sat indoors for close to a year. She lost weight and "cried a lot after the kids had gone to bed." Finally, she realized that "I had to do it for myself. No one else would." She became determined to press on with her life, learning to drive an automobile and to perform household tasks such as changing fuses, none of which had been a necessary concern to her when her husband was alive.

The emotional void left by her husband remained. She tried to block her pain by trying to convince herself that the murder had never taken place. Once as she was walking along the street she noticed a man in front of her and it seemed to her that it was her husband. She ran toward him and touched his hand before realizing what she was doing.

The psychological ill effects of Fletcher's death were

also evident in the children, all of whom attempted to bury their emotions about it as the years passed, each with limited levels of success, she said. Her youngest son, Jason, became "quite bitter at having been deprived of a father." Wandsworth Cemetery, where Fletcher's body is buried, was a ten-minute walk from where the family lived. Jason would often go there late at night, climb over the fence because the gate was locked, and sit silently by his father's grave. Jason developed a surrogate father relationship with his grandfather, who died when Jason was only eleven. These deaths in quick sequence, Mrs. Howard believes, resulted in the delinquent behavior in her son that led to his eventual expulsion from school.

For years, even though Fletcher had been treated as a hero, his widow wondered about the simple bad luck of his passing by the bank at that unfortunate moment. She remembered that he had once jokingly made the comment to her that "I would love to catch a bank robber."

Following his death, Fletcher's family received mostly tributes from around the country, although there was a scattering of vicious mail. One anonymous correspondent wrote to Mrs. Fletcher, "Your husband deserved it. It was his own fault for poking his nose in where it didn't belong." That the incident had touched a good part of the nation was shown by a letter that arrived from Buckingham Palace, signed by an aide to Queen Elizabeth, which read, "The Queen has learned that your husband, who was so tragically killed whilst gallantly pursuing a bank robber, served for some years in her Company of the Grenadier Guards, and was also on duty in Westminster Abbey at her Coronation. Her Majesty commands me to send you her sincere sympathy in the great loss you have suffered."

The elevation of her husband to posthumous hero was not comfort enough for the loss. The widow lamented that he had involved himself. "It was just one

of those whims I think some people have. 'If they ever
come your way' sort of thing. He was very caring. Very
caring,'' she said later. While she was buoyed by the
laudatory headlines of the newspapers praising Fletcher's action, she was "surprised" when, a year afterward, the Queen's Commendation medal recognizing
his bravery arrived unexpectedly and without ceremony
in the mail. The package contained the medal, consisting of two small laurel leaves, and was accompanied
by a proclamation:

> By the QUEEN'S Order the name of
>
> Anthony Robin Fletcher (deceased)
> Contractor, London, S.W.19.
>
> was published in the *London Gazette* on
> 14th May, 1968,
> as commended for brave conduct.
> I am charged to express Her Majesty's
> high appreciation for the service rendered.

The document was signed by "Harold Wilson, Prime
Minister and First Lord of the Treasury."

Listening to Mrs. Howard talk of this moved Detective Harrison, adding further incentive for him to devote
full energy to this project.

At the same time that Harrison was intensifying his
efforts in London, in Los Angeles de Becker and Saldana were a single-minded duo, either uninformed or
unconvinced according to their public statements of the
strength of Scotland Yard's case. The result was that
they rejected the London option in favor of whatever
course they could find to keep Jackson incarcerated in
California. They, too, looked to June 15, 1989, but with
more trepidation, not opportunity as Harrison viewed it.

Arthur Jackson himself provided de Becker and Saldana with a means to extend his California imprisonment beyond his sentence for the 1982 assault. This

series of events had its genesis in late winter of 1988. Jonathan Felt, an associate producer for the Tribune Entertainment Company, was working on a Geraldo Rivera television special about murder in America. Felt contacted Jackson at Atascadero and asked the prisoner whether he would talk about his attempt to kill Saldana. Felt provided Jackson with a Federal Express account number so that the prisoner could easily communicate with him at the show's production office in New York City.

During March of 1988, Jackson sent eight letters to Felt, which he signed "Arthur Richard Frank." In many respects, they were similar to all of his past literary wanderings. They also contained some fresh elements that would eventually allow Saldana and de Becker to act against him. Interspersed in the lengthy handwritten documents were specific, seemingly hateful threats against Saldana, promises that Jackson or accomplices would complete the task of killing her.

Felt, who later testified that the serious tone of the threats concerned him, passed the letters on to de Becker in early April 1988.

De Becker's assertion that Jackson remained obsessed with killing Saldana, as he said in one letter to a state official, *was* well founded: "While I recognize that much of this content is the rantings of a delusional psychotic, we cannot ignore the dangerous nature of Jackson's ideation." In one letter to Felt, for example, Jackson had written:

I am capable of alternating between sentiment and savagery. Police or F.B.I. protection for T.S. won't stop the hit squad men, nor will bulletproof vests. The revolutionary terrorists involved, like me, possess the kamikaze spirit.

Saldana would later say that learning of the fresh threats caused a terrible relapse in her long emotional recovery from the 1982 attack. "I was terrified. And what progress I had made in the years before in getting over the attack, both physically and emotionally, were set back. I started to have severe stress symptoms the moment I read excerpts of the letters. I had insomnia, nightmares. I went for therapy, psychiatric counseling, after not having been in therapy for years, because I was so fearful. I had such an extreme stress reaction that my feet and hands went numb. The stress put complications on the herniated discs I had from 1982 which led to the numbness. I was hospitalized in 1988 shortly after these death threats for a period of five and a half weeks. I was walking with a cane. I needed to take sleep medication. I was in fear for my life at all times."

Jackson, unquestionably, had expressed some tough-minded thoughts:

> Don't assume that time or sentiment will make me less, will lessen my resolve in this matter. In other words do not labor under the misapprehension or the illusion of psychological false security that sentiment will weaken my resolve and determination to impose the ultimate penalty on schedule (only a few weeks from this juncture), which threatens the lives of Theresa Saldana and over a dozen other people. . . . I foresee a Greek-tragedy style apocalypse the more time we waste. Theresa and other people are under death contracts. The hit-men are kamikazes like I am. Police protection won't stop them. I shall give the signal to terrorist death squads to proceed with the murders of Theresa Saldana, public officials, U.S. Military personnel and staff at Atascadero lunatic asylum.

Once de Becker received the threat-filled letters via Felt, he and Saldana instituted a number of safety precautions. A photograph of Jackson was given to the manager of the apartment building where Saldana lived in Los Angeles. She was provided security escorts. She used an alias in some circumstances, to make tracking her through public records more difficult.

The most grievous effect of Jackson's threats was visited upon Saldana's father. "My father was literally sickened by the thought that Jackson would murder me or have someone else kill me," Saldana would later testify. "I know that my father felt helpless and agitated by the threats and by the knowledge that I was living in a state of terror. Although he had no prior history of heart trouble, my father died of a stress-related heart attack only weeks after learning of Jackson's death threats. As far as my family and I are concerned, Arthur Jackson killed my father."

For several months after receiving the letters, de Becker and Saldana contacted various state and federal officials, seeking help to keep Jackson incarcerated beyond his scheduled parole date, using the threats in the letters as proof of his continuing danger to Saldana and others.

Finally, in the spring of 1989, as the June release date approached, they launched a concentrated publicity campaign. Saldana would later refer to this effort as a "strenuous national campaign to raise public awareness," of "having to tour the nation begging for my life, literally." A number of the news stories generated by this effort noted that Saldana, then thirty-four, was six months pregnant with her first child and living in southern California with her second husband, actor Phil Peters. In her autobiographical television movie, the terrible stresses the aftermath of the attack placed on Saldana and her family were shown to have caused an estrangement with Feliciano. The two later divorced.

People magazine, in its June 5, 1989, issue, ran a lengthy and dramatic account of the case. Saldana was quoted as saying, "I've asked everyone—the district attorney, prosecutors, judges, lawyers. There are absolutely no plans to protect me. Period. Period. Period. And there will be none. None at all.''

An Associated Press article distributed from Los Angeles on June 5 ran in newspapers across the country, including *The New York Times*, which published the accompanying headline: ''DESPITE THREATS TO ACTRESS, PRISON TO RELEASE ATTACKER.'' None of these stories placed any emphasis on the deportation procedures in place or the fact that Jackson faced pending murder charges in London. Many reports, adopting an alarmist tone, didn't mention these elements at all. Many readers could only have been left with the impression that Jackson was about to be released to freely roam the streets of Los Angeles or any other place he chose to go.

De Becker and Saldana had cut a wide path in their search for help. One important place the two had not gone was the Los Angeles County District Attorney's office, and the publicity appearances had engendered resentment among some there. Everyone in the office viewed Saldana as a fully innocent victim of Jackson's obsession, but there was certainly not universal appreciation of the aggressive tactic of pursuing justice through public relations. There was particular upset because the district attorney's office was one government agency with the jurisdiction to handle the matter. California statutes included a law providing punishment for those convicted of sending threatening letters to victims of certain crimes, witnesses, or their immediate families:

> . . . any person who has been convicted of any felony offense specified [in previous sections] who wilfully and maliciously communicates to a witness to, or a victim of, the crime for which the person was convicted, a credible threat to use force of violence upon that person or that person's immediate family, shall be punished by imprisonment in the county jail not exceeding one year or by imprisonment in the state prison.

Curious to some prosecutors was that de Becker had known about the threatening letters since April 1988, but with Jackson's June 15, 1989, release date only weeks away he had not yet asked the district attorney in Los Angeles County to prosecute Jackson, although he had contacted many other state and federal officials who did not have jurisdiction in the matter. These same lawyers believed that the existence of the law was undoubtedly known to de Becker and Saldana. The actress and her organization, Victims for Victims, were publicly credited with being instrumental in the lobbying effort that led to adoption of the law by state legislators several years before. Some county attorneys viewed the law as having been designed specifically to help Saldana, who had received a disturbing eighty-nine-page letter from Jackson in 1984, after his incarceration. At that time, no state law existed to sanction the authors of such threatening messages.

Even the man who had prosecuted Jackson in 1982, Michael Knight, thought that the de Becker–Saldana team had taken the wrong approach by not coming to the district attorney to file a complaint as soon as the letters had been received in 1988. "They went all over the place trying to get somebody to file charges. The problem is, they didn't come to us," Knight observed later.

The first inquiry Knight received about the matter had come from a member of the California State Assembly, to whom the prosecutor replied, "All I know is what I see on TV. Nobody has come to the district attorney and said this is happening in L.A. County. I'm not even sure we have jurisdiction. I'll do some research."

Then, on June 5, ten days before the disheartening release date all had been awaiting, Gavin de Becker filed a formal complaint with the Los Angeles County District Attorney's office. The simple form stated, "It is requested by complainant that an investigation be conducted into allegations that California State Prison inmate ARTHUR JACKSON convicted of assault on actress THERESA SALDANA has threatened to commit bodily injury to her. These threats were contained in written letters mailed from Vacaville State Prison to several persons.''

Supervising Investigator Gerald Loeb assigned Senior Investigator Dennis Stults to the case. Stults, who had been with the office for fifteen years and a policeman for three years prior to that, is a soft-spoken, serious man with a literary bent. In his spare time he was writing a crime novel. He, like others in his office, had not taken well the public criticism, implying negligent inaction, that had been levied by de Becker and Saldana.

The next day Stults went to de Becker's office in Studio City where the security consultant provided the investigator with the history of the threatening letters. De Becker, however, did not give Stults originals of the letters Jackson had written. For the time being, he only provided copies to the district attorney's office.

The investigation was given a priority status in the DA's office, attention Stults and others say the case would have merited had the complaint been filed there in the first place, prior to the publicity campaign.

When Stults interviewed Saldana's 1982 rescuer, Jeffrey Fenn, the former water delivery man who was now a Los Angeles County deputy sheriff, Fenn said that he, too, had received threatening letters from Jackson beginning in March of 1987, all of which had been mailed to the sheriff's office. Fenn, however, told Stults that he had not been aware that the threatening letters violated any California statute and he believed he had thrown them away. He later confirmed for Stults that he had not kept any of Jackson's messages. The sheriff's deputy, according to later statements, had not doubted Jackson's seriousness but was not especially concerned because he thought it was unlikely that Jackson would ever have any opportunity to carry out the threats.

A search warrant was obtained which allowed Stults to examine Jackson's personal belongings at the prison medical facility for "evidence which tends to show that a felony has been committed or a particular person has committed a felony." Specifically, Stults said in an affidavit presented to a Superior Court judge in Solano County, where the Vacaville institution is located, that he would be looking for "any letters, documents, diary, or writings of any type which relate to threats of harm to Theresa Saldana, Jeffrey Fenn or other persons, any writings or notations which tend to relate to past letters written to Theresa Saldana, Jeffrey Fenn or other persons." The investigator was not proposing to make the search just on a hunch. Stults had already been advised by a security officer at Vacaville that Jackson was "in personal possession of a quantity of written matter which [he] habitually keeps in his immediate possession."

In his affidavit, Stults also explained to the judge why the investigation was beginning so long after the letters had been written: "de Becker did not make these letters known to any law enforcement authority at the time."

The search warrant was signed in the northern California courthouse on June 8. On the same day, back in Los Angeles, Loeb obtained the original versions of the letters from de Becker and they were marked as evidence. On June 9, four days after de Becker's complaint had been filed, Stults was at the California Medical Facility at Vacaville confronting Jackson.

When the prisoner was brought into a conference room, Stults showed him the court-approved search warrant and read the portion stating the purpose of his search.

"You don't need a warrant, here's all that I have," Jackson said. Then the prisoner pulled a small brown paper bag from his pants pocket and handed it to Stults. The investigator was not there to interrogate Jackson, and he asked no questions.

"If there were threatening letters, I would have mailed them, wouldn't I?" Jackson said.

Stults thought that Jackson was the most bewildering person he had encountered in his years as an investigator. The prisoner seemed "fairly intelligent," was "extremely focused," was "not intimidated by prison," and disturbingly, appeared to be in the full, mysterious grip of his obsessions.

Four documents, none of which contained threats, were confiscated from Jackson's paper bag. Eventually, prosecutors used them as handwriting samples for comparison with the letters that had been sent to Felt.

With a formal complaint from de Becker and the evidence of the original documents now in hand, Knight filed criminal charges against Jackson on June 10, alleging eight counts of threatening a victim and witness to a crime, each count with a date corresponding to those on the letters Jackson had sent to Felt:

> On or about,   1988, the crime of threat to use force on a witness, in violation of Penal Code, Section 139, a felony, was committed by Arthur Richard Jackson, who did wilfully, maliciously and unlawfully communicate to Theresa Saldana in the County of Los Angeles, who was then a victim and witness to the crime of attempted murder with intent to commit great bodily injury, for which the defendant was convicted, a credible threat to use force and violence upon said victim and his/her immediate family.

The next day, a Los Angeles newspaper, the *Daily News*, ran a lengthy article with the headline "SALDANA GOT ACTION WITH PUBLICITY—OFFICIAL PLEA GOT NO-

WHERE, BUT NEWS STORIES OF THREATS MOVED
BUREAUCRATS.''

Unlike his role in the 1982 prosecution of Jackson,
Michael Knight found his new dealings with Saldana,
who was now accompanied by de Becker, unpleasant.
''I was upset because they were blaming us for not
doing anything and it wasn't until they came to us that
anything was done. I found cases that said we could
file it here. I filed the case. I appeared on TV and said,
'We're going to go after this guy and we're not going
to let him out, and even then Gavin de Becker and
Theresa were upset because it took so long.''

Since the belief was common in the district attorney's
office that de Becker had long been aware of the proper
way to utilize the statute, some came to believe that de
Becker had merely employed a stalling tactic. *Los
Angeles Times* reporter Edwin Chen noted in his article
about the filing of the charges that Saldana's own
group, Victims for Victims, ''in 1984 persuaded As-
semblyman Richard Katz ... to sponsor the law that
was invoked in Thursday's filing against Jackson.'' The
case against Arthur Jackson would be the first court
test of that law.

Chen also reported that the de Becker–Saldana lobbying campaign had made quite an impact on a number
of public officials who were responding to the pleas of
the now well-known actress and her security consultant.
Chen wrote, ''Jackson's impending parole has caused
an uproar, prompting the Los Angeles City Council and
60 members of the State Assembly to ask the State
Board of Prison Terms to block his parole. Gov. George
Deukmejian also sent a letter on Thursday asking the
board to prevent the release of Jackson, whom he called
a 'singularly obsessive and dangerous person.' ''

Prosecutor Knight was also certain of Jackson's obsessive determination. ''One of the reasons I worked
so hard on the case is that I did feel a danger,'' Knight

said afterward. "I thought all along that if this guy ever gets out, he'll kill her."

Rankling Knight and other career prosecutors, though, was that the politically ambitious elected district attorney, Ira Reiner, a politician whose sights were clearly set on higher office, was among those who seemed to take self-promoting advantage of the publicity Saldana was generating. Knight was not pleased that Saldana and de Becker publicly thanked the district attorney instead of the staff members who had actually done the work. Reiner, Knight grumbled, had not been involved in the lower-level office decisions and "had nothing to do with it," but, "of course," accepted the congratulations in front of television news cameras. Reiner had told the *Los Angeles Times*, "It takes care of the problem for now. But it doesn't take care of it in the future. He's going to get out of prison in some years and undoubtedly he will be as deranged then as he is now."

In Los Angeles, many viewed Ira Reiner as a man too often making prosecutorial decisions with an eye toward his own publicity. The Los Angeles District Attorney's office, with more than eight hundred lawyers at that time, was said to be the largest local prosecution office in the country. Reiner, obviously, could not involve himself in every case. He was known, however, to quickly call press conferences on those issues arising in his office that would generate publicity. His distinctive basso profundo was often heard on the evening news. Reiner's chief press officer was blunt about the district attorney's reasoning behind personally involving himself in the Saldana matter. "It was a high-publicity case," former newspaper reporter Sandi Gibbons said later.

Reiner, who can be a charming man and commands a certain impressive presence on television and in public speaking engagements, admits that there was some public relations pressure connected to this case. He sug-

gests, though, that he viewed his personal participation
as more a burden than the exploitation of a politically
advantageous prerogative of office to involve himself,
as some of his subordinates have assessed his role. "By
the time I was there it was a celebrated case," Reiner
said. "But that would be a reason why a case would
come to the attention of the district attorney . . . it can
be a small matter, but if there's a tremendous amount
of public attention, it goes right up to the top. . . . Political isn't the word."

Reiner is a Los Angeles native, born there in 1936
and a graduate of the University of Southern California
and Southwestern University School of Law. His wife
is a Superior Court judge. Reiner's career was, for a
time, one of political upward mobility. He began public
life as a Los Angeles deputy city attorney, later served
on the Los Angeles City Fire Commission, and was
elected successively to the positions of city controller,
city attorney, and in 1984, district attorney, defeating
Robert Philibosian, who had been district attorney in
1982 when Jackson was prosecuted for the attack on
Saldana.

Reiner was off to a good start in his new job, a post
that has launched other men to higher office. In an
assessment of his first year as district attorney, the
headline on a *Los Angeles Times* article read, "AS D.A.
a quiet zeal has replaced maverick's high-visibility tactics." Reporters Robert W. Stewart and Paul Feldman
wrote that "most prosecutors interviewed by the *Times*
gave Reiner high marks for what they regard as the
quiet, professional manner in which he and his top aides
have managed the office. If Reiner has been less vocal,
he has hardly been silent. Like a cagey prizefighter
biding his time in the early rounds, he continues to
throw his share of stinging jabs."

However, by the time the newest case against Jackson was opened in 1989, the media coverage of Reiner
was not so temperate or positive. With more than five

years in office by then, the district attorney had been pummeled with criticism for employing bad judgment in a number of cases in which prosecutions were lost. Some of these trials gained national attention, including the McMartin Pre-School child molestation case and the so-called *Twilight Zone* criminal negligence case, concerning the movie-set deaths of actor Vic Morrow and two children in a helicopter crash.

The *Long Beach Press-Telegram* editorialized that "District Attorney Ira Reiner should review the marching orders he gives—or fails to give—his prosecutors. They don't do his office proud." The (Los Angeles) *Daily News* referred to "Reiner's Rumpus Room" in an editorial that said in part, "there's enough turbulence in Reiner's fiefdom to satisfy anyone's taste for bureaucratic bungling and backstabbing." Still, Reiner had won reelection in 1988. In January of 1989 he announced that he would run for California attorney general in 1990.

As various parties worked toward Jackson's scheduled June 15, 1989, release date as a deadline for action, timeliness again became a moot point. The California Board of Prison Terms added extra insurance that Jackson would continue to be held.

On April 14, 1989, while being moved from a dormitory-style room to a two-man cell, Jackson had become belligerent. When he refused to enter the room, a guard pushed him in and locked the door, trapping Jackson inside. Using a broom handle, Jackson broke nine small square windows in the cell door. Guards entered again, subdued him with handcuffs, and took him to another locked cell. Later, he was charged with two counts of physically resisting staff and one count of destruction of state property.

Jackson later said that the move was a "set-up" designed to disturb him and create a problem for which he could be charged. A Vacaville staff member familiar with the incident also told the authors of wondering whether the timing of the incident was more than coincidental to the pending parole date. The staff member said that the incident was especially curious because Jackson's claustrophobia was well known and there was no compelling reason to move him from the open dormitory setting to the more confining cell. Jackson contended that his reactions to the prison guards had been in self-defense. Afterward, he asked that two prison staff members, including a psychiatrist, neither of whom had seen the incident, be called as character witnesses at his hearing. Prison officials denied the request.

On April 22, a senior hearing officer at the facility found Jackson guilty, "based upon written report." Sixty days of credit Jackson had received for good behavior were disallowed and a total of $46.35 was assessed against his prison trust account for the broken windows. Then on June 13, two days before his scheduled release date, the Board of Prison Terms conducted a parole revocation extension hearing and found evidence to substantiate the April charges. He was penalized an additional 270 days of incarceration.

In May, prior to the district attorney's filing of charges and the rescinding of Jackson's June parole eligibility date, Harrison made his second trip to the United States, "quite confident" that he would soon be returning with his murder-suspect prisoner. Extradition papers had been filed and Scotland Yard had already purchased Jackson's plane ticket, an expensive "club class" seat in the section of the plane that would provide the most security for Harrison. The British detective also carried with him the arrest warrant issued by the Horseferry Road Magistrate's Court:

> For that he, the said Arthur Richard Jackson, on the 29th day of June 1967, within the jurisdiction of the Central Criminal Court did murder Anthony Robin Fletcher. Contrary to Common Law.

Four additional charges were for wounding John Charles Morriss "with intent to resist the lawful apprehension of himself," and three counts of armed robbery.

It had long been overlooked by California authorities that Jackson had made reference to the London murder, albeit vaguely, as early as the fall of 1981 when he wrote his execution petition. Even then he held the confession as a trump card to play in exchange for his state-sponsored execution:

> I will give myself up and I will confess and I will tell *all of the things I did* and I will even surrender myself and make a full confession if they agree to the terms of this thing and whereby I am going to be executed for killing this person or persons.

Jackson had also talked about the incident to his defense attorney, Steven Moyer, who remains bound by law and ethics not to divulge any of the information imparted to him by Jackson in 1982. Jackson had even told Moyer the secret of Fletcher's last words, which the prisoner thought would be so enticing to Harrison: "All right fella, let's have the gun."

As he headed for America, Harrison thought his major problem would be ensuring that deportation was handled properly. He was prepared for any testimony he might have to offer to a judge. He had also worked out a procedure for the physical transfer of Jackson from the U.S. Marshals Service. The plan called for Jackson to be brought on board the airplane by Federal marshals, who would then formally transfer him into the custody of Harrison three miles out over international water.

Soon after arriving in Los Angeles, however, Harrison came to realize that his biggest obstacle to bringing Jackson back was being constructed by de Becker and Saldana.

Government investigators and lawyers in Los Angeles who believed that they were working in Saldana's best interest felt unduly pressured by de Becker. Harrison heard comments bandied about the district attorney's office that he considered quite unsubtle in their criticism of the security consultant's manner. De Becker's lobbying style was not appreciated by some in the office, and sometimes was deeply resented. Some felt unfairly abused by the critical publicity he and Saldana had generated, and others were insulted at being bypassed because of his seemingly unusual access to Reiner.

Even after the charges had been filed, Harrison's proposal was still given serious consideration by the district attorney's office. The filing did not require the district attorney to follow through with prosecution. At any point the Los Angeles case could have been dropped in deference to the London prosecution. But as long as the charges were pending in Los Angeles, Harrison would be prevented from taking Jackson into custody and returning him to Great Britain. And, in accordance with the plan pushed by de Becker and Saldana, Harrison would have to wait until Jackson finished his new sentence if he were convicted of the pending charges.

Los Angeles prosecutors launched a study to determine whether justice would be better served by allowing Jackson to go back to London with Detective Chief Inspector Harrison. In early June, John Lynch, the DA's office director of central operations, assigned one of his best lawyers, William Hodgman, to meet with the British detective to assess the quality of the murder case.

After an initial briefing over the telephone from FBI Agent Dan Payne, Hodgman met with Harrison and Payne in Santa Barbara, about ninety miles north of Los

Angeles. Typically methodical and thorough, Harrison recounted his entire investigation. "I was very impressed with the professionalism of the investigation," Hodgman said later. "If only all of our murder cases here in Los Angeles County could be of that caliber."

Hodgman continued his research, and sought advice from the U.S. State Department, several officials with the British Crown Prosecutor, and experts in other British government agencies.

He weighed the strengths and weaknesses of the British case against those of the Los Angeles County case. He knew, for example, that Jackson's defense attorney in the letters case would quickly challenge whether the county even had jurisdiction to prosecute because of the circuitous route that the letters had taken, including the fact that they were not addressed to Saldana and had been sent to New York State to someone who was not directly connected to the actress.

Some legal research led Hodgman to conclude that jurisdiction was a solvable legal problem. He soon developed the opinion, though, that a greater dilemma rested in "factual weaknesses in the threats themselves." After studying the letters he determined that the alleged threats "were not as explicit and particularly directed towards Saldana as I was first led to believe," and that a defense attorney could construct a credible argument in Jackson's favor. Taking an objective view of the clarity of the potential prosecution argument, Hodgman realized that "the language that was threatening was contained in much longer correspondence which had all sorts of ramblings in it and I thought it was debatable whether it was ever intended for Theresa Saldana to become aware of, or be the recipient of."

Ultimately, Hodgman concluded that the Los Angeles case was probably winnable. In addition to the facts at hand, the background of the case, including the 1982 attack and conviction, carried with it an emotional component that weighed heavily in favor of the prosecution.

Hodgman assumed that the trial judge in this case would allow at least some testimony about the 1982 attack because the link between that incident and the pending case was solid. Putting aside legal technicalities, Hodgman believed that the Los Angeles case would boil down to this: "Here's this poor woman who was nearly killed some years ago and here's this guy who appears to be crazy as a loon. Here are some letters that appear to be threatening."

Hodgman, though, believed that his assignment was not to determine just whether the county prosecution was a potentially successful solution, but whether it was also the *best* solution for everyone involved. His analysis rested on a simple notion. "We had a choice," he said afterward. "And relative to the British case, I thought the L.A. County case was the much lesser case, which offered a far less punitive impact on Jackson than the British case, which was stronger factually and gave us a very good likelihood that he would be put away for years, perhaps for the rest of his life in a prison from which he could not communicate."

Jackson's inability even to send letters from a British prison would benefit Saldana, the prosecutor believed. Detective Harrison had offered the argument, accepted by Hodgman as correct, that in England, even more so than in the United States judicial system, the psychiatric opinion that Jackson is a continuing danger to others would be a strong, determining factor in a judge's decision to keep Jackson incarcerated beyond any possible parole date. Hodgman had learned that if convicted on the murder charge, Jackson would have to serve at least fourteen years before being eligible for parole, a term that would put Jackson at least in his early seventies before he would face his first chance for release. Certainly by then Jackson would pose a greatly diminished threat, if not a nonexistent one.

Under California sentencing guidelines, Jackson's potential term on the threat charges, unquestionably, would be far shorter than a sentence for murder in England, creating in a few years the necessity to deal with the matter again.

De Becker's logic—that the London murder still could be prosecuted even years from now after Jackson had served more time in California—was well understood by Hodgman and Harrison. Both men believed, however, that further delay could only decrease the chances for success in Great Britain. Even the best cases can weaken with age, and Harrison felt that each passing year was more critical. There was also the possibility that in the coming years unknown and unanticipated legal complications could arise concerning either Jackson's incarceration in the United States or his extradition for prosecution in England.

Harrison believed he could easily counter de Becker's strongest criticism of his case, that the eyewitness testimony was clearly insufficient to categorically place Jackson at the crime scene in 1967. Harrison and prosecutors both in Los Angeles and London had confidently concluded that the lack of witnesses to positively identify Jackson was irrelevant to winning a conviction. "We would not even ask the eyewitnesses in court whether they could identify Jackson," Harrison said. "All they would say is 'I saw a murder by a man of that [general] description.' We made that very clear in the extradition papers."

Neither did Harrison think that Jackson's confession, which the suspect could recant, was a vitally important building block of the case. He maintained that the heart of the case was the physical evidence of fingerprints, palmprints, and demand note handwriting, all of which could be shown with scientific precision to belong to Arthur Jackson.

Still, Harrison worried that people who were important for courtroom testimony were getting older. Some had already died, depriving British prosecutors of helpful corroboration of their physical evidence. For example, the pathologist who had done the autopsy on Fletcher, documenting that he had died from a single gunshot wound to the chest, had died. In place of this witness, British prosecutors planned to use the testimony of two police officers who attended the autopsy and transcripts of all the testimony taken at the 1967 coroner's inquest.

Completing his research, Hodgman offered his analysis to his supervisors in the district attorney's office. "I came to a personal conclusion that the best course of action was to have Jackson extradited back to Great Britain, for the long-term physical and psychological security of the victim, Theresa Saldana," he said.

Both Hodgman and Harrison tried to convince Saldana and de Becker to quit their opposition to the extradition. "I didn't make any headway," Hodgman said. "They were adamant that they wanted the matter prosecuted here and they expressed that in absolute and no uncertain terms. A phrase that was used repeatedly by de Becker was 'A bird in the hand is worth more than two in the bush.'"

District Attorney Reiner said that he, too, tried to convince de Becker and Saldana that Hodgman, whom he called "an excellent lawyer," was right. The prosecutors secondarily added an economic argument, that government money would, in some sense, be wasted by a trial in California. There wasn't a prosecutor in the office who had looked at the case, as Hodgman's recommendation worked its way up the chain of command to Reiner, who disagreed with the proposal that the best course was to have Jackson sent back to London. Reiner himself had concluded that the Scotland Yard case "was about as solid as it could get." Reiner was struck by Saldana's stubbornness, even though he recognized that the source of her adamance was an immutable, fear-based drive from deep within her. "You can't always be clear as to why she felt that way, just viscerally," Reiner said. "She was not trusting of the idea that he wouldn't come back, because he had come back into this country before. And you're sometimes faced with trying to be logical to somebody and you can just talk yourself blue in the face. . . .''

Saldana's efforts were not unique, according to the district attorney. The lives of many victims who suffer terribly traumatic events ''begin to revolve around advocacy in connection with what has happened to them. . . . And that's what you saw with Theresa, that this became, clearly, a huge part of life and dealing with it. . . . What she wants is to have him in prison until he dies and she's not going to be completely comfortable, nor should she, until that happens,'' Reiner observed later.

Some lawyers and investigators in the district attorney's office had come to believe that opposing extradition was actually counterproductive to Saldana's long-term safety, as well as unjust to Jackson's other victims.

Even Jackson himself had recognized that a painful part of mourning by Fletcher's friends and relatives was that they did not know who the killer was. In a departure from his usual schizophrenic avoidance of emotion, Jackson mentioned in his 1981 death petition some concern for the peace of mind of Fletcher's survivors. In an oblique reference to the bank-robbery killing, he wrote:

> For if I had died at that early stage, certain secrets may likewise have died along with me, at worst, or, should [the secrets] have survived, owing to some ulterior reason, might never actually be proven in the strict legal sense, at best. I am referring to unsolved major crimes, and an assortment of undisclosed information. . . . Appreciate also the fact that in my doing the right thing by getting matters of such gravity as revelations on murder, and armed robbery in a European Country declared prior to paying the supreme penalty for a capital offence here in the

United States ... providing ... a quasi-humanitarian service to members of the family belonging to a murder victim who have probably wanted to know the identity of the killer for a certain period of time, including the context and motive behind the crime, and who have now resigned themselves to abandoning hope of ever finding out.

In the face of Saldana's obstinance, Harrison tried an extraordinary method of persuasion. "I even had Fletcher's wife write to [Saldana] to [express] hope that she wouldn't oppose the parole." Mrs. Howard had told Harrison that she believed Saldana had had "her share" of justice. The terrible event that had sent her life on a new course more than twenty years before was not closed for her, and would not be until Jackson stood trial in London.

"I wonder if it would do any good if I was to write?" Valerie Howard had asked Harrison.

"By all means, try," the detective responded.

Mrs. Howard later said that she had believed at the time that a personal appeal from her directly to Saldana might be effective because "I thought [Theresa Saldana] might have a bit of compassion. I feel very sorry for what [Jackson] did to her. I really can sympathize. It must have been terrible. And I thought the fact that he's still going to be locked up would perhaps satisfy her. He's not going to be left roaming the streets where he could possibly go back and harm her anymore."

Writing the letter was not an easy task for Mrs. Howard. Later, she would recall that she worried about the letter's beginning for a long time before realizing that the best way to begin was with the simple truth of her feelings. She did not keep a copy of the letter, but remembered the beginning to be: "Dear Miss Saldana, This letter is very difficult for me to write. We don't know each other but the only thing we have in common is a person called Arthur Jackson."

Mrs. Howard knew from Harrison that Saldana "was fighting very hard and she desperately wanted to keep him over there, she would do anything to keep him over there. I just went on and said that he killed my husband a number of years ago and could she not see it in her heart to stop what she was doing and let us have him back over here."

Sometime later Mrs. Howard was told by Hodgman that he had personally delivered the letter to de Becker. The security consultant has since acknowledged receiving it, although he was unsure whether Saldana had ever seen it. Valerie Howard remains disappointed that she has never received a word in response from Theresa Saldana or Gavin de Becker.

De Becker said later that Saldana failed to respond to Mrs. Howard not out of callousness but because both he and Saldana felt that the actress and Fletcher's widow were "not in the same boat." Applying the cautiousness he advises all of his celebrity clients to use with communications from strangers, de Becker said the question of whether to respond to Mrs. Howard created a dilemma for him and Saldana. "How far do you go to involvement with people's attempt to communicate with you?" he asked. The security consultant said he did not recall that the letter required or requested an answer. Saldana, he said, "was fully aware of the [Fletcher] family's wishes."

Harrison's instinct that he would lose the extradition battle became stronger as he felt the intensity of the political dynamics of the situation, particularly the impact of publicity being generated by de Becker and Saldana. "It was good media by Gavin de Becker and Saldana. Can't blame her. One has to sympathize with her. You could never eliminate the possibility that he would someday want to go back and complete his 'divine mission.'"

The British detective wanted to talk to Saldana himself, to offer his assurance that no problems would be likely to arise if his proposal was put into action. "She refused to see me," Harrison said with disappointment.

Harrison saw that the potential for critical publicity bothered many people involved in the decision-making. "I realized that it was a hot potato. I think everyone was pretty worried, because de Becker would have jumped on the bandwagon. But de Becker didn't realize that we had all the evidence. When I saw the Board of Corrections, they were amazed with the evidence we had."

But the agency that ran the prisons was different from the body that approved prisoners' paroles. The California Board of Prison Terms was apparently not as impressed with Harrison's lobbying. "They wanted me to guarantee that he'll do twenty years. I said, 'I can't *guarantee* anything. I can guarantee you he'll stand trial. I can almost guarantee you he'll be convicted. But I can't guarantee you how many years he'll serve [in England]. You can't do that in America either.' "

The director of Scotland Yard had written an open letter to American authorities in which he fully supported Harrison's assessment of the strength of the murder case. Copies were delivered to appropriate officials in California.

De Becker later said that he had not been convinced by the "one-sided" Scotland Yard evaluation of the murder case. He also conceded that he had never spoken to Harrison directly, obtaining his information about the proposed British prosecution only through "FBI contacts." Pushing for prosecution in Los Angeles was "a weighty, cautious decision," he said. "It was the devil we knew versus the devil we didn't know. [Saldana] has to live with Jackson one way or another. The decision was a scary one to Theresa." In the end, they were unwilling to relinquish Jackson to a situation that "would be out of our hands."

Harrison had come to believe that de Becker "controlled things,'' at least in Ira Reiner's office. Similarly, Hodgman realized that Saldana's wishes ''in this particular instance were a very important concern for [Reiner].'' And everyone recognized, Reiner admitting so himself, that Saldana's access to lobby him personally was most unusual in a county in which cases involving thousands of violent crime victims were prosecuted each year.

Saldana's celebrity was a focal point of Reiner's attention to the matter, but it was de Becker's persistence that impressed Reiner. ''I was drawn into that and spent a lot of time on it because of Gavin de Becker. . . . Gavin is very bright and very determined. And Gavin is one of these people who correctly assesses a situation that you must go to the very top in terms of being an advocate. And so he did. . . . You talk to Gavin about questions of law in areas where he is particularly involved, you just assume he's a lawyer, which he isn't.''

Certainly, Reiner, de Becker, and Saldana appeared to share some prosecutorial philosophies. For example, Jackson's schizophrenia was not a relevant courtroom issue as far as Reiner was concerned. ''I tend, except in exceptional cases, to take a position that mental illness by itself is not significant in the criminal justice system . . . in the sense that I can't see the criminal justice system as a treatment center. I think it's ineffective as a treatment center.'' Reiner argues that focusing on issues of mental health when someone has been charged with a crime usually is ''subverting what should be the focus . . . to protect the public. So, if somebody is dangerous, the question should be the protection of the public, which means the incarceration and separation of the person from the public.''

In Jackson's case, according to the district attorney, ''He's crazy as a loon. Which means, and maybe that's a good illustration of it, because he's so crazy any question of treatment, to me, is just a preposterous notion. It may be very important to Mr. Jackson, but in terms of society the critical factor is simply to warehouse him so he is not a threat to other people."

Reiner also agreed with Saldana that, in a sense, in the 1982 trial Jackson had been "rewarded" for failing to kill her because attempted murder carries a much lesser penalty than murder, no matter how close he came to actually succeeding. Reiner had lobbied in the state legislature to increase the penalty for attempted murder, "to equate it with the crime of murder. To bring it down to a simple phrase, the person should not be rewarded for being a bad shot."

Whatever strong opinions Reiner may have held in this case were apparently kept largely to himself throughout much of the debate over it in the office. Hodgman's view was that Reiner had been completely unrevealing of his position until the last moment. Hodgman did not see evidence that the district attorney had supported extradition.

Indeed, Hodgman was taken aback· by the curt method in which he was informed that Reiner had reached his decision. Just before a scheduled meeting with Reiner and de Becker, Hodgman was called in his office and told that he "need not attend." Soon afterward, Hodgman received a one-sentence memorandum from Reiner that said, "We shall proceed in accordance with the best interests of Theresa Saldana."

"I give a lot of deference to the sensibilities of the victim," Reiner said later. "In this case you really had a situation where the victim could not be persuaded to the contrary."

Hodgman, as a member of the office's elite and highly independent special trials unit, began preparation for the Jackson trial but soon was assigned by Reiner to prosecute Charles Keating, a major figure in the national savings and loan scandal that had rocked the end of the Reagan administration. "Taking [Hodgman] off Saldana and putting him on Keating was hardly a punishment," Reiner said. "Saldana was an interesting case, Keating was vastly more significant. What you had was the greatest financial scandal in the history of the United States ... and this is the flagship case in that scandal.''

(Hodgman won a conviction in the Keating case and in 1992 was named the office's ''Prosecutor of the Year.'' During the same period, Reiner's political fortunes tumbled. In 1990 he was defeated in the Democratic primary for California attorney general by Arlo Smith, who lost in the general election to Republican Dan Lundgren. De Becker, according to records, contributed $1,250 to Reiner's campaign. Reiner later said that the contribution from de Becker was ''no big deal.''

In 1992, Reiner ran for reelection as Los Angeles County district attorney and was beaten in a nonpartisan primary by his longtime chief deputy turned adversary, Gilbert L. Garcetti, whom Reiner had demoted under questionable circumstances some months before the election. During the primary campaign, added to the other high-profile losing cases for which public opinion held Reiner responsible was the failure of his office to gain any convictions against the four Los Angeles police officers who were tried for the videotaped beating of Rodney King. The acquittals were held up for worldwide attention as a classic case of miscarriage of justice. Still eligible to run in the general election later in the year, Reiner, then fifty-six, faced seemingly insurmountable odds, and he withdrew his candidacy. (He told *The New York Times* that he didn't ''have the stomach'' for a negative campaign.)

With Hodgman's departure from the Jackson case, Deputy District Attorney Susan Gruber was assigned to the prosecution.

Harrison returned to London, disappointed at going back ''empty-handed.'' He did have the satisfaction of his belief, small consolation that it was, that he had provided Reiner and other California authorities with a better long-term solution than anything they were attempting. He held no antagonism toward Saldana. "I can't blame Saldana. [Jackson] could never reform his character." Dismayed by the turn of events in the United States, other Scotland Yard officials contemplated asking the California governor to intervene. They were advised by their legal department against such international lobbying. "You're not getting involved in politics in America, we'll just wait," Harrison and his colleagues were told. The Britons weren't about to approach American authorities "cap in hand," forced to beg for Jackson.

CHAPTER TEN

|￭￭￭￭￭|

The Second Trial

On a June morning in 1990, in a holding cell of the Los Angeles County Criminal Courts Building, Jackson sat quietly with his thoughts.

He wore a drab blue jailhouse jumpsuit. Just before he was taken out, to make his first appearance in court to answer to the charges that he had written letters threatening Theresa Saldana, sheriff's deputies wrapped chains around his ankles and padlocked the shackles so that they could not slip loose. The restraints shortened his gait, allowing him to walk only by slowly shuffling his feet. Each of his arms was secured close to his body by handcuffs linked to another chain around his waist. The uneasy reality that Jackson remained a potential danger filled the downtown courtroom with a sense of tension and confrontation as Jackson was escorted in for this preliminary hearing.

Just before the start of the proceedings, a court bailiff entered the spectator area of the room and directed his comments over the heads of some people in the first few rows of seats to a cluster of two dozen young people who listened intently to his firm instructions. They appeared to be friends of Saldana's. They wore pink armbands matching the ribbon she wore in her hair that day. They seemed to exhibit both a repulsion of Arthur Jackson and an air of vengeance toward him.

"When the defendant is brought out I need everyone

to stay seated,'' the bailiff said to this group of people who, up to this point, had been behaving well. The young people, somber and tense with a determination in their faces to match that expressed by Jackson, stiffened in their seats at the warning from the bailiff that ''this is a highly sensitive matter of security.'' Some of the group expressed premonitions that were probably melodramatic. ''If all hell breaks loose, jump under there,'' one young man whispered to his female companion while pointing to some rows of empty benches. Because of Jackson's chains, the concern that he might harm anyone at that moment was overwrought. The bailiff seemed to be warning that he would not allow the slightest movement by the victim's friends toward the defendant they reviled.

In contrast to the intensity of Jackson's writing, in person he looked dazed. His eyes made contact with no one as he was directed to his seat at the defendant's table. His uncombed brown hair was thick on the sides and back of his head. The color of his skin was unnaturally pale. He sat hunched slightly forward in a peculiar huddle, the chains making it difficult for him to sit back in his chair.

His new attorney, Deputy Public Defender Norman Kava, leaned over and said ''Good morning'' to his client. Jackson looked up with some alertness but he appeared as though his mind was trapped in some distant place. Soon, the judge entered and began the hearing.

''Could you state your true name?'' the judge asked.

''Say 'yes,' '' Kava said to his client, who then answered the judge's question.

Kava began his presentation by arguing a question of jurisdiction, suggesting that the case was not being properly tried in Los Angeles County because the letters had been written in another California county and sent to New York State. Deputy District Attorney Sterling Norris, a senior staff lawyer temporarily handling the

case for the prosecutor, Susan Gruber, countered that
Los Angeles County jurisdiction was proper because
the effects of the defendant's actions had been "felt"
here. Precedent cases demonstrated that when alleged
criminal actions were taken in one California county,
they could still be prosecuted in another under the
proper circumstances. The case law prevailed and Kava
lost his jurisdictional argument.

The lawyers stipulated to some facts, including Jackson's October 1982 conviction for attempted murder,
and the fact that he had written the letters in question
while incarcerated at Atascadero and had then sent them
to New York. The hearing moved forward with testimony by Gavin de Becker confirming the process by
which he had received the letters from a television
producer.

Then, yet again, Saldana was called to a witness
stand to face her attacker.

She entered the courtroom from a side door not open
to the public and, passing in front of Jackson without
turning to look at him, she was led to the witness chair
by de Becker, who walked close to her. With seriousness on her face, she held her head high and rigid,
although her gait seemed to divulge some nervousness
in her.

The start of her testimony was shaky. Six years had
passed since the last courtroom encounter and there
were fresh emotions coupling with the old feelings. "I
can't answer questions with him in the room," she said
tearily, soon after sitting down. Immediately, the judge
declared a recess and Jackson was escorted out, the
chains around his body clanking as he shuffled. From
the other side of the courtroom a television technician
followed Jackson's movements with his camera. Then
Saldana returned to the anteroom from which she had
entered the courtroom a few minutes earlier. The door
was closed behind her but she could still be heard as

she loudly repeated her distressful complaint to de Becker, "I'm afraid to talk in front of him."

The courtroom was silent for another ten minutes before Jackson was brought back into the courtroom and Saldana, appearing calmer, returned to the witness chair. Displaying fresh resolve, she began to answer the prosecutor's questions firmly.

The new threats, Saldana told the judge, had come at a time when she and her husband "had regained equilibrium and were over the [1982] attack."

She obviously had made great strides in moving her life forward. The year 1986 had marked the publication of *Beyond Survival*, the book she authored in which she had eloquently charted her torturous path to recovery after Jackson had "hurled [me] into an entirely new reality devoid of the comfort and normalcy of the past. I now shared with other victims of violent crime the bond that sets us apart from the rest of the world: the personal, shattering knowledge of the depth of pain and trauma one human being is capable of inflicting upon another."

Through a television movie produced after the 1982 trial and in the book about her experiences, Saldana testified, she had tried to show "how essential it is to create something positive out of an ugly, wrenchingly painful experience."

Because of Jackson's latest assault on her psyche, she said, she had developed debilitating psychosomatic symptoms. "I considered the threats extremely credible especially in light of the fact that he already tried to murder me."

That her psychological torment was extreme, even though Jackson was currently incarcerated, was not in question. She had written that "the most vivid and horrific memory I have of the event is one not of physical suffering but of psychological anguish. . . . It is difficult to put into words the uncontrollable, bone-chilling terror one is left with after a life-threatening attack. It is an insidious fear, awesome in its intensity and destructive power—hard to live with and harder still to break free of. In the hospital I was plagued by flashbacks which catapulted me backward in space and time and shook the bedrock of my sanity.''

Her recovery had been a series of seemingly simple steps which, at the time, may have appeared insurmountable but eventually were viewed as triumphant successes when each challenge was overcome. One such moment included the first time that she felt comfortable simply sitting in a restaurant again. Another event came when she walked on the street for the first time without someone protectively close beside her. That moment didn't happen until nine months after the attack and, even then, a friend was posted a block away to stand watch.

Jeffrey Fenn, Saldana's rescuer, testified about his receipt of letters from Jackson, all of which he said he had discarded. Because that evidence had been destroyed, the judge promptly dismissed three of the eight counts against Jackson, all of which had related to Fenn.

During most of the hearing Jackson sat staring at the wall, his body hunched over and constricted by the chains and handcuffs. He seemed to expend a lot of energy just trying to rest his elbows on the chair arms. From time to time, he strained to read documents on the table in front of Kava.

Kava was as mystified by Jackson's thought process as everyone else who dealt with him. The defense attorney thought that his client was full of strange contradictions. ''I found him to be rather intelligent in certain ways, but very complex, and not particularly interested in what his fate was in the case.'' Kava believed that Jackson's primary interest in the courtroom was to ''see Saldana, to see how she was reacting to the proceedings and to have his day in court, not so much to get acquitted but rather to state his desire about [his future].''

In preparation sessions, Jackson had answered Kava's questions only indirectly. ''He was constantly interested in being in a 'higher court,' which could be interpreted in several ways, but it certainly didn't include a court in the California state system,'' Kava said later.

There was little surprise that after the brief hearing, the judge found the evidence and the law sufficient to send the case to trial. Six months later, on December 3, 1990, the proceeding began, presided over by Superior Court Judge James A. Bascue on the fifteenth floor of the Los Angeles County Criminal Courts Building.

Defense attorney Kava recognized that with the matter going to a jury, the chance of an acquittal was ''essentially hopeless,'' particularly because Judge Bascue had decided to allow the panel to hear detailed testimony about the 1982 attack.

The prosecutor, Susan Gruber, was a deputy district attorney experienced in cases involving stalking crimes stemming from obsession. A few years before, she had successfully prosecuted a woman who had stalked and harassed the actor Michael J. Fox. Because of Gruber's background, Hodgman had consulted her when he was handling the case before moving to the Keating trial.

Gruber also knew de Becker, who had been Fox's security consultant, and well remembered her difficulties with him. The prosecutor believed that de Becker had tried to unduly direct her handling of the Fox case. Because she had not given in to him then, she had looked forward to a smoother relationship with him during the prosecution of this case. ''I had already gone through that route with Gavin, how cases should be prosecuted and who the prosecutor is. I basically had to go through Gavin to reach Michael J. Fox.''

Gruber's previous uncomfortable experience with de Becker was not all that made her apprehensive about this assignment. She also believed that de Becker had a special relationship with her boss, Ira Reiner, which could make him review her performance more critically than normal. Reiner had not done anything overt to acknowledge that he would be looking over her shoulder. In fact, she had had no conversations at all with Reiner during the course of the prosecution. Her suspicions had been raised only by comments made to her by de Becker, who, Gruber said later, "told me he had made large [campaign] contributions to Ira Reiner."

Gruber was well aware that Reiner had already overruled Hodgman and others in the office over whether the case should even be prosecuted in Los Angeles. Gruber had agreed with the assessment that the murder charge in London was a better course to follow. At the time, she also had not yet met Saldana and she believed that Saldana's publicity campaign raised questions about the actress's sincerity. That doubt, however, evaporated when Gruber met the actress for the first time. "I felt that her response was tremendous and far greater than any type of emotion I've seen exhibited from any victim I've worked with. I've dealt with very emotional victims. I questioned it initially because it was so overwhelming. But I met with her numerous times, hundreds of hours I had spent with her, and [her fear] is absolutely genuine."

Gruber was a southern California native, a graduate of Beverly Hills High School, the University of Southern California, and Southwestern University School of Law. She had been a deputy district attorney since 1982. She had also developed special concerns about taking on this case because she was due to give birth in several weeks. Gruber came to the realization that in all the years that Jackson had been in the California criminal justice system, she was the first woman, apart from Saldana, who was an antagonist to him. She worried that he might transfer his murderous obsession with Saldana to her. She sought advice from Dr. Markman, whom she knew from other cases. He advised her that largely because of the apparent lack of any schizophrenic symbolism expressed by Jackson toward Gruber, the likelihood that Jackson would make such a switch was highly improbable. People like Arthur Jackson do not easily transfer their obsession from one person to another, the psychiatrist explained. Satisfied with that analysis, Gruber pressed on with the prosecution.

While studying Jackson's letters to Jonathan Felt, the television producer, Gruber had concluded that the hardest part of preparing her presentation would be to determine which portions of the writings constituted "credible threats" according to statutory definition. Eventually, she was confident that she had isolated real threats in the messages. "There were parts of the writings that I believed showed his mental state. Not in terms of a psychotic state or a schizophrenic state, but in terms of his mind-set on being intent on killing this person."

In her opening argument to jurors, she said, "It has been proven, and he has been convicted of a violent attack on Theresa Saldana with the specific intent to kill her. . . . He has been able to express his desire of assassination to people outside of those prison bars who can, in fact, effectuate those threats."

Jackson sat and listened, his head tilted back a bit, revealing a balding spot on the top of his head. He combined the look of a sad, benign character with that of a terrifying, uncontrollable creature. His quietness gave no clue to what bizarre thinking might be swirling through his mind at that moment, or what interpretation he might be giving to the proceedings, of which he was the central and most unsympathetic participant. He sat in the courtroom, the product of forty years of delusional thinking and a few minutes of brutal violence.

Kava made two main points in his opening argument. First, he questioned whether there was any evidence to prove that Jackson had intended to communicate the messages to Saldana when he sent the letters to Jonathan Felt. Second, he asked the jurors to consider whether Jackson actually had the ability to carry out the threats. He said he doubted whether the section of the statute that required that the threats be ''credible'' could be supported by the facts.

Saldana's entrance to the courtroom on the second day of the trial brought a hush. A United Press International writer in his dispatch referred to one striking clothing accessory, ''her signature chiffon scarf tied in a bow at the top of her head to keep her long, dark hair off her face.''

Sitting in the witness chair, Saldana took deep breaths. Her responses were filled with determination. She was, as always, movingly dramatic in her retelling of the 1982 attack and her long recovery from the injuries she had sustained.

At one point, as a matter of routine, Gruber asked Saldana if she could identify the defendant. The witness's body movements revealed that this was a most unpleasant task. She turned her head only slightly in the direction of the defense table, her glance toward Jackson hardly perceptible, before verifying that Jackson was the man who had attacked her in 1982.

Gruber had placed all of the letters to Felt into evidence. When she handed the documents to Saldana and asked her to read portions of them, news photographers at the side of the courtroom became more animated as they recognized a telling picture. Saldana examined the dozen or so documents methodically, occasionally taking sips from a glass of water as she studied. When she was reading the excerpts, Jackson pursed his lips and stared at the ceiling lights above the judge. Then he began to write, filling a tattered piece of yellow paper completely, right to the four edges.

Saldana told the jurors that the first letter she had received from Jackson, which was not part of the evidence in this case, was an eighty-nine-page document he had begun writing after his arrest in 1982, although it did not reach her until 1984. ''I remember him saying that he swore 'on the ashes of his dead mother and the scars of Theresa Saldana that he would complete his divine mission' of killing me. And I recall he made references to friends he had made in prison, including the late John Holmes, and that he had discussed with them better ways of killing me so that he wouldn't fail the next time. . . . It included the fact that he only regretted not having used a gun because he couldn't get access to a gun."

Saldana said that she had not actually seen the letters Jackson had written to Felt until a year after de Becker had received them, simply because she had not asked to see them sooner. Initially, de Becker had read portions of the letters to her over the telephone, and "I was already under enough terror from the excerpts alone . . . I especially recall that [Jackson] said that there was no police protection or FBI protection or bulletproof vest that could save me. That if certain demands of his weren't met by a certain date, that my life would be forfeited. I was referred to repeatedly as 'assassination target Theresa Saldana' and it said that he had arranged with other people to have me murdered."

Gruber pressed Saldana with more questions to emphasize to the jurors the depth of Saldana's fear that had been revived by the letters.

"The most frightening aspect about them was that for the first time since this happened, he stated that he had other people who were in place to murder me," Saldana said.

"Did you believe that?" Gruber continued.

"Yes, I did."

"And why is that?"

"Because I was aware, especially after reading the letter I received in 1984, that he had befriended other criminals and had spoken to them about means of murder."

Kava shared a problem with Steven Moyer, Jackson's defense attorney in the 1982 trial. Neither man was able to conduct a vigorous cross-examination of Saldana for fear of alienating jurors, who would likely view such questioning as an unfair attack on a sympathetic and innocent victim. This was particularly confining to Kava, who needed to prove that Jackson's threats could not be taken credibly. The best way to demonstrate that would be to try to push Saldana into admitting as much through tough questioning. That was a dangerous path for him, though, and he did not embark upon it.

Kava did elicit the admission from Saldana that, of course, she wanted Jackson to spend as much time as possible in prison, and that was why she was pursuing this case. "I was happy that he received the maximum [sentence in 1982] and I was unhappy that the maximum was so low." Indeed, in 1982 and after, Saldana made public statements questioning a legal system that did not allow a life sentence, the sentence Jackson could have received had she not survived her injuries, just because he had failed in his attempt to kill her.

Kava then turned the questioning to the London murder case. Saldana said something curious when considered in light of de Becker's previous arguments that the British murder case seemed weak. Saldana offered a different viewpoint.

"You were aware that the defendant confessed to murder?" Kava asked.

"Yes," Saldana replied.

"Did this play any role in your interpreting the 1988 letters as real threats on your life?"

"Yes. I believe that his confession was valid and I believe that in addition to his attempting to murder me, he killed at least one other person."

In describing the 1982 incident, Saldana said that her assailant had "kept aiming for my heart." As she said this, Jackson nodded affirmatively to himself, not raising his head to look at her or anyone else. Then, as she continued talking, he raised his head and fixed his gaze above the judge's head to stare at the Great Seal of the State of California on the wall for a few moments. Most of the time, though, he just stared at the table before him, seemingly bored by the proceedings.

Once, as Kava paused to construct a question in his mind, Saldana smoothly turned from side to side in her chair. She glanced at Jackson once, then quickly whirled back in the opposite direction, closing her eyes tightly for a second.

When de Becker took the stand, he was asked to summarize his background. He talked about a serious, solid beginning to his now-successful security business, not mentioning the show business connections to Elizabeth Taylor referred to in *Premiere* magazine. He told the jurors that he had incorporated his business in 1980. "At the time I was director of the special services group for President-elect Reagan, and then in that capacity also assessed threat material which was directed toward political public figures. Following that in 1982, I was appointed by President Reagan to the advisory board at the U.S. Department of Justice."

Under his supervision, de Becker said, some 175,000 threatening or bizarre communications directed to "media figures" had been assessed by his firm. "Our office has been pioneering research into predicting dangerous behavior and assessing people who are commonly called 'star-stalkers' or 'obsessive fans.' "

After studying Jackson's writings for years, de Becker had come to at least respect the defendant's accuracy. "Insofar as to everything I have been able to corroborate, he is an excellent witness to events in his life. He is very credible and very accurate and extraordinarily detailed and clear."

"After receiving the 1988 letters did you feel that the life of Theresa Saldana was, in fact, in jeopardy?" Gruber asked him.

"Yes. I felt it was before. We always knew we would be facing the threat of Jackson. We could only hope that he might direct his attentions elsewhere. But after the 1988 letters it was clear that that was too hopeful.''

In his cross-examination, Kava attempted to demonstrate that the letters were too rambling to be considered clear and legitimate threats.

''You'd have to come to my office to see letters that are rambling,'' de Becker replied. ''These are not what we would call rambling letters.''

As Gruber's expert witness, de Becker was unwavering in his analysis and ability to fend off the defense lawyer's cross-examination parrying.

''All communications, even the one we are having now, are clothed in all kinds of language,'' he said to Kava. ''You really need to get to what is the core issue. And in Jackson's letters it is the core issue that I concern myself with. And the core issue had to do with threatening to kill her or use others to kill her if he didn't get certain conditions met. And that kind of threat is sometimes wrongly called a 'conditional threat.' That's not what these were. These were what is called an 'intimidating threat,' which means it sets forth conditions that must be met in order to avert harm.''

Kava questioned de Becker's motive for waiting almost a year from the time he received the letters from Jonathan Felt at the television production company before finally filing a formal complaint with the Los Angeles County District Attorney's office.

''Your first contact with the DA's office about these letters was in approximately mid-May 1989, is that correct?'' Kava asked.

''Yes, that is correct,'' de Becker replied.

''Is it fair to say that you believe Mr. Jackson was about to be paroled in June of 1989?''

''About to be released actually.''

''You know for a fact, Mr. de Becker, that he wasn't going to be released June 15, 1989, that he was going to be extradited to England, don't you?''

"No, absolutely not."

"It's your testimony that Mr. Jackson had no holds from England?" Kava asked.

"He had an immigration hold, but we had no verification that Jackson walking out of Atascadero and going to England was in any way relevant as to whether or not he could still harm Theresa," de Becker said.

"Without going into any details, had you ever during the year of 1989, had you ever had any contact with representatives from Scotland Yard about the matter?"

"No, I had not. I still have not."

"No direct contact?"

"No."

This testimony seemed to demonstrate that by previously refusing to meet with Douglas Harrison, de Becker may have effectively insulated himself from having to admit to detailed information about the London plan, information which could have weakened his position against extradition. Kava tried to probe further into de Becker's strategy.

"Why did you wait over a year to give the—to notify the district attorney's office about these letters and give them copies of them?"

"When the letters arrived, within six to seven days of my having all the letters, I contacted the people that I thought were the appropriate people because Jackson was in their custody. Given that no one else, the Department of Justice nor the Department of Health, nor the Department of Corrections, nor anyone else who knew about these communications had gone to the district attorney at that time it seemed appropriate that we do that. . . . It is my testimony that I had no reason to make contact with the district attorney's office until May of 1989."

Kava, however, privately had formed a cynical theory about de Becker's action. He believed that the security consultant had knowingly waited until the last possible moment because that aided his plan to maximize Jackson's California prison time. De Becker had done this without considering the problems it might cause for prosecutors in either Los Angeles or London, Kava believed. Under state sentencing laws, de Becker obtained an advantage by filing new charges against Jackson at the last moment possible. Every day Jackson remained imprisoned on the 1982 sentence while the new charges were pending would automatically be deducted from any sentence he received upon conviction of the new charges. Thus, waiting until the old sentence was virtually completed reduced the amount of incarceration the courts would view as concurrent, effectively stretching out any new sentence to its full limit.

Prosecutor Susan Gruber concluded her presentation with technical precision, calling Jonathan Felt to verify that he had spoken to Jackson, that he had then received the letters and sent them on to de Becker. Senior Investigator Dennis Stults discussed his search of Jackson's materials at Atascadero, and Georgia Hanna, a "questioned document examiner" for the DA, verified that the letters were, indeed, in Jackson's handwriting. Then Gruber rested her case.

Defense attorney Kava now faced another dilemma. His client wanted to take the stand. However unwise that might be, there was nothing Kava could do to prevent it. "I have advised Mr. Jackson that it is not in his best interest to testify," Kava told Judge Bascue.

"It's his constitutional right he's exercising and I do appreciate the fact that you will cooperate with his choice to testify," Judge Bascue responded.

During this exchange, Jackson seemed to be expressing his eagerness to talk. He sat on the edge of his seat, apparently anticipating that his time to explain himself was approaching.

"I cannot guarantee that I will be able to stop him in terms of his answers," Kava warned the court.

"I think we both appreciate that," the judge replied.

"The court will do its best. Counsel will too, to keep it in a question-and-answer format."

Arthur Jackson walked to the front of the courtroom and took the witness stand. This moment was tinged with some absurdity, but at Judge Bascue's insistence, the courtroom was maintained in dignity. A system of laws and procedure would endure and accommodate the craziness.

Jackson was impatient with Kava's matter-of-fact opening questions. The defense attorney did not reveal the considerable discomfort he actually felt conducting this exchange. Jackson was pressing to make a speech because he believed he had an important message to impart. Kava, who knew that by expressing his beliefs Jackson would be incriminating himself, was persistent in his effort to control the flow of testimony coming from his client.

Asked if he remembered receiving a Federal Express number from Jonathan Felt, Jackson replied, "This is seemingly insignificant, but it was an item of mail. He wanted me to respond to his inquiry about what I just recently was reminded, it came under the title of 'Murder in America.' "

Asked if he had been incarcerated at Atascadero at the times he sent the letters to Felt, Jackson quickly said "Yes," emphasizing that he had a different agenda for this moment. "I don't want to sound cynical, but it's just that I am anxious to get some issues stated here of my own."

Kava tried to stay on track, asking Jackson why he had sent letters of such content to Felt.

"Well, now, we're getting to the essence of the matter I have been trying to get at for a while now," Jackson responded, "and that is my chief objective, my true hope. Hopes and dreams were based on the anticipation that Mr. Felt would think logically and submit these letters to the proper jurisdictional authority in

New York or Washington, D.C., which would be the federal authorities.''

Felt's transferral of the letters to de Becker had brought ''the worst of both worlds,'' Jackson told a fascinated room of spectators, judge and jury included.

''I admit that they were rambling and that's where the fatal error lies, that I should have been more concentrated in my efforts to interpret specifically what my intentions were when I wrote those letters. . . . I had a grievance. . . . For six years, from 1982 to 1988 I constantly campaigned to have my right to volunteer as a candidate for state-administered execution under the First Amendment of the United States Constitution which provides for free—the exercise of religious freedom . . . and that is still my intention to this date. And that was the reason why I wrote those letters. And, as we have mentioned also, Mr. Kava, the motive, or rather the moral behind the whole idea was a red herring, a red herring strategy to attract the attention of the U.S. Department of Justice in Washington because they had denied me my right in February of 1985 when they turned down my civil rights case. William Bradford Reynolds was then the assistant attorney general.''

Jackson seemed genuinely distraught that his motive for the tone of the letters to Felt had been misunderstood. Of course, his perception of reality differed from that of everyone else in the courtroom and his opinions would have little bearing on the conclusions others would reach about what he had done.

''But had I known that Jonathan Felt was going to go in a roundabout way without me knowing, I would have avoided like the plague sending those letters to Jonathan Felt because he messed everything up. Look where I am today because of that.''

The letters did contain specific, threatening language, a fact that Kava could not ignore. For example:

Assassination target Theresa Saldana and the aforementioned other persons, together with the U.S. military personnel in Europe will be focused on and their lives will be forfeited by terrorist hit squads associated with my revolutionary past.

"Did you, in fact, mean to carry out those threats when you wrote it?" the defense attorney asked his client.

"No."

"Why did you write that?"

"Well, as I just explained, the red herring factor covers the whole answer, really. That was to divert attention towards the true destination I wanted these letters to be sent to. And to draw attention to my hopes and dreams. The whole thing with regard to my threats was pure bluff."

"Did you have any particular means or ability to carry out such threats?"

"No. I wish I had the means and ability to have perhaps been contacted by a true, real revolutionary organization that could have sprung me from Atascadero and perhaps airlifted me up to the San Francisco Bay area so that I could have carried out my mission without, perhaps, government assistance ... to offer myself as a martyr in the name of Divine Providence. . . . That is the special covenant I made within my religious doctrines."

So desperate was Jackson's desire to leave the prison system's mental health facilities, he said, that he had purposely adopted a theatrical-style role in the letters. "I didn't mean to play the part of a villain but I had to. I had no other alternative but to create the impression that my threats were genuine so I could get the most maximum attention from the federal government [to execute him]."

If he had been moved to a federal penitentiary, and allowed to leave the state's psychiatric facility, he said, "that would have helped my morale for one thing, and would also have been of some documentary interest to me because I read up on penology in books and movies and saw various world-famous prisons and so on. Prior to that I was interested in ancient castles of England and Europe. Then I took an interest in prisons.

"You know, there is a certain similarity between castles and prisons. You know what I mean?" he asked without receiving a response from anyone.

While imprisoned, Jackson had been wide-ranging in his entreaties to government officials for help in carrying out his petition to be executed. He testified that he had sent letters to California Supreme Court Chief Justice Rose Bird, William Bradford Reynolds at the Department of Justice, Judge Rittenband who had sentenced him in 1982, the International Court of Justice of the United Nations, Amnesty International, and California Governor George Deukmejian.

Jackson had carried to the witness stand a page-and-a-half-long statement which he wanted to read. Titled "Statement to the court, message to the news media, Arthur Richard Jackson, December 4, 1990," the document's central point was that his mission no longer required him to kill Saldana. His comments, though, brought little comfort to anyone concerned with Saldana's safety.

"You see, I did say at the beginning of my [1981] petition that I wanted her to join me in heaven but you must remember that, as I've explained to you, I believe strongly that I have been a victim of witchcraft all of my life since childhood."

Jackson, of course, was only proving to the jury how deeply disturbed he was. Susan Gruber, through simple, factual questions on cross-examination, was able to further demonstrate Jackson's true danger.

"Mr. Jackson, in 1982, you tried to kill Theresa Saldana, isn't that true? she asked.

"That's correct," he replied without hesitation.

"By the use of a knife?"

"Yes. Unfortunately. I would have much preferred a handgun."

"Because you didn't want to hurt her? You just wanted to kill her?"

"Yes. And besides, in addition to being more efficient it would also have been more humane."

Jackson used some of his extensive movie knowledge to answer Gruber when she asked him about writing over and over again in his diary that he wanted to kill Saldana.

"I wouldn't say to such an extent that it was pathologically morbid where I just kept repeating it in the diary all the time like I was Jack Nicholson in *The Shining* where he couldn't stop writing the same thing over and over again. No. Not like that."

As Gruber asked her questions, Jackson furrowed his brow and tilted his head slightly forward, making him appear to stare at the prosecutor with ominous, hooded eyes.

Jackson said he was not unemotional about Saldana. "There was one occasion about March 1984, that she appeared on *Good Morning America*, I think it was, and when I heard that she was going to come on I suddenly felt a rather cold, icy feeling come over me. And I walked out of the TV room. I just didn't want to watch it."

When Jackson's extraordinary testimony ended, the judge announced that he needed to explain for the record that however bizarre the proceeding may seem to those reading it in transcript later, Jackson's appearance conformed to the requirements of law. "During the testimony of Mr. Jackson, Mr. Jackson testified to some statements that this court feels an appellate court might review from the record and not understand really what happened in the trial court. This court wants to make the observation that Mr. Jackson appeared thoroughly competent during this trial, that he has communicated freely and openly with his counsel. He appears alert. He testified in a very forthright, direct manner.''

When it was over, Gruber said that her cross-examination of Jackson had been a rigorous experience. "As the prosecutor, I found it extremely difficult for him to be on the stand because he is very smart.''

As the judge prepared the jurors for their deliberations, the possibility existed that this trial was already over, as had happened in the 1982 trial. Subtleties of law might not mean much to jurors who couldn't help but be stunned by what they had just witnessed.

The judge instructed the jurors that three elements were required to prove that Jackson had committed the crimes charged. The first was that the defendant had to have been previously convicted of attempted murder or another felony in which the defendant inflicted great bodily injury to another person. The second was that "the defendant willfully and maliciously communicated to the witness or victim of that crime to which he was convicted of a credible threat to use force or violence upon that person or that person's immediate family.'' And third, the crime had to have occurred within the county of Los Angeles.

Gruber's final argument to the jury, because Jackson's appearance as a witness had proven his craziness and potential for violence, needed only to focus on Saldana's fear of Jackson.

"We know he is determined. We know he is intent. We know in a very strange way he is a very clear thinker. A bizarre motive does not mean that he cannot plan, that he cannot execute his plan. And what is of the utmost importance is something else we know about the defendant Arthur Jackson. That he is vicious and he is brutally dangerous. He has proven that to us. He is without morals. He is without rationale. And he is without a conscience. And this can be summed up by a quote from Arthur Jackson: he would have preferred a gun, it would have been 'more efficient and humane.' ''

Then she turned to the victim's plight. "This terror that no human being should ever have to experience is exactly what Penal Code 139 was designed to prevent. That no victim, no human being, should be made to feel what she has been feeling."

"And you ask yourself, 'Was Theresa Saldana's fear, was her terror real?' And after you look at this, remember what she has been through, the only answer is 'yes.' "

Norman Kava's job, which included his plea to the jury that they put aside emotion to look only at the letter of the law, may have been impossible to accomplish at this stage of the proceedings. Everyone recognized that this case existed only because of the horror of 1982, and Kava was forced to argue that the brutality of that attack was not necessarily relevant to the current charges.

"There is an overwhelming sympathy, compassion, maybe even sorrow for Miss Saldana in this case. On the other hand ... you may dislike [Jackson], you may find contempt for him. Some of you may even hate him. It doesn't matter. You're not deciding this case based on what you feel about the parties relating to the 1982 incident. You've got to look at it separately."

There were sound legal questions concerning the propriety of jurisdiction and whether Jackson harbored the proper intent under the law, but they were of little help to Kava in convincing the jury.

"You heard Mr. Jackson's testimony and it is your job to judge him as a witness. He, I will concede, is different from you, from me, from Mrs. Gruber and the judge. He is a different kind of person. He is not insane, not legally insane. He is not legally incompetent. However, he has a mental problem. He came across as being honest as to what he was testifying to, as horrible as some of it was."

The jurors did consider the law and sent relevant questions about technicalities to the judge during their deliberations. They asked, "Which letters pertain to which count?" and "Does the communication or threat have to have been direct, i.e., if the communication went from Jackson to Felt to de Becker to Saldana could this apply to element number two?" To this important question, Judge Bascue answered back in writing, "The law does not require direct communication."

On December 14, the jury returned with its verdict, convicting Jackson on all five counts.

That day, Gruber saw District Attorney Reiner for the first time regarding this case. "He held a press conference and asked me to join him at the podium," she said with a hint of sarcasm in her voice.

Sentence would not be levied by Judge Bascue until after the New Year. As the holidays approached, Jackson, who was being held in the Los Angeles County Jail temporarily, continued his correspondence with others. The judge was not pleased with a Christmas card he received from the prisoner. The message inside read in part:

Before I sign out I wish to caution against being sent back to the California Department of Corrections or the CDMH on a punitive basis over the false conviction that the jury brought in with their verdict. It would be a tragic mistake because I would be a heavy liability risk, ten times greater in magnitude than I was from 1982 to 1988 inclusive.

On January 7 the parties returned to the courtroom for the sentencing hearing.

Saldana pleaded for the maximum term. "As you can see, my sister is in the courtroom crying. My husband is in the courtroom having anxiety attacks. My mother is in New York City on the verge of who knows what. This has never stopped since 1982. He has literally trampled not only on me but on my family, and has continued to do so. The thought of any leniency being shown on him as regards the number of letters or how I received those letters is truly ridiculous in my opinion.''

She reiterated her argument that Jackson not be extradited to London until his full California sentence had been served. ''If Jackson is deported and forfeits all or part of his sentence here, it is our belief that this trial and everything it entailed would have been a sham. As you can see, Mr. Jackson is sitting and reading some kind of newspaper while I do this. I can't imagine why.

''My family and I ask for what is routinely given criminals—what we would like is some time off for good behavior. We have fought long and hard. What I would like more than anything in my life is to shed my image as a victim, once and for all, and just be able to return to my own life and to my career without being further harassed by a person who, first, almost murdered me, and then went on to continue to threaten my life again and again.''

Then she directed her words directly to the prisoner in an astonishing verbal confrontation, likely to be the only time in her life when she would ever choose to talk to him directly. ''Arthur Jackson,'' she said firmly, ''I ask you to please leave me and my family alone. Take me out of your thoughts. I do not know you. You are a stranger. You do not know me. I am not your victim. I am not anyone's victim any longer. You have caused not only me but my entire family tremendous suffering for many years. I ask you to forget about me. I ask you to give my family some peace for once and for all. That's all I have to say.''

Jackson did not reveal his reaction to being addressed by the object of his obsession. He was concentrated for the moment on his own agenda, which included his desire to serve his sentence in the Los Angeles County Jail rather than to be returned to a state prison psychiatric facility. He, too, was allowed to make a statement to the court before the sentence was announced.

''I have here a testament of truth and justice and also

assurance by the defendant, I, Arthur Richard Jackson, on this day, Monday, January the 7th, 1991, there is absolutely no intention on my part to endanger the life of Theresa Saldana and that any reports or impressions to the contrary are based on misunderstanding and also distortion of the context and the relationship.

"If I am ordered to be sent back to the California Department of Corrections other than by way of the fourteen-stage arrangement, I would regard it as a declaration of war. I am a reasonable person. I am not looking for trouble. It is the people who want me to stay locked up in California who are looking for trouble."

"Who are you threatening, Mr. Jackson?" the judge asked. "Are you threatening someone at this time?"

"No. This is really precautionary advice."

"Mr. Jackson, are you threatening the court? You say you are declaring war. What are you talking about?"

"I'm saying it's a declaration of war against me if the court sentences me to further time."

"Very well."

Jackson continued, "I classify myself a victim of special circumstances and also as a victim of witchcraft. At the same time I also regard myself as God's chief representative for truth and justice. Also for honesty, perfection, prudence, moral conscientiousness, for total separation from all association with the evils of the world as well as a candidate for gaining human independence from the entire human race altogether by way of execution at a prison of my own choice, total independence from California's custodial jurisdiction and total independence from the entire human race which I see as a victory for the Kingdom of Heaven over the forces of Hell.

"Now, the jury finding me guilty is calling me a liar, and by calling me a liar, convicting me of the charges, you might as well call God or Jesus Christ a liar. I challenge anyone on earth to prove that I am not worthy of being called one of God's chief representatives for truth and justice.

"You may, of course, wish to call me a schizophrenic, but my answer to that is that you're all members of the biggest schizophrenic social culture in the world in which lies, cheating, tricks and games are a way of life. At least I don't deal in lying, cheating, falseness and tricks and games. That's all I have to say."

"The court disagrees, Mr. Jackson," Judge Bascue said sternly. "She was in danger, is still in danger. It is my opinion, Mr. Jackson, that you are a danger to yourself. You are a danger to Miss Saldana, but you're also a danger to everyone about you. I find you to be extremely—"

"I wasn't going to kill her," Jackson said, interrupting the judge in mid-sentence, which apparently did not please the jurist. These exchanges between Jackson and the judge are valuable illustrations of the difficulties inherent in trying to understand and communicate with a schizophrenic. The men were on different verbal wavelengths and neither understood the other. Bascue, though, was sound in his determination that Jackson posed a great threat to others.

"I find you to be an extremely dangerous person," the judge said while looking down at Jackson. "I'm asking that these matters be forwarded to the Department of Corrections and the attorney general's office. If you should be released I'm putting people on notice that I find you to be a danger. I want them to evaluate whether you should remain in some custodial setting, and I am ordering an evaluation based on your articulated threats in this letter, which I see as additional threats; your declaration in court about warfare."

"Not my warfare. The court's warfare against me."

"You are sentenced forthwith to five years, eight months."

That was the maximum sentence possible.

"Corrupt American justice. Most crooked country in the world," Jackson said.

"Court will be in recess," the judge said.

CHAPTER ELEVEN

| ▌ ■ ■ ■ ▌ |

Vacaville

The California Medical Facility at Vacaville is a collection of flat-roofed, ugly concrete buildings, each three stories high, all surrounded by strong chain-link fence topped with multiple curls of razor wire. Desolate brown hills form the backdrop in the distance. This bleak inland northern California scene is the antithesis of the charm of Aberdeen's architecture and natural coastal beauty.

Within the walls of the Vacaville facility, the picture is even darker. There, the psychotic and other severely mentally disordered of California's prison population are housed, sometimes in hellish situations. One psychiatrist who works there has told the authors of inmates so hopeless that they purposely inject themselves with AIDS-tainted needles, using drug paraphernalia illegally smuggled into the prison. They expose themselves to a fatal disease because the AIDS ward offers more television time than other places in the facility. A certain death sooner than necessary is traded for whatever extra short-lived pleasures they can obtain, even a few more hours of television a day.

Arthur Jackson has received virtually no psychiatric treatment while in custody in California, a prison staff member has told the authors. The system is overloaded. Furthermore, Jackson refuses medication, as the law allows him and every other psychiatric prison inmate or state hospital patient to do. There are new medications that might alter his thinking process, as Thorazine has done effectively during other short periods in his life. Jackson, however, has never taken psychotropic drugs for any substantial, effective period of time.

There is a universal menace inside Arthur Jackson, one that is not limited to his obsession with Theresa Saldana. He would be a threat to society if he had never learned of her existence. His schizophrenia was well formed almost thirty years before he knew that she was alive. Inevitably, he would have focused his obsessions on someone else. He still might do so in the future.

One day in 1992, Dr. Markman sat in a visiting room at Vacaville, confronting once again the strange thoughts of Arthur Jackson. The prisoner's hazel eyes looked at his visitor expectantly, because he labored under the delusion that perhaps, finally, this person would help him to be transferred into the custody of federal authorities, his escape from what he believes is the "insult" of being labeled a psychotic by state authorities and housed in a mental health prison facility. Jackson sought a deal: he would exchange answers to an author's biographical questions in return for help in maneuvering through the bureaucracy and speeding his placement in a British prison. It is beyond his comprehension that such a contract is just not possible.

He had a day's growth of stubble on his face. The sickly skin pallor displayed in the Los Angeles courtroom was replaced with a bit of tan, from his daily exercise walks in the prison yard.

A constant in Jackson is his inability to perceive his actions as wrongful, not only in the legal sense but also in the moral context that innocent people have been hurt by him. This mental process is at the core of the legal definition of insanity. Jackson believes that his motivations are generated externally by forces beyond his reach and control, which in a sense is true. He views the results of all that he does egocentrically, or autistically, measuring the world around him only in relation to his own grand schemes. To him, direction comes from the soul of Joseph Cretzer, or perhaps the spirit of Saint Michael the Archangel. The truth is, his behavior is much more the product of bad body chemistry affecting the neurotransmitters of his brain.

Jackson was distant and cool during the conversation, as he had been in previous sessions with the forensic psychiatrist, the first a little more than ten years before and a few months after his attack on Saldana. This continuing demonstration of an inherent inability to display any interpersonal warmth is one aspect of the blockade his schizophrenia has erected, precluding any normal relationship for him.

"I'm a peace-loving, law-abiding individual," he told Markman as a guard stood outside the room watching through a window. "I was somehow ensnared, entrapped into a dangerous situation beyond my control— a vortex," he explained, rightly recognizing that his behavior is beyond his control, although he has no logical perspective on its real roots, or what medication might accomplish.

His attack on Saldana, he claimed, was the direct result of Hollywood's previous abuse of him, when, in the mid-1970s, he sent a forty-nine-page "semiautobiographical" manuscript to Gregory Peck. He unquestionably assumed that his writing would be purchased, providing enough money for a "free holiday" to the United States for a friend and himself. Later, while watching *Defiance*, he concluded that pieces of his story had been stolen and incorporated into the movie.

As he talked, he quickly crossed over from presenting merely strange logic to proffering truly crazy thoughts. His mother, he said, "was a spiritual medium, she received messages from the world of the dead." Later, he likened Saldana to the biblical character Delilah. "I'm like a moral Samson, the standard bearer of truth and justice."

His entire focus in life had become a single-minded effort to return to Great Britain, knowing full well that he would be incarcerated in a British prison and certainly would not go to Aberdeen. "I'm depressed and homesick," he says. He could not be considered suicidal, though. Reminded that England abolished the death penalty in 1959, he employed his psychological avoidance mechanisms and abruptly changed the subject.

He repeated the argument that he had unsuccessfully offered in his pitiful appearance on the witness stand in Los Angeles a year and a half before. The threats in the letter, he continued to profess, were "not real. They were pseudothreats. The letter was a call for help. There has never been a desire to make a second attempt on Theresa Saldana's life." Accepting this declaration of his would be foolhardy. There is no way of confidently knowing whether he truly believes this or if it is merely part of his tactical posturing. He soon states that if he is tried for murder in London, he plans to use a "secret defense" that would ultimately allow his return to the United States, although he does not elaborate on why he would want to come back.

He refused to talk about the 1967 London bank robbery and the killing of Anthony Fletcher. He did offer to reveal the location of the murder weapon, the gun he had purchased in Italy and which he fired at Fletcher, but only in an attempt to bargain the information in trade for help in getting transferred to the "prestige" of federal custody.

During the interview his lucidity receded and minor obsessions transfixed him. He became preoccupied with a sugar container on the table. Then he concentrated on the "luminescence" of some sheets of notepaper. The conversation ended.

Arthur Jackson's story highlights the dilemma the justice system faces in dealing with the violent mentally ill. Certainly, Theresa Saldana and her advisers would not have to have been so tireless and determined in their efforts if public policy offered greater assurance of long-term protection.

There are still the murder charges pending in London, and extradition will be mandatory for this prisoner. Frighteningly enough, though, it should not be forgotten that if those conditions did not exist, and Jackson had won a legally mandated parole from custody of the California Board of Prison Terms, upon release he might not even fit California's civil code criteria for involuntary hospitalization.

He *might* fit current standards for being a danger to others, but that classification remains difficult to prove in court. It is not enough to say that a person is a *potential* danger in some undetermined future. The law requires proof that there is an *imminency* of danger. And even then, the person can only be held for ninety days. During that period there must be a *demonstrated danger* to extend the confinement for another one hundred and eighty days, and so on. Each court hearing requires a substantial effort of time and money. During each one hundred and eighty-day period the person being held is entitled to one habeas corpus hearing of his own. The events become a continuing soap opera.

When the California legislature held hearings concerning the proposed adoption of involuntary hospitalization statutes, neither the four forensic psychiatrists nor the judge then associated with Department 95, Los Angeles County's busy mental health court, were asked to testify. The state government committee that established the criteria was not always provided with sound medical advice. Lawmakers heard from one psychiatrist who made the incredible claim that he could cure schizophrenics in seven days. Out of this grew a provision for a fourteen-day treatment period, an absurdly short amount of time.

Originally, the rules for involuntary hospitalization were based on common sense. Eligible for such action were people who suffered from a mental disease, disorder, or defect and were in need of care, treatment, supervision, or restraint. Then, in an increasingly common clash of law and medicine, civil libertarians forced redefinition. Critics of forced hospitalization, citing examples of abuse, claimed that citizens were being unfairly put into "pharmacological straitjackets."

To be hospitalized involuntarily under current California guidelines, a person must fit one of three categories as a result of a mental disorder. The person must be gravely disabled, which is defined as an inability to provide for food, clothing, or shelter; must be physically dangerous to himself or herself; or must be physically dangerous to others.

While the new definition on the surface might seem inclusive enough, legal interpretation has made the criteria extremely exclusive, resulting in astoundingly few involuntary hospitalizations on the basis of danger in Los Angeles County, the most heavily populated and dangerous region in the state.

In essence, the law has taken decision-making about hospitalization away from competent psychiatrists who should be empowered by the courts to make such determinations. Instead, such authority has been given to lawyers and judges. In the process, a legal bureaucracy has burgeoned to support the activities of the Los Angeles County mental health court.

There are ripple effects in other associated institutions as well. Across the nation, according to studies by the Public Citizen Health Research Group and the National Alliance for the Mentally Ill, jails, prisons, and public shelters are inadequately housing more mentally ill than are being properly treated in hospitals. One report by the two groups said poor treatment of the mentally ill by the early 1990s had reached its worst level since the early 1800s. In 1992, Dr. Sidney Wolfe, director of the Public Citizen organization, told *The New York Times*, "We were shocked to find that 29 per cent of the jails we asked admitted to holding people in jail with no charges at all, solely because they are mentally ill.''

A series in the *Los Angeles Times* written by Hector Tobar classified the Los Angeles County Jail as the ''largest mental institution in the United States,'' a ''hospital of last resort.'' Manuel R. Mora, head of mental health programs in the Men's Central Jail, told Tobar, ''People who just a few years ago were in a county or state psychiatric hospital, now you'll find them here.''

The frustrating irony of the Arthur Jackson case is that had the prosecution agreed to an insanity plea in 1982, and had Jackson been willing to enter that plea, his mental condition—coupled with the extra oversight his case would have generated—would undoubtedly have resulted in his confinement in the state hospital system until at least 1994, eliminating the parole problems that began in 1987. Beyond that date he would have been required to undergo an annual psychiatric examination to determine whether he continued to be demonstrably dangerous.

Theresa Saldana and others with legitimate reason to fear harm from mentally ill people deserve freedom from those worries.

On a national level, risks are attached to many of the freedoms that we enjoy. In the competition between freedom of the individual and the welfare of society we must take some rights from one side when we give in to the other. Usually, our courts attempt balance with a juggling act between the two. Still, Americans are victims of more violence not because we are necessarily a more violent society, but because we are a freer society whose legal community is mesmerized by the abstract notion of rights and freedom without analyzing full societal impact of laws and court decisions.

In the case of Arthur Jackson, the best interests of all would be met if this man remained confined against his will and was administered drugs to control the symptoms of his schizophrenia. His situation suggests provocative and hard-to-answer questions about the competition of constitutional rights. In truth, a man like Arthur Jackson is no more dangerous, or more predict-able, than an urban street gang member who commits random, drive-by shootings. The callous gang member functions within his own social code at the expense of society. We know from statistics that even after a prison term most of these young people will again commit serious crimes. Yet they are consistently released from institutions.

A gang member *might* be deterred if he is punished consistently and repeatedly for his behavior. For the most part, this offender recognizes that his actions prob-ably will not send him to jail because only about 2 percent of all crimes result in actual incarceration of the perpetrator. Potential punishment as a means of in-timidation is a message that seems never to get across.

Jackson, too, is undeterred by the threat of punish-ment, in his case not because of an instinctive sense of the weaknesses of the legal system but because such eventualities are irrelevant to his thought process. The difference between Jackson, who is a psychotic, and the gang member, who is most likely a sociopath, is that society holds out some *hope* that its system and institutions can deter the sociopath. There is recognition that excepting proper therapy and medication there are no proven means of deterring the psychotic.

Nonetheless, the courts have increasingly viewed the involuntary confinement of psychotics and criminally convicted sociopaths as identical deprivations of rights. The civil commitment of dangerous people is difficult because the interpretive criteria used by judges are civil rights–oriented and, too often, judges make decisions based only on fragmentary understanding of psychiatry and mental states. In California, for example, the crisis in mental health care is at least partially attributable to the 1967 Lanterman-Petris-Short Act, the legislation that made involuntary commitment of an individual to a state psychiatric hospital a difficult task.

In Los Angeles County there may be thousands of people who should be categorized as "dangerous," but for the last year in which statistics were compiled, less than a dozen people were adjudicated to be a danger to others and, as a result, were involuntarily confined to a psychiatric institution under the code.

The legal reforms that led to this situation were the result of an unusual coalition of interests. The political left supported reform on the basis of furthering civil rights. In California a man was confined for seventeen years before someone finally discovered that he was not insane but simply could neither speak nor understand English. There was adequate proof that some people were unjustly confined, and many state institutions *were* poorly run human warehouses. The political right looked at the economics of such institutions—it was too expensive to house people in publicly supported mental institutions.

Many ill effects of the changes wrought by this coalition continue to haunt us in every American city. A population of mentally ill people was released onto the streets, people incapable of taking care of themselves properly who are now deprived of community support. An absurd example of detrimental action by this political movement was a lawsuit filed by the American Civil Liberties Union in New York City to prevent New York Mayor Ed Koch from implementing his program of forcing the most helpless of the mentally ill into city shelters, particularly in times of bad weather.

When the law equates confinement for treatment with punishment it is both illogical and counterproductive. In every state hospital there is a patient-rights advocate, properly tending to the civil rights of his or her clients but unfortunately also causing the necessary treatment of some patients to be curtailed. Court interpretations of the laws have concluded that a person has the "civil right" to refuse treatment and remain ill. Many patients initially take their medication voluntarily and see their conditions improve. Because of the significantly distressful side effects of psychotropic drugs, though, many of those same patients discontinue the use of the medications, leaving doctors incapable of forcing the patients to take the drugs, despite the benefits.

Helping the helpless can mean suspension of some rights. A person on the street talking to himself, filthy and emaciated, unaware of what is happening around him, may not be a danger to others, but society can be a danger to him. He might be better off being placed in a hospital.

A society can only be evaluated on the basis of how it treats its lowliest members, of which Arthur Jackson is one. Jackson should be institutionally confined and properly treated medically.

But there is little likelihood that legislative or judicial action will, in the absence of a criminal conviction and prison sentence, make confinement of people like Jackson easier in the foreseeable future. The debate has not yet been properly framed as a question of medicine and remains a question of law.

In mental hospitals throughout the United States and Great Britain there are people who are diagnostically similar to Jackson, although not necessarily as dangerous. When they refuse treatment, doctors are left powerless to do anything about it. A physician's bias is toward eradicating illness. A lawyer's philosophy emphasizes individual freedom.

By 1993, as Jackson served his term at Vacaville, with completion possible sometime in 1996, Saldana had achieved a level of celebrity from her acting but still was inextricably intertwined with that singular, disastrous moment in her life. "SHE HAS REASON TO SMILE" read the headline accompanying the attractive photograph of Saldana on the cover of *Parade* magazine, the most widely circulated newspaper Sunday supplement in America. A subheadline read, "After overcoming a harrowing attack, the star of TV's *The Commish* has grown beyond survival." The article by contributing editor James Brady focused on Saldana's current major role, on the television show *The Commish*. The article concluded with the adulation that "One reason 'The Commish' works so well on television is Theresa Saldana—wife, mother and real-life heroine."

Scotland Yard's Douglas Harrison stayed on the job a year longer than he had planned, always hoping that he could bring his Scottish suspect back for a murder trial. Throughout, he had regularly written to the witnesses, keeping them up-to-date on the progress of the case. He retired in 1992 at age fifty-five, "a bit disappointed" that Jackson was still in America. Before leaving he briefed his replacement. The plan still holds that whenever Jackson is available for extradition to London, British police officers will fly to the United States to escort him back in their custody.

In London, Valerie Howard, the widow of Anthony Fletcher, says she waits for her justice, understanding of Saldana's motivation to block Jackson's extradition but nonetheless thinking of the actress as a "little bit selfish." She balances her knowledge that a murder trial will "recall buried memories" with her strong sense that Jackson "must be convicted in the U.K. and go to a British prison. As far as I'm concerned, he's served no sentence for anything that he did to us. I know my boys would be very relieved if he came back over. That man's caused a lot of upset in our lives."

In Aberdeen, Scotland, a city where violent crime is virtually nonexistent, a random survey of residents demonstrates that Jackson, because of his aberrance and his ignominy, is remembered by many. At the central library where he spent so many hours, his own story is on file, in a folder stuffed with newspaper articles chronicling the twists and turns of his life.

From his confinement in America, Arthur Jackson continues his writing, moved by the delusions that give him hope that through Joseph Cretzer and Theresa Saldana he will find a place for himself of greater contentment:

The overriding and exclusive factor which drove me to do what I did was this torturous love sickness in my soul for you, combined with a desperate desire to escape into a beautiful world I have always dreamed of, the palaces and gardens of sweet paradise.

Index

295